EYEBALL TACOS
AND
KANGAROO STEW

Life-Changing Meals in Far-Flung Places

Anna Cohen Kaminski JB

EYEBALL TACOS AND KANGAROO STEW

Life-Changing Meals in Far-Flung Places

First published in the UK in October 2021 by
Journey Books, an imprint of Bradt Guides Ltd
31a High Street, Chesham, Buckinghamshire, HP5 1BW, England
www.bradtguides.com

Text copyright © 2021 Anna Cohen Kaminski
Edited by Samantha Cook
Photographs © 2021 Anna Cohen Kaminski
Cover design and illustrations by Sonia Leong (fyredrake.net)
Layout and typesetting by Ian Spick
Production managed by Sue Cooper, Bradt & Zenith Media

The right of Anna Cohen Kaminski to be identified as the author of this work has been asserted by her in accordance with the Copyright, Designs & Patents Act 1988.

All rights reserved. All views expressed in this book are the views of the author and not those of the publisher. No part of this publication may be reproduced, stored in a retrieval system, or transmitted in any form or by any means, electronic, mechanical, photocopying, recording or otherwise without the prior consent of the publisher.

Some of the content of this book is based on articles published previously on the BBC Travel, Lonely Planet and Rough Guides websites. Most events in the book are described according to the author's present recollections, though some timelines, locations and dialogues have been altered. The names and identifying details of certain individuals depicted have been changed to protect their privacy.

ISBN: 9781784779900

British Library Cataloguing in Publication Data
A catalogue record for this book is available from the British Library
Digital conversion by www.dataworks.co.in
Printed in the UK by Zenith Media

To find out more about our Journey Books imprint, visit www.bradtguides.com/journeybooks

To all who've shared my journeys and my meals

And to Salvador Ortiz-Carboneres (1942–2019),
without whom my present life
wouldn't have been possible

ABOUT THE AUTHOR

A freelance travel writer for nearly fifteen years, **Anna Cohen Kaminski** has contributed to dozens of travel guidebooks, covering destinations across six continents. She's the co-author of several editions of the *Rough Guide to Chile* and Rough Guides to South America, Central America, Europe and Southeast Asia on a Budget, as well as the Trailblazer *Trans-Siberian Handbook*, and Lonely Planet guides to Mexico, Jamaica, Borneo, the Baltic States, Central Asia, Kenya, West Coast Australia, Wales, Canada, Nicaragua, Argentina, Brazil, the Philippines, Vietnam, Greek Islands, Costa Rica, Papua New Guinea and Mongolia, among others. An incorrigible foodie, Anna is prepared to travel great distances in search of memorable meals. Her other favourite pastimes include corresponding with death row inmates, trekking in the mountains and attending Bruce Springsteen gigs. A career in criminal law is her 'road not taken'. She presently calls Cómpeta, Andalusia, home.

ACKNOWLEDGEMENTS

A massive thank you to the Bradt team – Adrian Phillips, Claire Strange, Anna Moores, Susannah Lord, Samantha Cook, Ian Spick and Hugh Brune – for making this book possible and for all your hard work. I'd also like to thank Zora O'Neill for being a tremendous 'story therapist'; Sonia Leong for illustrating my book cover; Mike B, Celeste, my sister Genie, Heather, Georgia and Dawn for the proofreading and thoughtful critique; my parents for the encouragement; and, finally, Nicolas, for telling me that my writing was 'good' rather than 'interesting'.

CONTENTS

	Foreword by Zora O'Neill	*xi*
	Introduction	*1*
Chapter 1	**DEATH ROW** – *United States, Egypt*	*9*
Chapter 2	**ON TRIAL** – *Ukraine*	*39*
Chapter 3	**ISLAND IN THE SUN** – *Jamaica*	*75*
Chapter 4	**WANDERING JEW** – *Israel, Lithuania, Latvia, Estonia*	*100*
Chapter 5	**RIDING THE RAILS** – *Russia, Kazakhstan, Uzbekistan*	*123*
Chapter 6	**AMONG THE TSAATAN** – *Mongolia*	*145*
Chapter 7	**JUNGLE DEEP, MOUNTAIN HIGH** – *Chile, Nepal, Peru, Colombia*	*164*
Chapter 8	**RAINMAKERS AND CROCODILE SKIN** – *Papua New Guinea*	*179*

Chapter 9	**THE BLESSING OF BARON KRIMINEL** – *Haiti*	*213*
Chapter 10	**HONORARY WONGUTHA** – *Australia*	*245*
Chapter 11	**DINNER WITH TOM JONES** – *Thailand, Laos, Vietnam, Malaysia*	*268*
Chapter 12	**THE ARCTIC CALLS** – *Canada*	*286*
Chapter 13	**EYEBALL TACOS AND RENEGADE SAINTS** – *Mexico*	*307*
Chapter 14	**ACCIDENTAL IMMIGRANT** – *Spain*	*323*

FOREWORD

As the author of a memoir about living and travelling in the Middle East, I have become very good at answering a single common question: 'What's it like to travel alone as a woman?'

My answer is always, 'Great!' This short answer confounds people – it goes against all the usual fears and admonitions and news stories of freak violence – so of course I explain. It's a pleasure to go alone, without a companion as a buffer. Utter strangers approach you and look out for you; they tell you their secrets and show you places you'd never see otherwise. (It helps, I must acknowledge, to be middle-aged and white, which smooths the path in ways I probably can't even see.)

Unfortunately, my experience is not very well represented in travel writing, so I'm always on the lookout for people who share my mindset. Probably not coincidentally, most of the like-minded women I know are also fellow guidebook authors; we have a practical streak a mile wide, and we go to all the bad places out of a sense of duty. Among these women, probably the most remarkable is Anna Kaminski.

Here I must confess I still have not met Anna in person. A major quirk of guidebook writing is that, for logistical reasons, we authors are almost never in the same place at the same time as any of our colleagues, so we communicate through message boards and social media. Even more than most of us writers, Anna is almost always sending bulletins from remote and intriguing places, such as deep rain forests or a Caribbean island I hadn't even known existed. From the time I started seeing her posts around 2010, I had her mentally logged as a minor legend, at the very least.

In the summer of 2016, I had just published my memoir and was beginning to field all those admiring-but-concerned questions when an issue of the Lonely Planet authors' newsletter arrived. It included a short 'Meet a Writer' interview with Anna in which she compounded her legendary status. She made tantalising reference to Papua New Guinea and Mongolian reindeer herders, work as a lawyer's assistant in Jamaica and a Philippines ferry trip that required a life jacket. But what stuck out to me most in that interview was her comment that the *worst* travel advice she'd ever received was 'Don't travel alone; it's not safe.'

On the contrary, she explained, 'I find that precisely because I am alone (and a diminutive female to boot), locals take me under their wing and I interact with people far more.'

I was so grateful to see my precise experience written by someone else, though I am less diminutive. I especially loved how she'd relegated the fact that she was a woman to literal parentheses. It mattered, sure, but it didn't define where she went and how.

As it happened, the very next day Anna wrote to me with compliments on my book – she had, among all her other interesting life experiences, also studied Arabic for a time. In return, I had the chance to tell her how much I appreciated her travelling attitude, and we compared notes on our positive solo experiences. I refrained from deluging her with the bucket of questions the interview had raised, nor did I tell her that I was now mentally labelling her the Most Interesting Woman in Travel Writing.

Years passed, and Anna's posts from far-flung locales continued. When all of us professional travellers were grounded during the Covid-19 pandemic, she managed to make her little home in Spain look intriguing. She posted about her various souvenirs from her travels and all the ambitious recipes she was trying out, to capture the remembered tastes from trips. Locked down in New York City, I travelled vicariously through her stories. At last I was delighted to learn that Anna was finally at work on her own travel memoir – all those questions I harboured would be answered!

What I've read in this book is even more interesting than I could have guessed. I'm most fascinated by Anna's life before guidebooks. Nearly all of us authors have surprising career paths (mine is through pre-Islamic poetry and tech journalism, for instance), but I think it's fair to say Anna is the only one who came via the exceedingly strange land of the American justice system. The lens through which she sees the world was sharpened by writing to and meeting inmates on death row, then by translating for Scharlette Holdman, the woman who established the field of death-penalty mitigation research. After these experiences, the rest of the places Anna has visited are rightly coloured by questions of justice and fairness.

Perhaps this explains a darker thread in Anna's travel stories. Throughout, there's the lurking awareness that no matter how far you travel, you can't escape yourself. People fail; connections fray; death is everywhere. Fortunately, though, the wider world can also teach different ways of dealing with inevitable tragedy. A transporting Haitian Vodou ceremony, for instance, or a quiet moment in Mexico City with Santa Muerte, the unsanctioned patron saint of the marginalised and desperate.

Which is not to say this book is grim or morbid. Anna lunges for the opposite poles of travel pleasure: on the one hand, the thrill of seeing the supposed 'exotic' up close and marvelling at the boggling diversity of human expression; on the other, the delight of going to an entirely foreign landscape and language, only to find people exactly like yourself. Anna is adept at finding both these experiences, the strange and the familiar, even in the same locale. Her Mongolia tale is perhaps the perfect example.

And then of course there's the food, another great pleasure of travel. Like Anna, I value food as a way of making connections in new places: one compliment to a cook, and a door opens. Unlike Anna, I have a terrible memory, so I envy her ability to conjure past meals with a crystalline clarity. Through her descriptions, I'm hungry for everything from Ukrainian dumplings to eyeball tacos.

Anna recounts a life in travel, but the meaning and experience of that travel has shifted over time. Those of us with the right passports have the ability to jet off to sample delicacies in other countries, to check boxes on our bucket lists. The world is our oyster. But we're recognising, especially in this past year, with so many people grounded by the pandemic, that travel has long-term consequences. At the same time, many of us steady travellers still want to push – and encourage others to push as well – against the political forces that encourage separatism, division and fear. So, I ask myself now, just as travel is starting again: to go or not to go?

Anna's book provides one possible answer: Go, and be brave. And when you go, go further. Go for longer. Go to visit those who might benefit from Santa Muerte's grace or the intercession of a good lawyer. And go alone, so that you're better able to meet new people and learn new lessons – and of course, so that you eat new foods.

Zora O'Neill, 2021
Author of *All Strangers Are Kin: Adventures in Arabic and the Arab World* (2016).

INTRODUCTION

There used to be this nondescript restaurant on Calle Bernardo O'Higgins in Punta Arenas, Chile. It was single-storey, low-key and identified only by a simple wooden plaque: 'Brocolino'. Easy to walk past it without noticing it. Yet on occasion, it served me some of the best meals of my life. When Hector – the large, shaven-headed, bespectacled owner/chef – was on form, he'd whip up remarkable, inspired dishes in his domain: a cluttered kitchen ('organised chaos', as he put it), with pots and pans haphazardly dangling from hooks, along with bunches of dried herbs, strands of chillies, garlands of garlic.

'Sweetbreads in champagne sauce – Hannibal Lecter's favourite!' read one of my favourite menu items. Hector would plate and serve them to me himself, humming cheerfully, then loiter, leaning on the back of the chair opposite me, shooting the breeze, catching up on the lives of our mutual acquaintances. He'd fill me in on the inspiration behind his dishes and their names. '"Steak in the style of Paris Hilton", ha ha ha!' he'd chuckle conspiratorially. 'Has nothing to do with her. I just wanted something catchy.' It worked, too, with many customers ordering the dish because of the name. And the sweetbreads were spot on: tender, perfectly seasoned, lightly floured, pan-fried till crispy, the richness offset by a creamy sauce with sharp notes of sparkling wine. Lecter himself would have approved, I'm sure.

An experimental chef whose freestyling approach I'd emulate when teaching myself to cook properly, Hector had his share of disasters. On an off day, he didn't hum or linger, an oppressive silence reigned in the mostly empty dining room, and a plate of gloopy rice topped with sad-looking abalone would sullenly land in front of me. I'd argue with one of my travel writer colleagues, who'd leave Brocolino out of a rival guidebook. 'He's inconsistent, unreliable,' she'd say about Hector, and she was right. But I'd always included his restaurant in the *Rough Guide to Chile*, relishing the Russian roulette aspect of eating there. For a foodie, for a traveller, there are few things worse than an utterly forgettable experience. And chef Hector's meals were nothing if not memorable. One way or another.

* * * * *

This is a book about memorable meals. I have one rather useless talent: an excellent memory for what I've eaten, where and when. Useless, that is, until I became a travel writer, at which point it became very convenient indeed, helping me to remember dozens of dining experiences when it came to writing up my research.

Before I started writing for Rough Guides, then Lonely Planet, I'd worn various hats: nursing assistant, translator, investigative assistant and interpreter for an attorney-at-law, general dogsbody at a law-related NGO. But every stage of my life has been framed by the memories of meals consumed, from my visits to America's death rows as a backpacker to research trips as a guidebook writer that would carry me across six continents. My recollections of my life's experiences cannot be separated from the flavours they conjure up, and vice versa.

Food loomed large in my life from a very young age. I was born in Moscow in 1981. Both my parents were physicists, and the first eight years of my life were spent in the *akademgorodok* (purpose-built academic community) of Chernogolovka in the former Soviet Union, an hour's bus ride from the capital. As kids, my sister and I never went

INTRODUCTION

hungry, largely due to the Herculean efforts of my parents. Moscow was always well supplied with food, but the rest of the country wasn't, so you had to be prepared to act at a moment's notice when a foodstuff became available and rumours spread like wildfire. One time, a surprise shipment of Hungarian tinned green beans arrived in our town and my mother and sister ferried several dozen tins home through the snow on our sledge. I'd help my mother carry bottles of milk and kefir (fermented yoghurt drink) from the 'milk kitchen' that prioritised families with children, decades before the latter became a Western hipster staple. Sometimes, I'd accompany my parents to the Izmailovo Market in Moscow, a day-long venture on the bus and the metro; my father with his massive rucksack, sewn by a friend of his from orange parachute silk, and my mother with her large bag on wheels. They'd buy me some *churchkhela* (a crimson Georgian sweet consisting of solidified grape juice on a string, with lumps of walnut inside) as a treat.

Though shortages were a fact of life, I was the only family member for whom food became a constant preoccupation. Our culinary repertoire was rather limited. My mother – a strict vegetarian since she'd read Gandhi's autobiography in her early twenties and reached the conclusion that other creatures needn't die in order for her to live – didn't particularly enjoy cooking and quality ingredients were hard to find. In our kitchen, I'd hand-crank the meat grinder for my mother in order to turn cuts of gristly meat into palatable mince. Slabs of 'Cheddar' required soaking, then melting, in order to become edible, while the good stuff – Lithuanian cheese with lots of tiny holes – did not. There was plenty of bread and butter in my childhood, too, plus porridge on a sliding scale of desirability (running from millet to oat, with buckwheat and rice in the middle). On rare occasions, there'd be an entire roast chicken; I enjoyed extracting the heart, liver and kidneys once the carcass had been mostly stripped of meat, and munching on the dark flesh that bounced so pleasingly between the teeth. Occasionally, someone (possibly my grandmother or my aunt, since my mother would never have been that cruel to a small child) would torture me with pig's liver – powdery, brown-grey and with the uric tang of overcooked offal. Sometimes, my mother would bread and fry defrosted lumps of miscellaneous white fish. By this point, the Soviet Union had long since overfished its waters and so I didn't have to contend with my mother's childhood nightmare of live fish, flopping around convulsively on the kitchen counter, followed by scales and eyeballs and entrails everywhere, and fish bones stuck in her throat.

Long before the terms 'seasonal' and 'locavore' entered the Western foodie lexicon, our edible delicacies were seasonal and/or local: Turkish pomegranates in the autumn and oranges in winter; cherries, apricots and sweet, fragrant watermelon from the Central Asian republics in the summer. In June and July, we kids had axe murderer hands from all the wild strawberries and blueberries we consumed in the forest. Other families made fruit preserves for the winter and were prolific mushroomers, but not mine. We only went mushrooming when my cousin Sasha came down from Moscow, though I did know the difference between the edible porcini and chanterelles and the poisonous toadstools and fly agaric. Unlike my kamikaze sister, who at the age of three informed our mother that she'd eaten a toadstool and had to be rushed to the doctor.

There were other infrequent treats: *pelmeni* (boiled meat dumplings), smoked salami. The clandestine consumption of crumbly dark 'Red October' chocolate at friends' houses, and 'Eskimo' ice cream – even in -20° winter temperatures – because I wasn't allowed sugar at home. The equally furtive gobbling of cold frankfurters – sometimes brought from Moscow by my aunt – which I'd hide in a napkin in order to later combine my two favourite activities: eating and reading. One time, Masha K and I shoplifted some pickled garlic from the Co-op store with its sad assortment of mummified vegetables, and then each blamed the other when our parents could smell the pungent stench a mile off. And very seldom, several fathers, including mine, would get together for the day and take us kids to the Far Lake in the forest, and cook potatoes in the hot coals of a campfire, infusing my childhood memories with their almost sweet, moreish taste and the smell of wood smoke and pine.

The late 80s brought unsettling transformations. My father and my friends' fathers were travelling abroad for work and returning with blue jeans, Casio watches, Juicy Fruit chewing gum. Pepsi-Cola tasted prickly and exotic and foreign: of America. My father brought kiwi fruit and a mango back from Switzerland – alien fruit never seen before by anyone we knew. Other aliens appeared: in 1989, the first two foreigners ever – two American physicists – were allowed to visit Chernogolovka, even though my home town was located near Star City, and they could've somehow stolen Soviet space secrets. They looked exceedingly ordinary, with their beards, suits and ties – hugely disappointing to an eight-year-old who'd expected Native Americans with tomahawks and feathered headgear. When my parents' friends would gather in our kitchen some evenings to drink strong, sweet black tea, words like 'glasnost' and 'perestroika' were being bandied about freely. Change was in the air.

And on May 15, 1990, we upped and left – for good, as it turned out later. From 1989 onwards, scientists attending conferences abroad were allowed to take their families, the latter no longer kept behind as de facto hostages. I didn't even say goodbye to my friends, assuming we'd be coming back. Three flights followed: Moscow–Frankfurt, Frankfurt–Cincinnati, Cincinnati–Minneapolis. I remember the half a slice of rye bread with some sort of green spread and a chicken leg that tasted sweet on the flight to Frankfurt. The chocolate brownie that I was – amazingly! – allowed to eat on the interstate flight. Speeding through the night in the car belonging to one of my father's colleagues, then sitting in our new apartment at the One Ten Grant apartment complex, at 4am, eating peanut butter and bologna and vanilla yoghurt. Compared to my beloved Soviet food, this was a spectrum of brand new flavours on an entirely different scale. And the supermarkets! My god. The first time we went to the Red Owl, I thought I'd entered some sort of temple of light – all brightly lit shelves and fridges brimming with symmetrical, colourful mountains of food. I stared at it all, slack-jawed, the same way that in later years I'd gawp at Machu Picchu, the Taj Mahal, and other wonders of the world.

Four months in Minneapolis were followed by four months in Highland Park, New Jersey, and then, on January 2, 1991, we found ourselves emigrating to Cambridge, UK, where my father was offered a permanent position at the university. At the age of nine, I'd attend my first British school, my face scarred by chicken pox, what little English I spoke pronounced with a Noo Joisey accent.

The wanderlust that propels me owes no small part to my family's immigrant experience and my upbringing that encouraged the pursuit of knowledge for knowledge's sake. It's a deep-rooted compulsion – to chart new horizons, to seek out ways of life that differ dramatically from my own. My father, the bibliophile, collected books of folk tales from different countries before I was even born, as if in anticipation

INTRODUCTION

of my arrival. I devoured them as soon as I learned to read, and would spend hours poring over the map of the world on our wall. My mother would tell me about my grandmother, Esther, who very much wanted to see the world, but never found herself beyond the confines of the Soviet Union. Sometimes, when I'm on the road, I like to think that I'm channelling my indomitable grandmother.

'Must be a dream job,' fellow travellers would sigh wistfully, when discussing my profession. And to me, it definitely is. If you'd asked me in my late teens what I wanted to do with my life, I would've told you that I wanted to travel and to write about it. Some of my friends took a gap year before going to university. 'To get it out of my system,' they'd say, as if hodophilia is some troublesome medical condition, a frivolity that one must get over before attending to real life. But I couldn't. It was – is – my system.

It's not for everyone. In time, I'd learn about the darker side of being constantly in motion: missing great chunks of loved ones' lives, the long work hours, the loneliness of my chosen way of life, the difficulty of getting the work–life balance right. But I'd never stop appreciating the constant absorption of new knowledge, the steep learning curve.

When I was growing up, my family hardly ever ate out. In the USSR, there were few places to do so, and you were most likely to get severe gastric repercussions for your troubles. In the UK, a few grudging visits to McDonald's and Pizza Hut aside, my parents saw dining out as an unnecessary extravagance. Until my mid-teens, my idea of culinary sophistication was ordering the blackened catfish at Chili's, or the Four Seasons pizza at Pizza Express. But once I began travelling independently, aged seventeen, I found this entire new world of edible discoveries to be made, which fuelled my wanderlust just as much as my hankering for new cultural horizons. The more I travelled, the more I talked about food at home, bewildering my mother, who couldn't understand how an academic with but a passing interest in nourishment found herself with a food-obsessed bon vivant for a firstborn.

What's the difference between a memorable meal and a life-changing one? Is there such a thing as a meal that's *not* life-changing, given how our lives are being irreversibly altered with every passing moment? I'm not entirely sure, but I think it's this: memorable meals revolve largely around the food involved. Life-altering ones may also do that, while simultaneously signalling a shift in your life's trajectory, or subtly altering your perception of the world. From the myriad meals that jostle each other for space inside my head, I've pared my life down to fourteen parts, each seen through the prism of an edible experience that has left an indelible mark.

CHAPTER 1

DEATH ROW

'Are you wearing any underwear?' The uniformed woman runs her hands along my back, my sides, and down my thighs and legs in a manner rather more intimate than I'm used to or am entirely comfortable with. In a nearby building, the man I am meeting is stripping naked so that the accompanying guards can check his bodily crevices for contraband. They will do the same once our visit is over. I am inside Florida's notorious maximum security prison, Union Correctional Institution. This is standard procedure.

Once I've been frisked, I get a visitor's badge and pass through a metal detector. The electric door disgorges me outside, into a tunnel of electric wire fencing. I press the buzzer at the end and another gate opens. Once it shuts behind me, I am ushered into the visiting room.

I take my first mental snapshot of Marvin – a barrel-chested, 6ft 5 shaven-headed, bearded black man. He catches sight of me, grins broadly and makes a beeline for me. He towers over me when I shake hands with him.

'Hey, I've been looking forward to your visit all week,' he says.

His orange uniform is impeccably clean. I compliment him on this. Marvin tells me he's washed his uniform by hand in anticipation of my visit. Soon he is laughing at himself: 'This little woman I've never met before has me as nervous as a schoolkid sent to the principal's office!' It tickles me that he's more jumpy than I am, and I tell him so. He laughs. But then, it's my fifth visit to America's death rows, and I'm beginning to get the hang of this.

Marvin and I pick a table far away from the other visitors. We exchange small talk at first, sizing each other up.

'How'd you get here, by the way?' Marvin knows that I can't drive.

'Christian and Richard gave me a ride.'

My friends – a couple I'd met when I was an exchange student in Puerto Rico – now live in Gainesville, Florida, and have gallantly taken the day off in order to help me meet Marvin.

I complain to Marvin about having been felt up by the guard on the way in and compare the visitor entry procedure here to that of San Quentin. My first prison visit didn't involve any hands-on frisking, but was considerably more terrifying, because I was entering the unknown.

* * * * *

San Quentin State Prison – California's oldest and, barring Alcatraz, its most notorious penitentiary – is a sandy-coloured fortress that sits on a peninsula jutting out into San Francisco Bay. I was early, so I strolled slowly along the quiet main street of the small community that services the prison, and watched a couple playing with their Labrador retriever on the small beach. This domestic tableau was at odds with the fact that a mere five-minute walk away almost seven hundred condemned men and women exist in four massive cell blocks, under unrelenting neon light and with round-the-clock surveillance.

California has the largest death row in the United States. The closest runners up, Florida and Texas, have about half as many death row inmates apiece, though that's partly because inmates there spend eight to ten years on death row before being dispatched to the other side, whereas in California, some have been on death row for longer than I've been alive.

The nerves really kicked in when I entered the one-storey annexe by the main gate, where the inmates' families and friends awaited their turn. I deposited my belongings in a locker, filled in a visitor's form. Eventually, I was buzzed in, and the officer asked me who I had come to see.

'William Clark.'

I showed that there was nothing in my pockets. Producing dollar bills in a clear plastic bag, which were then counted to make sure they didn't exceed $20, I removed my shoes and watch, placed them in the tray provided on the conveyer belt, and then stepped through the metal detector.

As I was yet to meet Scharlette Holdman, and yet to hear her San Quentin Bra Story, I was deeply dismayed when frantic beeping ensued.

'Are you wearing an underwired bra?'

'Yes. Is that a problem?'

Apparently so. Maybe the guard was having a slow day or was intrigued by my accent, or perhaps I looked particularly unthreatening – skinny, 5ft 0, androgynous-looking, frequently mistaken for a teenager – because she was less brusque with me than with the regulars. She explained that it's possible for a visitor to slip the wire out of the bra during a contact visit and slip it to the inmate as contraband, and that they could potentially fashion a weapon out of it. Though how the inmate would then get the wire back to their cell remains a mystery, given the full body search after the visit.

* * * * *

'Anyway, I'm directed to this store cupboard which is The Place where Bras go to Die,' I tell Marvin. There was a large garbage bag there – a veritable sartorial graveyard full of sad, skanky, non-supporting bras of questionable cleanliness for me to choose from. I'd get my underwired bra back upon exiting, I was told.

'Can you imagine having to put on another person's underwear?' I ask. Marvin screws up his face. He's one of the most fastidious, most cleanliness-conscious people I know. In reply to one of my letters, when I asked him how he passed the time of day, he wrote:

'I have a daily regimen of cleaning my floor and walls with soap and rags, as I cannot stand filth. I wash everything by hand. I keep everything in order. My military training taught me that I can find anything in the dark or a smoke-filled compartment if I keep things orderly, which could save someone's life in an emergency situation.'

For Marvin, one of the biggest horrors of prison life is occasionally having to move cells. The last time that happened, Marvin ended up scrubbing every inch of his new abode with a toothbrush because its previous occupant lived in filth. Also, sometimes there are rodents.

'Some of the guys here feed the filthy creatures, à la Green Mile,' he tells me. 'And my neighbour is terrified of them, so he wakes us all up with his hysterical screaming whenever he sees a mouse.'

As we chat animatedly, I catch one of the guards looking at us curiously. To him, Marvin and I must look like a really odd pair. By this point, we've been friends for about a year. And yes, at first glance, we are vastly different. From his letters, I know that Marvin comes from a small town in Georgia, and is the second oldest of four children – three boys, one girl. I'm the oldest of two girls. Marvin grew up in a wooden four-bedroom house, with gables, a shaded porch and a back yard. Until my sister was born and we were given a three-room apartment, my parents and I lived in a cramped studio in planned Soviet housing.

Marvin hails from a deeply religious, Christian background, and on Sunday mornings he'd have been off to church with his entire family, dressed in his best clothes. My family is broadly atheist, and religion was deeply discouraged in the USSR. And I didn't own any 'best' clothes; most of mine were hand-me-downs from my older cousins.

Marvin was a model student and a star basketball player, whose young life was fairly regimental, and whose extracurricular activities comprised sports meets and little else. By contrast, I enjoyed much greater freedom. We Soviet kids were allowed to roam anywhere within our small town and the forest that began where my street ended. I had rhino skin on the soles of my feet from going barefoot all summer, skinned knees during the warmer months from falling out of trees, and often a bloody nose in winter – either from falling flat on my face while ice skating at the rink behind our apartment building, or from being hit with a well-aimed snowball. With torches made from sticks or plastic carpet-beaters that we set alight, we trespassed in the basements of our multi-storey apartment buildings in search of ghosts and rats if the caretakers forgot to lock the door. We built secret hideouts in the woods and played at being spies and cowboys and Indians. While Marvin only had male friends, growing up, with his parents making sure he stayed away from girls, we Soviet kids ran as a mixed pack – with Kolya, the Redkozubov boys, Masha T, Masha K. We went swimming in the lake together, fought other neighbourhood kids, threw water balloons from balconies at passers-by, shoplifted onions and then cooked them over makeshift campfires, eating the charred bits and all.

There's one thing Marvin and I have in common, though: Soviet or American, we were expected to be self-sufficient from an early age and to help out. We ran to the grocery store for our mothers, did the chores at home and looked after our younger siblings. Nowadays, social services would've been called, but back then, Soviet parents thought nothing of leaving a three-year-old in the care of a six-year-old for the evening, bragging to their friends about how independent and mature their kids were. Meanwhile, Marvin would find himself helping his younger brother and sister with their homework and making dinner when his father worked late and his mother had extra church-related duties.

Speaking of dinner... 'I'm sorry. Where are my manners?' I interrupt Marvin. 'You must be hungry.'

'You came to see *me*... you're my guest. So it should be me treating you...' He's momentarily downcast. Marvin is very traditional in his outlook when it comes to gender roles and Southern hospitality. He's mentioned several times in his letters how difficult it is for him to be dependent on the charity of others. Unlike inmates in general population, who are 'privileged' to work for a few cents an hour, death row inmates aren't allowed to work at all and must depend on family and friends for financial support.

Food is a major preoccupation for prisoners on death row. Partly because they are fed slop – often made from expired ingredients, and just enough to keep them alive until they are executed. 'In my twenty years behind bars,' Marvin wrote, 'what I've missed the most is the food from my childhood.' His mother, a prolific chef, cooked up the full repertoire of Georgia dishes for the family on a daily basis: grits with pimento cheese or shrimp, fried okra, fried green tomatoes, crispy-skinned fried chicken, sweet, dense cornbread, corn on the cob and barbecued ribs whenever Marvin's father fired up the barbecue in the summer and the neighbours came over; peach cobbler and pecan pie for dessert. All of which sounded impossibly exotic to me.

Until he joined the navy, Marvin lived pretty much in one place his whole life, whereas I've been on the move since I was eight years old. When we emigrated to the UK, I missed Russia and my friends terribly, and failed to appreciate that I wasn't the only one in our family having trouble settling in. Though made welcome by my father's new colleagues, my parents found themselves very isolated – far from friends, family and, in the case of my father, the lively, passionate community of physicists that he had surrounded himself with in Chernogolovka.

In the years that followed, our house became a volatile place. I never knew what I'd be coming home to, and often found myself escaping by wandering the streets of Cambridge at night, plugged into my Walkman. Marvin's teenage years in his outwardly exemplary, devout Christian household were also troubled. His father was a serial philanderer, and sometimes he'd catch his old man out on the town, with a woman on his arm. It was a small town. People talked. Because Marvin had been raised to respect his parents unquestioningly – the Bible said so – he couldn't bring himself to confront his father, even though he knew how unhappy the infidelities made his mother. So the burly teenager confronted the women instead.

But I digress.

* * * * *

Since proper junk food, plus anything with vitamins in it, is the subject of wistful daydreams, nostalgic conversations and final wishes on death row, I'm glad that it's in my gift to feed Marvin properly, at least during my visit. We wander over to the vending machines and Marvin picks out cheeseburgers, trail mix, apples and fruit juice to keep us going for five hours. As I warm up the burgers in the microwave, I tell Marvin how much the visitation room reminds me of my high school canteen. Picture a large hall with welded metal tables and stools, vending machines and microwaves along the side. But instead of schoolchildren, the room is awash with the orange uniforms of inmates, and all the furniture is nailed down. A relaxed atmosphere prevails: visitors and inmates are sitting around their tables, talking earnestly, sharing meals.

Marvin and I bite into our burgers. From the age of seventeen, until this prison visit, I've been visiting family in New York and then spending my summers traversing the United States and Canada by long-distance Greyhound buses, which have tended to stop for breaks exclusively at fast food joints. I've got them ranked in order of preference: Arby's, Carl's Jr., Taco Bell, McDonald's, Burger King. My taste buds are not yet the refined tools of trade of a jaded foodie and travel writer, and this prison burger, topped with the ubiquitous square of plasticky orange cheese that bears little relation to dairy products, scores somewhere in the middle.

Marvin leans closer to me across the table and gives me a searching look. 'I've been wanting to ask you this in person. Why would someone like you want to get to know someone on death row? Do you like "bad boys", or do you just oppose the death penalty?'

There is no short answer to this. It's difficult to pinpoint exactly how or when my journey to America's death row began. Like many teenagers, I railed against the many injustices of the world. Obsessing over the idea of crime, punishment and incarceration, I voraciously devoured accounts of life behind bars in Stalinist gulags and elsewhere – from *Crime and Punishment* by Dostoyevsky and *Journey into the Whirlwind* by Evgenia Ginzburg to *Dead Man Walking* by Sister Helen Prejean. Most people I know believe that if you're behind bars, you must've done something to deserve it. But my parents, though considerably more conservative than me, actively encouraged me to write letters on behalf of prisoners of conscience through Amnesty International.

Family background played a part in it. Pretty much every Soviet family had friends or relatives who'd done time behind bars during Stalin's Terror of the 1930s and 1940s. My maternal grandfather was imprisoned in the 1940s as an 'enemy of the people', convicted on falsehoods from his co-workers, and escaped death by the skin of his teeth. If it hadn't been for a prison nurse risking her life to get word to my grandmother, and if my grandmother had been marginally less resourceful, and hadn't managed to somehow cross the Soviet Union during wartime – from Almaty, Kazakhstan, where my maternal family was evacuated during the war, to Moscow – and prove my grandfather's innocence, I wouldn't be here to tell this story.

There was a surprising amount of tolerance from my parents when my death row mail started arriving. 'You've got another letter from one of your murderers,' my mother would say. Tolerance up to a point, that is. When my university friend Steve, a local journalist, wrote a tongue-in-cheek article on me for the *Cambridge Town Crier*, describing me as 'courageous', interviewing my mother about me and rustling up a half-presentable photo ('It's the only one your mother could find in which you're not half-naked or on a camel or something'), my folks were less than pleased because of the attention the piece generated. They didn't feel that I'd done anything deserving of fanfare.

EYEBALL TACOS AND KANGAROO STEW

* * * * *

'Okay, so you've been interested in criminal justice for a long time,' Marvin says. 'But what exactly made you decide to write to a bunch of death row guys?'

Well.

It was a wet March afternoon at the University of Warwick in 2004. I was procrastinating, putting off a rather urgent essay on plantation slavery in the Caribbean by idly googling people I knew. I typed in 'Forrest Albert Carter', a troubled man I'd been entangled with for a while, and found myself staring in shock at his downcast face, looking at me from 'San Diego's Ten Most Wanted' bulletin.

When you look back on your life, can you pinpoint pivotal moments – tiny decisions that seemed utterly inconsequential at the time, but in hindsight, ended up irrevocably altering its path? In my case, it all began with a haircut.

It was the year 2000, and I was backpacking across the States. I enjoyed planning my solo journeys almost as much as the travel itself, poring over maps, booking hostel dorms. I'd allocated myself three days to explore San Diego and Tijuana. But that haircut threw everything. Impulsively, I wandered into The Gallery on Broadway, a barbershop catering largely to an African American clientele. Forrest – think Morgan Freeman, but almost skeletally thin – cut my hair. We got talking. Turned out he spent time in Iran as an engineer in the military forces, before they all got kicked out in '79. He was a draft dodger, too; supposed to have served in Vietnam, but didn't, then spent years waiting for that ominous knock on his door. I sensed a bigger story. He invited me to dinner. I accepted.

I hardly remember the food at all. It was mediocre Chinese at a food court. But that dinner was the domino that toppled all the others. Or perhaps the haircut was the domino. Without it, maybe there would've been no death row pen pals, no getting banned from the United States, no travel writing career.

Dinner turned into a movie. Movie turned into breakfast. I ended up staying in San Diego for three extra days, upending my carefully planned travel itinerary, rebooking hostels, changing bus tickets. And that should've been that. A glimpse into a tortured soul. A short fling. But I made the mistake of trying to turn it into way more than it actually was.

So I went back to San Diego twice in subsequent years, surprising Forrest and learning a bit more about him. A Riverside, California native, the youngest of ten kids. Two children, estranged. Two bitter divorces; in the last one, he lost his business, his house, his car. When I saw him in 2002, he seemed pleased to see me but distracted. He disappeared for hours at night, offering no explanation. I got angry and left, and gave him little thought until I saw that 'wanted' page.

What the hell did he do??

I frantically googled Forrest's case.

'Possession of a controlled substance.'

The nocturnal wanderings suddenly made sense. I was new to the world of addiction, coming from a sheltered, solidly middle-class background – but I'd read enough crime novels for the penny to finally drop. Still, being jailed for mere possession? Not even 'with intent to distribute'? San Diego PD must've been having a really slow month. But that was before I learned that in the States, addiction is treated as a crime rather than an illness. And there's greater stigma attached to some drugs than to others. Different degrees of shame. It's fine if you're a celebrity and can afford to check yourself into some fancy private clinic for your coke habit. But if you're an impoverished crack addict and a man of colour, you're likely to end up behind bars. Both are derivatives of the same plant, yet penalties for crack possession are much higher, because it's a poor person's drug. And if you befriend a crack addict, you're tainted by association.

When I told this story to a friend, many years later, I involuntarily blurted out: 'Please don't judge me!' And then smiled ruefully at the ridiculousness of my own words. If he had been going to judge me, he'd have done it regardless. And if he hadn't, there was no point in telling him not to.

* * * * *

A mission formed in my head. I must find Forrest. Help him. Save him. And so I did, that summer. Find him, that is. I rode a Greyhound bus to San Diego, found out which jail he was held in, make my way there and flung myself into his arms.

Clichéd cinematic gestures a relationship do not make. But it would take me several years to figure that out.

* * * * *

Somehow, googling Forrest's case turned into googling 'death row', and I came across websites featuring pen pal profiles of condemned men and women. They ranged from brief two-liners – name, age, height, star sign and a couple of interests – to in-depth essays. Some proclaiming their innocence.

The statistics were damning: out of America's condemned, at least ten percent turn out to be innocent. Some spend years or decades on death row before being exonerated. Some are executed before they are able to prove their innocence.

What compelled me to write to these individuals? Curiosity, mostly. I wanted to be the keeper of their stories. I wanted to know what it was like to be incarcerated for years with a death sentence hanging over you. How these men were shaped by their lives' paths and found themselves behind bars. Whether they were innocent. And if they weren't, I wanted to know if there was more to them, as individuals, than the worst act of their life. Sister Helen Prejean, who served as a spiritual advisor to many condemned men and accompanied them to their executions, has led me to consider something that hadn't occurred to me before. That perhaps it's not just the wrongfully convicted who are deserving of dignity and compassion; maybe all people are. I was willing to hear them out, should they trust me enough to confide in me.

In the book *Silence of the Lambs*, during her interview with Hannibal Lecter at the asylum, Clarice Starling admires the detailed sketches of Florence that he has on his cell wall. She asks him if he drew them from memory, to which he replies: 'Memory, Officer Starling, is what I have instead of a view.'

By the time Starling encounters him, Lecter had spent a decade in a basement cell, deprived of natural light, listening to the screams and jabbering of the insane, and often deprived of his books and other tools of distraction by a sadistic warden. When his immediate surroundings become overwhelming, Lecter retreats to the memory palace inside his own head, free to wander the streets of Florence, or listen to classical music, or peruse centuries-old texts.

I wanted to know how death row inmates keep their sanity and manage to survive under circumstances that break others. And

I wanted to know what they'd choose for their final meal, were they to have one.

* * * * *

Slowly, based on how intriguing I found their cases, I put together a list of names.

Bill Clark, the only man on San Quentin's death row to be sentenced to death for two murders. It's fully acknowledged that he wasn't the triggerman, but he's accused of masterminding both. Maintains his innocence.

James Anderson, accused of kidnapping and murdering two women whose car stalled in the desert, even though from the evidence presented, it seems far more likely that the murders were committed by the brother of a girl he was accompanying at the time. James received dreadful legal representation. Sentence overturned in 1987, reinstated in 1991. Maintains his innocence.

Melvin Turner, accused of taking part in an execution-style robbery at a gas station. His co-defendant put all the blame on Melvin, who has an IQ of 87, and got life without parole, while Melvin was sentenced to death.

Both Melvin and James have been on death row longer than I have been alive. While California allows more time for appealing a death sentence, in many cases it means a lifetime of incarceration before potential execution.

José Medellín, in Texas, convicted for participation in a gang rape and murder of two teenage girls when he was eighteen. Witty, funny profile, and his photo reminds me of a woman I worked with when I was seventeen and on whom I had a crush. I even briefly took up playing rugby to impress her, before arriving at the conclusion that no woman, no matter how cool, was worth broken bones or a concussion.

Marvin Jones, a former US Navy officer in Florida, accused of murder and robbery. His profile describes his wide range of interests and his desire to correspond with people from around the world.

The same desire is expressed by Rasheed Simpson, of Pennsylvania, particularly keen on pen pals from outside the US in order to broaden his horizons and to find out what the rest of the world thinks of America's foreign policy. He comes across as someone I could have debates with.

Bernard Smith, of Arizona, sentenced to death for armed robbery during which someone got shot and killed. He states that his community ties are practically non-existent and sounds lonely.

* * * * *

On the day I penned my first letters to them all, it was a scorching hot April afternoon in Luxor, and I was on a mission to find a jalabiya (a loose-fitting traditional robe and marvellously practical garment for hot climes) to fit my short stature. I was travelling with my friends, Dawn and Heather, as part of a two-week breakneck stampede through Egypt's highlights. While the others were having a siesta, I was too restless and excited (I'm in Egypt!!!), so I made my way along the waterfront in the direction of Luxor Temple in search of the souq.

A young man speaking excellent English hailed me from the water's edge and persuaded me to come for a ride in his felucca. Once we were in the middle of the river, he treated me to cold hibiscus tea, but things got a bit weird when he offered to wash my feet in the Nile, 'So that you come back to Egypt.' I informed him that I'd spent two days swimming in the Nile, behind my group's felucca, crocodiles be damned, and if that doesn't bring me back to Egypt, nothing will. Back on dry land, we dodged a cacophonous jam of cars, bicycles and horse-drawn carriages on his motorbike, he duly deposited me in front of a tailor's shop, and I proudly showed off my custom-fitted snow-white jalabiya at dinner.

Buoyed by the success of my acquisition, that evening I took the plunge (carpe that diem!) and scribbled furiously late into the night while listening to the sepulchral tones of Leonard Cohen's 'By the Rivers Dark'. I fretted about getting the balance right – a mix of personal introduction, interests and background, plus some questions – not too probing, but enough to start a conversation. I didn't mention their cases, not at first, thinking of my potential pen pals as skittish gazelles whose trust must be earned. Mustn't scare them.

What I didn't consider at all was that all or most of these men may eventually die a particularly unpleasant death. When I told my mentor Jolyon about my new pen pals, he told me that he took my hat off to me, since he couldn't bring himself to befriend people destined for the death chamber. But I was twenty-three, yet to experience grief and loss, and I brushed the thought aside, just as years later, I'd dismiss a caution from a terminally ill man about befriending someone living on borrowed time. Surely, justice would win out and everything would be fine.

I didn't think that everyone would write back, but most did. Bill was charming and witty, and wrote in all caps. James, an artist and one of life's natural networkers, was keen to connect me to his other pen pals with similar interests. Melvin drew me cards with cute puppies and kittens. Rasheed shared photos of his family. Marvin asked me to send him photos of my travels, so that he could roam the world vicariously.

Bernard didn't write back because he happened to be already dead. Of natural causes. My letter to him bounced back. The pen pal website clearly wasn't updated terribly often. And since I was coming to the States for several weeks to visit family and friends after graduating from university, it made perfect sense to meet these men face to face, to get a proper measure of them as human beings.

* * * * *

'Why me in particular?' Marvin asks.

'Well, your profile caught my eye because you're not the stereotype of a typical death row inmate. You know, a drug addict and murderer off the streets,' I confess.

He nods.

'True. I wasn't abused, or neglected. I didn't grow up in dire poverty. I am not violent or mentally ill, and I can form rich, close relationships with people.'

'Which must make it harder, being in here…'

'You have no idea. Being surrounded by guys who are so badly damaged, who've been in and out of prison their entire lives, who can't imagine anything different.'

Marvin's solidly middle-class, traditional-values upbringing sets him apart from the rest of my guys.

Little Melvin comes from a violent home with an alcoholic father, who used to assault the mother and the kids, sometimes landing them in hospital. Until Melvin and his brothers got old enough to fight back and returned the favour.

José's parents are undocumented Mexican immigrants, working menial jobs. José had run wild on the streets of Houston since he was a kid, joined the Black and White gang when he was twelve; if he hadn't gone to prison when he did, he figures he would've been long dead.

Rasheed ran away from his stepfather's drunken rages when he was fourteen, and sold drugs on the streets of Philadelphia until he became a father at the age of eighteen and wanted a better life for his baby son. He decided to leave the underworld and go into the construction business, but the cops caught up with him, and told him that if he didn't divulge the names of his former associates, they'd pin a murder on him. He thought they were making empty threats. They weren't.

While getting to see Marvin was straightforward because my friends drove me, with the others, travel arrangements varied. To see Bill and Melvin, I had to make my own way to San Quentin Prison by bus. Meeting Rasheed had me rocking up at the Greyhound bus station in Philly at 4am on a chilly March morning and then running up to strange men to ask them if their name was Shawn. Rasheed's younger brother then drove me all the way across the state to Pittsburgh, PA – a five-hour drive each way. With James, the moment I walked out of the San Francisco Greyhound bus station I was accosted by his then girlfriend Marlene, a buxom, smiling woman who reminded me of Oprah Winfrey. Not only did she drive me to and from San Quentin, but James also found me a place to stay – with his friend Carolyn, the only African American goth I'd ever met and someone who'd also done time on death row – at the Bangkok 'Hilton'.

* * * * *

Marvin stuffs the last remaining burger bite in his mouth. 'Not necessarily something I'd choose for my last meal,' he tells me, 'but this is great.'

I'm surprised he's able to joke about a rather heartless custom – granting death row inmates a final dinner of their choice the night before their execution. As if that's adequate compensation for taking their lives. In some states, this can be anything within a hundred-mile radius (within a set budget); in others it will be whatever can be rustled up in the prison kitchens. Most of the condemned opt for comfort food – quarter-pounder burgers, bucket-sized milkshakes, fried chicken, pizza.

I seize the opportunity: 'So what would you have for your final meal?'

Marvin doesn't even need to think about it. 'My mother's fried chicken. With mash, and gravy, collard greens. Or chicken and dumplings.'

'Would you be able to eat, though?' I'm thinking of inmates who choose nothing at all, since the spectre of impending death presumably sucks all the joy out of the meal.

Affirmative.

'If I knew it was my last night, I'd want to remember all the good things in my life: my family, my daughters, my crew in the navy, you, Kristen.' Unlike some inmates who attract kooks with a fetish for incarcerated men, Marvin has managed to meet a wonderful woman who genuinely fell in love with him.

'Not me,' I tell him. 'If I knew for sure I was going to die, I don't think I'd be able to eat.' I've given the subject some thought. 'Now, near-death experiences – that's different,' I continue. I've had a few close calls during my travels, and found that after I'd recovered from the initial fright, my appetite came back with a vengeance, and not just for food, but for life. Eating – like getting drunk, and getting laid – is a life-affirming impulse.

'Like what?'

So I tell him about getting mugged in New Orleans the year before. How I was too frugal to pay for a cab, and walked from the west end of North Robertson Street, off Canal Street, to my hostel, located somewhere along the same street. I passed cemeteries on my left, and derelict, boarded-up buildings on the right. The street was practically deserted, and the fact that it looked like a really rough neighbourhood should have clued me in.

I asked a passing teenage boy for directions. He left, then returned with a slightly older, dreadlocked friend. 'We'll take you to where you want to go.' So what did I do? I followed them deeper into the ghetto to where a young man in a dirty vest and sweatpants was leaning on a wreck of a car, watching me.

'… And so this other guy came up behind me and grabbed me in a choke hold, crushing my windpipe. My eyes were bulging out, but it felt like time slowed down. I knew for certain – can't remember where I read that – that I'd pass out in about forty seconds. The other two made me turn out my pockets, got thirty bucks. Then the other guy let me go and then the two teenagers gave me directions.'

Marvin shakes his head in exasperation. 'What were you thinking? You're supposed to be an experienced traveller. That was such a "green" thing to do.'

Shamefacedly, I agree. He's right. It's embarrassing.

There was no fear during the mugging itself. It happened too quickly. The shock, the anger, the shaking, my painful throat – that all hit me afterwards. I found a payphone to call my friend Jak whom I was supposed to meet later, and hoarsely croaked that I'd been mugged. Come evening, Jak took me Brennan's, a fancy restaurant where he used to work as a waiter. It was my first ever experience of a truly fancy meal: white linen tablecloths, seamless service by Jak's former colleagues, and dish after dish of creole deliciousness. As the earthy, gamey turtle soup and seafood gumbo, rich with oysters, slithered down my bruised windpipe at Brennan's, I recovered my composure and good humour. So *this* is what proper food is supposed to taste like.

Marvin, who has long assumed the role of my protective big brother, continues to berate me for what he considers to be my utter disregard for personal safety and my lack of communication for several months: 'I didn't realise how much I care about you until the silence, young lady. I imagined a bunch of scenarios, ranging from you being kidnapped to you being beaten and robbed!'

I promise to be more careful and to write more frequently.

* * * * *

'This feels a lot more "normal" than San Quentin,' I observe, looking around Marvin's visiting room.

In the San Quentin visiting room, there were vending machines and microwaves as well, but visitors and inmates couldn't wander freely. There were eight visitors' cages in the room, each with a door at both ends and a table and chairs in the middle. When James's girlfriend Marlene and I got the coffee, the burgers, the cookies and the fruit, one of the prison guards led us to the allocated cage, let us in, and locked the door behind us. Then James – wiry, 5ft 8, goateed, wearing thick glasses – was led in, his hands cuffed behind his back. He walked in through the opposite door, put his hands through the slot behind him, and was uncuffed for the duration of the visit. Both doors were then locked.

'It's a security thing,' James explained. 'Before, we used to be able to walk around. No cages. But some of the guys would take their girlfriends into the bathroom... ' ... thereby getting around the prohibition on conjugal visits, I finished in my head.

James was not good-looking at first sight, with a scar on his forehead and pockmarks from old acne, but as soon as he began to speak, his face became very animated and his grin was truly infectious. He'd lost an eye in a motorcycle accident when he was my age, and his artificial eye remained still, while the other one darted around, giving his face a permanently quizzical expression. His handshake and hug were strong.

A strange sense of domesticity reigned in the cages. A family was playing cards in the largest one. An old-timer was tenderly kissing her husband in another. The kiss was marginally too long and they had to be careful not to attract unfavourable attention from the guards (you're allowed a hug and kiss at the beginning and end of each visit). The couple in the adjacent cage were having an argument, which was eventually diffused by their seven-year-old son asking them not to fight. The father then taught him how to box; picked him up, threw him in the air, called him 'Puppy'. In the cage next to ours, Stanley

'Tookie' Williams – the founder of the Crips gang, soon to be executed by the then Governor of California Arnold Schwarzenegger – was engrossed in conversation with a middle-aged woman. 'His long-term partner,' Marlene confirmed.

* * * * *

'They wanted to change things here as well,' Marvin says. 'Put an end to contact visits. "Security concerns," they said.'

'Yeah, that's the reason they give in Pennsylvania.' When I went to visit Rasheed at SCI Greene, Shawn and I sat in a cubicle separated from him by plexiglass that was punched with holes for us to talk though. Rasheed sat there, wearing a bright orange jumpsuit and glasses, with his hands cuffed in front of him, despite the fact that he was securely locked in his cubicle. When he smiled, his boyish face reminded me very much of one of my school friends. There was no possibility of buying him food and he hadn't hugged any member of his family in over a decade.

Marvin agrees that contact-free visits are inhumane. And clearly, the 'security concern' is nonsense, since some prisons are perfectly capable of arranging contact visits.

'For us, visits are the most important privilege. Everyone goes out of their way to preserve it. We staged a mass hunger strike in protest.'

'Have you seen your family recently?'
Marvin shakes his head. His parents live in Georgia, and though he's very close to his mother and sister, most relationships feel the strain over the years, and for them, it's quite a journey to come down to Florida.

'How about your girls?'

'Saw my youngest recently. She's grown so much, is studying hard. Until Easter, I hadn't seen them in four years. My wife couldn't face me.'

When Marvin was first arrested, his wife told him that she'd stand by him, but his incarceration proved too much for her. She was left alone with two young children, and after several years, she served Marvin with divorce papers and married another man. Marvin finds it difficult to forgive her. He takes 'till death do us part' very seriously. A divorce, he maintains, is a sign that the couple simply didn't try hard enough.

I'm more sympathetic when it comes to Marvin's wife's situation. It takes considerable perseverance to maintain family relationships with someone on death row, especially if the prison is some distance away.

Marvin is not the only one with kids. Rasheed has a son, and his son's mother brings the boy to see his dad as often as time allows. 'I always told her that if worst came to worst I would understand if she could no longer wait for me… but when I was finally arrested, she made it her business to let me know that she would not leave me stranded.' Rasheed's wife, also a teenager at the time, made sure that Rasheed and his son had a bond. 'My son was only six months old when I came to jail,' Rasheed wrote. 'He took his first steps in the visiting room!'

José, whom I never get to meet in person, also has a daughter. He became a father at the age of fifteen, and his daughter visits 'when she remembers she has a dad.' He's made peace with the fact that the parents of the two girls whom he'd raped and murdered want to witness his execution to achieve closure. 'If it was up to me, I'd be happy to spend the rest of my life behind bars, find some way to make it up to them… but I get it. I'm a dad too.'

As for Bill, he's estranged from his son and daughter. Their mother put up with Bill's incessant womanising when he was a free man, but she had one rule: be home before the kids wake up. And he couldn't even do that. Bill would show me a letter from his estranged daughter, who reached out to him after a decade of silence, in which she blamed him for being absent, for Mom having to work three jobs, for his not loving her and her brother enough to stay, and in the next breath he'd assert what a great father he'd been, unable to take responsibility for his own actions or to engage with his children's anger in any meaningful way.

'The helplessness is the worst thing,' Marvin confesses. He's distraught about his eldest daughter, who has moved out of the family home and hasn't come to see him in a long while.

'She's living with a guy, she quit her job in a department store and now she is a stripper, taking pills. She is destroying herself and her life. I feel I'm to blame, being where I am. She wouldn't have done it if I'd been there, daily. Physically. I hope to be able to speak to her, not to get on her case, but just to be her father. Be supportive.'

'What about your friends?'

'I used to think I had lots of friends, but they disappeared over time. Would I forgive them if I had my freedom once more and if they apologised for abandoning me? Yes. Would I want them in my life? Not really.'

I myself have wondered whether my own friends would stick by me and visit me if I were incarcerated for many years.

'Some would,' my mentor Jolyon assured me. 'At least for a while.'

But the long haul is a lot to ask of anyone.

* * * * *

Towards the end of the visit, I broach the subject of Marvin's case. Since all prison mail is opened and read by mailroom staff, and Marvin's letters can be used against him, I've waited to speak to him in person. I know the bare bones. Marvin quit the navy to spend more time with his wife and kids in Jacksonville, Florida. A used car dealer sold his wife a shoddy car. Marvin went to return it and the two men got into an argument.

'He started threatening me with a gun. He didn't know I was armed too. I was scared, Anna. I'm sitting in a corner of a room, with this armed man going off. I wasn't going to let him harm me. I defended myself and no one can tell me I didn't have the right to do so.'

Marvin shot and wounded the dealer. In a panic – he'd never shot anyone before – he ran into the bathroom in the dark warehouse and was startled by someone emerging from a stall. The car dealer's daughter. His gun was still in his hand. He shot, reflexively. Later, she died in hospital.

Marvin swallows, hard. It's clearly difficult for him to talk about it. He looks away when I notice his eyes tearing up.

'Out of fear, panic and surprise I took an innocent person's life… *My* actions caused her death. I committed an act which I cannot make restitution on. This is what I have to live with for the rest of my life.'

The dealer shot at Marvin when Marvin returned to call an ambulance. Missed. Marvin got in his car. Drove around in circles for hours, then turned himself in to the police.

During the trial, the dealer portrayed Marvin as a potential robber and killer.

'I told the truth. He lied!' Marvin's face is animated. 'I'm black… he's white… the deceased victim is white… The jury believed the lying white person. And my lawyer presented very little mitigating evidence on my behalf.'

It's clear to me that it was manslaughter, but the all-white jury saw it as murder. Worse: as aggravated murder with robbery as the motive. Even though Marvin stole nothing from the warehouse. His lawyer could have called on numerous witnesses to confirm Marvin's absence of a criminal record, good character, could have cited his exemplary career in the navy. But he didn't. The jury was split on whether to sentence Marvin to death or life without parole, so the judge made the decision to impose a death sentence. Florida is one of few states where a hung jury can be overruled by the judge.

It's extremely difficult to reverse a conviction. Now all Marvin can do is wait, while his lawyer appeals the verdict. But he doesn't think it'll do any good. 'It's not about justice… as long as somebody is assigned blame.'

Marvin doesn't believe that he'll ever set foot outside these prison walls, but is determined to live out the rest of his days on the inside with as much dignity and self-respect as he can muster.

'I put in a lot of effort to remain who I am and to hold on to the humanity, compassion, love, respect and conscience which have been instilled in me.'

A guard comes over with a Polaroid camera and we pose for photos. The end of visiting time draws near. Marvin thanks me for coming to see him.

'The time just flew by as *you* talked non-stop,' he kids. I am enveloped in a long, bone-crushing hug, and then he is gone. As I move through the throng of orange-clad men exchanging long embraces with their families, I am struck by the tenderness and the humanity of the moment. Then I step back out into Florida's clammy heat.

EYEBALL TACOS AND KANGAROO STEW

* * * * *

In May 2005, Forrest lands himself in jail again. I decide to fly back to the States to try and help him and get stopped by an immigration official in Cincinnati.

'You've been coming to the States a lot,' he tells me. 'What is the purpose of your visit?'

'Tourism,' I tell him, figuring that it's probably unwise to mention that I'm returning to help a drug addict. But it's my second visit in one year, and the immigration official looks dissatisfied.

He goes through my luggage. He reads my journal in which I scribble down my innermost thoughts. My face burns as my privacy is violated by this boorish man. Prior to stopping me, he loudly told a weeping woman in a chador: 'Sorry ma'am, I don't speak Iranian.' Iranian!

He finally finds a copy of financial guru Suze Orman's *Money Book for the Young, Fabulous & Broke* in my bag. Apparently, the possession of this book suggests that I'm a penniless burden on America, rather than that I'm trying to learn good money management skills after accruing student loan debt. He then flicks through my day-to-day diary and finds that I've scribbled down several shifts I'd done in a hostel in San Diego. The smoking gun. I try to explain that I wasn't even staying at the hostel, that I was staying with a friend, and that I helped out for free, in order to hang out with other young travellers. 'Well, it's still work,' he tells me. 'You needed a volunteer visa for that.' Blood drains from my face as he and his colleague inform me that I may not enter the United States.

I'm then unceremoniously put on the first plane back to London, noting that there's a satisfyingly grim symmetry to it all. The airport that welcomed my family to the United States fifteen years earlier is the same airport that turfs me out of the country. Ironically, for working for free in a youth hostel, rather than fraternising with condemned criminals and drug addicts. I'm fingerprinted like a criminal myself, and an airport security official accompanies me to the bathroom and lurks outside my stall, just in case I decide to do a runner through the window. I return to London, convinced that my life is over. The Forrest saga doesn't stop there, though. It just migrates south of the border. It will take several more years of broken promises, terse phone calls, emotional exhaustion and disappearances before I'm able to admit that I cannot help him, and cut him loose for good.

Death row correspondence doesn't always run smoothly, either. I sometimes feel smothered by Marvin's protectiveness, and bristle at what comes across as condescension. We also bump heads over the issues of gun ownership. He's very much pro-guns, he owned guns to protect his family, and he is unable to acknowledge that if it hadn't been for guns, then he and the car dealership owner would have engaged in good, old-fashioned fisticuffs and then gone home. The young woman would still be alive and Marvin would be a free man.

Bill Clark and I fall out, irrevocably. It's not due to his prison lothario schtick – having numerous women pen pals and trying to encourage them to break prison rules to provide him with physical relief. Luckily, I'd only ever met him behind plexiglass and was never in a position to do anything truly regrettable. It's not even the fact that the tasteful headless nudes of myself that I've sent him, at his pleading request, wind up circulating among his fellow San Quentin inmates for a fee (though I'm not pleased when I find out). It's just that I discover my red line. And it's this: I would rather correspond with a man who's committed a grave crime, has come to terms with it and who strives to improve himself and atone for it, than with someone who hasn't killed anyone but who cannot be trusted and is utterly incapable of positive change.

But before Bill exits my life for good, he does two things. He introduces me to another inmate, Paul, destined to become a lifelong friend. And he indirectly lands me right in the middle of a high-profile federal murder case.

CHAPTER 2
ON TRIAL

'My friend David is looking for a Russian translator to help him out in Odessa, Ukraine. I can put you guys in touch if you like,' constitutional lawyer Stephen Rohde tells me as I sit in his office in LA and pore over Bill Clark's trial transcript. Stephen also writes to Bill, and Bill introduced us. Since Stephen is too busy with casework to leave LA, he asked me to do him a favour. He organised that I, acting as a de facto paralegal, should have a more private visit with Bill, reporting back on Bill's case proceedings and state of mind – sensitive subjects that are impossible to talk about under normal visitation conditions. *Some people do this for a living?* Fresh out of university and with the rest of my life a blank slate in front of me, an idea forms in my head that I'd quite like to visit prisons and help lawyers represent their clients. But how does one get into this?

A week after my visit to Stephen's office, I'm picked up at LA's Greyhound bus station by David Evans – a cheerful, bearded, bespectacled attorney-at-law in his fifties to whom I take instantly. I'm wearing the only formal attire I own, to try and make a good impression – a pinstripe suit from Bangkok, plus kitten heels that keep falling off my feet. I'm not used to wearing heels. The one and only time I'd worn heels to a wedding, my friends dubbed me 'Bambi on ice'. David doesn't seem to mind. Over the clatter of dim sum trolleys and the din of fellow diners in LA's Chinatown, he asks me questions about myself, jumping rapidly from subject to subject. I answer the best I can.

Yes, Russian is my mother tongue. Yes, I have Ukrainian roots on both sides. While my immediate family is Moscow-born, all my grandparents are Ukrainian Jews, hailing from Kobelyaky, Berdychiv, Chernobyl. Yes, although I was only eight years old when my family emigrated to the West, I have vivid memories of life in Soviet times, which could be helpful. And yes, I've been to Odessa. It was the first place I'd ever travelled to; at the ages of three and five, I accompanied my father to summer physics conferences there. Death row pen pals? Yes. My grandmother was a lawyer in the USSR; I'm considering a career in criminal law and I wanted to learn about America's death row from those on the inside.

David seems satisfied with that.

'So what's the job?' I probe.

'It's a high-profile federal death case. Two ringleaders, plus several others, have been kidnapping wealthy businesspeople, extorting money from them and then killing them. My client, who's from Odessa, is accused of having assisted them. He swears he's innocent.'

'Our job is to find out what really happened,' David continues. 'To interview family members and anyone else who'd known him. To try and understand how Petro Krylov might have ended up in that situation, and to persuade the jury that his life should be spared.'

Detective work, a chance to be useful, plus the possibility of saving a potentially innocent man's life? I'm in.

* * * * *

Shura's hands flutter nervously, like startled birds, as she bustles around the small kitchen, insisting on topping up our bowls with homemade borscht and sour cream, slicing bread, and refreshing the platter of open-faced sandwiches.

The kitchen is rather crowded. There are four of us there, making up the legal team: me – an interpreter; David Evans, the attorney-at-law; Scharlette Holdman, the mitigation specialist; and Natasha Khazanov, a psychologist, originally from St Petersburg.

The mother of our client is a stooped, anxious-looking woman with hennaed hair in a ponytail, and blue eyes that keep tearing up. Petro's entire nuclear family is there, too: Andrei, the father, with a florid face and a glint of Soviet gold dental work when he talks; Maria, the portly, quiet grandmother, and younger sister Anya, a slender, wary young blonde woman my age who snaps at Andrei for trying to speak English, fearing that he will miscommunicate what he is trying to say.

Scharlette gets me to translate our objectives: 'We'd like the jury to "be in your kitchen", to see Petro through your eyes.' Earlier, she instructed me to translate everything as literally as possible, because she picks up different things from what people say and a summary does not suffice. 'We cannot assume anything,' she taught me. 'We must abandon logic and not try to explain a family's circumstances through our own interpretation.' So I do my best.

Scharlette goes on to tell them that we would like to get to know who Petro really was, through their stories.

'Do you have any questions?'

They do, of course. Three years back, Petro dropped off the radar. The news finally came in confusing, frightening fragments. Arrested. Five murders. Until David took over as Petro's counsel, Petro wasn't even able to call his family.

'One day, there's a call out of the blue,' Shura tells us, looking at David with gratitude. 'Andrei picked up. "Hello, this is Petro." "Petro?

Petro who?" "Petro, your son." Andrei was overcome with emotion. He just froze. He couldn't speak.'

David and Scharlette fill the family in on the case, while Natasha and I translate.

In 2001 and 2002, five people – all prominent members of the Russian diaspora – were kidnapped for ransom in LA. Their relatives were extorted for considerable sums of money, but no matter how cooperative they were or how much ransom was paid, the victims were strangled, their bodies dumped in a reservoir near Yosemite National Park. The kidnappings and murders were masterminded by two businessmen from San Fernando Valley, LA – Iouri Mikhel and Jurijus Kadamovas, both of them immigrants from the former USSR. They wanted to amass $50 million before abandoning their extortion and killing spree. Petro, along with several others, is accused of having helped them. His fingerprints had been found on some plastic ties used to strangle one of the victims.

Natasha addresses the family in her measured, calm voice, explaining how the American justice system works. How the lesser co-defendants were given the option of testifying against everyone else involved in exchange for five-year sentences and life under the Witness Protection Program afterwards. Petro refused the offer, not least because his family in Odessa received an anonymous phone call after his arrest. The two ringleaders were mixed up with the Russian mafia, and he was under no illusions about what might happen to his family if he talked. The Russian mafia has longer arms than American law enforcement. Petro maintains his innocence, but the prosecution want to try him alongside the ringleaders, in which case the worst-case outcome would be the death penalty.

Shura and Maria cry quietly. Anya looks intensely angry. Andrei is silent, but his eyes are bloodshot. They all seem shell-shocked.

'How did he get involved with such people? Was it so that he could pay for my cataracts operation?' Shura is distraught. Petro used to wire money back home, to help his family. Scharlette assures her that she is not the cause of Petro's misfortune.

'We just can't believe it. It still seems like a bad dream,' the grandmother speaks up. 'Petro is not capable of committing a bad deed. He was always such a kind boy, always helping others.'

'We will do what we can to save Petro,' David promises them, and little by little, the family begins to look somewhat reassured.

To lighten the mood, Scharlette asks if they have any old family photos we could look through. They do, and I get my first glimpse of our client: an ordinary-looking young man with brown hair in a crew cut, and an open, friendly, guileless face. There's Petro as a boy, with his arms around infant Anya ('such a good big brother, protective, loving'); Petro wearing a cadet uniform, graduating from Odessa's naval academy; Petro at family gatherings; Petro in a smart suit, with his arm draped over the shoulders of a striking blonde woman in a wedding dress ('so happy, marrying Natalie', 'loved her so much', 'so many good friends', 'such a wonderful wedding'); Petro sitting on the couch in LA, with his newborn daughter in his arms, smiling at the camera. (Later, during the trial, the prosecutor would use that very photo to try and portray Petro as a heartless criminal, saying: 'Look at him. Five people have been murdered, and he's grinning.')

'He fell in love with a local girl here, Natalie,' Shura tells us. 'They got married. Then her parents emigrated to California. She went as well, of course. You don't pass up an opportunity like that. So Petro decided to follow her to America.'

She dabs at her eyes with a handkerchief.

'I tried to dissuade him – tried to tell him that there are plenty of other girls here, but he wouldn't listen. "Mama, I love Natalie and can't live without her," he'd tell me. "There is no other woman for me."' Guilt is weighing heavily on Shura. She's convinced that if only she'd been persuasive enough, then Petro would be here in Odessa, instead of in prison in California. It's weighing on Andrei, too, who sees America as a cruel, heartless and materialistic place, where it's every man for himself. A country that takes immigrants like his son, takes advantage of their trusting nature, chews them up and spits them out. Petro was unprepared, he tells us, whereas he, Andrei, much more worldly than Petro, could have protected his boy, if only he'd been in America with him.

They are deeply familiar to me, all those 'if onlys'. Taking responsibility for things entirely out of one's control, and punishing yourself for them, because in some ways, that's easier than admitting to yourself that you have absolutely no control over the chaos of the universe or calamities that befall your loved ones.

The Krylovs' own story is a rather commonplace one. When the Soviet Union collapsed in 1991, and Ukraine became an independent country, they lost everything, like so many others. Roubles became worthless paper, and Maria saw her pension and savings go up in smoke. She went back to work, while Shura and her sisters, Olga and Valentina, travelled to Poland and brought back household goods to sell. Andrei didn't go; he felt defeated and ashamed about being unable to provide for his family. Straight out of the naval academy, Petro helped out; he and a friend started a business, selling car parts at a local auto market.

But then Petro went to the States on a temporary study visa in the late 1990s. 'He went to LA first,' Andrei contributes. 'Then the next thing we know, Petro's in New York, telling us that there's no work in LA, that he's going to stay in New York and find work there.'

We make plans to meet up with various family members in the days to come. In turn, they promise to dig up more photos and documents, and to think of more stories that could be helpful to our cause.

* * * * *

The culture of hospitality is strong in Ukraine; it's inconceivable that a guest should go hungry, so much of our time doing interviews in Odessa revolves around being fed while talking to our client's family. In the days that follow, we split up into two teams to interview various relatives in their homes, or chase up relevant documents. We interview Olga and Valentina (Shura's sisters, Petro's aunts) and Petro the elder (Shura's brother) – all middle-aged, with kindly faces, anxious, solicitous of one another and of their sister. The string of cousins – Natasha, Larisa, Pasha, Roma – all young professionals in their twenties. Two of Petro's school friends. Other assorted relatives.

Our leisurely dinners as a team are an opportunity to debrief, to share what we've learned that day, to bounce ideas off one another, and to figure out what leads to chase up next. For me, it's also an opportunity to get to know the team members, sometimes together, sometimes one-on-one. All of them are fifty-something professionals of many years, at the height of their respective careers, whereas I'm a 24-year-old nobody barely out of university. I am honoured that they feel I have something to bring to the table.

Scharlette's reputation precedes her. On a reading list he gave me before the Odessa gig, David included *Among the Lowest of the Dead* by David Von Drehle, about capital punishment in the

United States, so I could get to know more about her. She is formidable. An anthropologist by training, the director of a tiny NGO and a self-taught expert in criminal law, Scharlette spent a dozen years or so in Florida from the mid-70s onwards, fighting the executions of condemned men and women on Florida's death row by rounding up lawyers at the eleventh hour for last-minute appeals. Capital punishment in the States being what it is, the condemned would overwhelmingly fall into economically marginalised, ethnic minority groups, unable to afford a lawyer. In America, the quality of justice often boils down to what you can afford. Just ask O J Simpson or Michael Jackson. Inmates assigned legal representation pro bono often found themselves with absolutely shocking lawyers – turning up to the trial drunk or unprepared, calling no witnesses, presenting no evidence and generally doing practically no work on behalf of their clients. Dubbed the 'Mistress of Delay' and the 'Angel of Death Row', Scharlette managed to scandalize the Florida Bar Association sufficiently for much-needed reform to take place, and death row inmates gained proper legal representation at least at the appeals stage, after they'd already been convicted. In time, the practice of presenting mitigating evidence on the behalf of the accused has become the gold standard in capital punishment cases across the States.

I'm fascinated by how Scharlette's discipline – mitigation specialist – combines detective work (gathering documents, inferring things from clues) with deep dives into the human psyche, and even some cloak-and-dagger action. You become part-psychologist, part-archivist, part-social worker, part-detective. You aim to explain, rather than excuse. To show that the perpetrator is a deeply flawed human being, but a human being none the less.

Given the sheer scale of her achievements, when she emerges from the airport alongside David, I find it difficult to recognise the defender of some of the biggest monsters in the American imagination in this short, plump, down-to-earth woman with glasses, mop of dark blonde hair and uproarious laugh. She'd represented the likes of the Unabomber, and Jared Loughner – the mass murderer who targeted Democratic Representative Gabrielle Giffords – Eric Rudolph, who bombed the Atlanta Olympics, and Khalid Sheikh Mohammed, one of the architects of 9/11. Petro is small fry in comparison to her more notorious clients. She's here as a favour to David, an old friend.

Still, I'm rather shy around her. But Scharlette has a knack of putting people at ease that transcends language barriers – something that I come to witness countless times in her interactions with the Krylovs. And it's hard to feel intimidated for long by someone who needs my help in shopping for oversized T-shirts and underwear at Privoz, Odessa's massive market, because her luggage has gone AWOL en route. Scharlette is very expressive in her use of mime, and the sellers love her, gathering around to watch the spectacle of her trying on clothes.

* * * * *

'So what did you make of the Krylovs?' Scharlette eyes me expectantly.

I share my initial impressions. They seem to be loving, close-knit, yet traumatised. (Nods all around in agreement.) Anya seems distrustful of us, much more so than the mother, father and grandmother. (More nodding.) They're trying very hard to be helpful. 'Yes,' interjects Scharlette. 'Unusually so, in our line of work.

It normally takes much longer to earn the family's trust, and few of our clients in the States have such a ready collection of documents – photos, proof of employment.'

I tell the team that visiting Petro's parents is like stepping into a time warp. The nine-storey apartment block – a typical 80s construction – is graffitied on the outside, and inside, the stairwell smells exactly like the one in the apartment building I spent my childhood in – of stale cigarette smoke and garbage. The elevator is tiny, dimly lit, and often out of order. The apartment itself is an exact configuration of the one my family lived in: three rooms, tiny bathroom, equally tiny toilet, and the kitchen that's at the heart of the Krylovs' social life.

'I don't know how familiar you are with Soviet architecture,' – I aim this at Scharlette and David, since Natasha is ex-Soviet, like myself – 'but this is actually a pretty comfortable set-up by Soviet standards.' Soviet housing could be divided roughly into three categories. Firstly, well-constructed pre-Revolution apartments, confiscated from nobility and turned into communal flats, with a room allocated per family (and woe betide you if you had to share the bathroom and kitchen with slovenly or racist neighbours). My mother grew up in such an apartment. Then there were the *Khrushchevki* (1960s apartment blocks named after Khrushchev) – low-cost concrete blocks with paper-thin walls and no elevators (but at least each family got their own apartment). And finally, there were apartment blocks like mine and the Krylovs'.

What I don't tell the team is that Andrei sparks emotional turmoil in me – more so than the familiar surroundings and home-cooked food. He calls me 'Annushka', an affectionate diminutive of 'Anna', just like my father, which makes me flinch, and arouses in me a mix of sympathy, apprehension and raised hackles. He strikes me as someone quite volatile and quick to anger, and I'm not sure why. I convey that hunch to the team, and they make a note to ask the parents and grandmother about whether they disciplined their kids.

'It doesn't sound like Natalie treated Petro very well,' I speak up. 'She basically left her husband when a more attractive economic opportunity presented itself.'

Scharlette, who's met Natalie in California, doesn't think much of her, either: 'When Petro followed her to LA, she turned him away. "You don't have a green card, you don't have any money, what use are you to me?" she told him.'

And so Petro went to New York, lived in someone's dank basement, and washed and repaired cars for a couple of years, saved money, applied for a green card, and then presented himself to Natalie again. This time she was willing to accept him, now that he'd proved himself to be a competent money earner. In LA, he worked all hours to provide for his wife and young daughter, and for relatives back home. Natalie has visited Petro in jail, which has surprised Scharlette, who expected her to dump him like radioactive waste as soon as he found himself in trouble.

'How did he cross paths with Mikhel and Kadamovas?' I ask.

'He started working with electronics, installing stereo systems in people's houses,' David fills me in. 'The two of them were his customers. Some relative of Natalie's introduced Petro to them.'

I judge Natalie. It's inconceivable to me how someone can be so motivated by material wealth. But then, while I have Soviet roots, I clearly lack the mentality required to survive in post-Soviet Ukraine. I speak the language, but I'm a stranger here.

* * * * *

Londonskaya Hotel – our base in Odessa – is worlds away from the Krylovs' apartment block. It's all nineteenth-century opulence, chandeliers, grand staircase and mile-high ceilings in plush, enormous rooms. Out front is the pedestrian Primorsky Boulevard, lined with stately beeches. Below it is the port. Around the corner from the Londonskaya is the striking Opera House, while the boulevard itself is bookended by the columned Archaeological Museum and the equally stately Vorontsov Palace. Pedestrianised, cobbled Deribasovskaya Street, a short stroll away, features some of the most expensive shops in town.

One Sunday lunchtime, we nab our favourite outdoor dining spot at Boulevard, an old-school restaurant with a fantastic view of the boulevard and some of Odessa's most photographed spots. Directly across from us are the famous Potemkin Stairs, as seen in the 1925 film *Battleship Potemkin*, designed as an optical illusion. If you look down from the top, the stairs look as though they are the same width all the way down. They are overlooked by the statue of the Duke of Richelieu, the first governor of the city. He is clutching a scroll in his left hand. 'Posmotri na duka s liuka' ('Look at the duke from the manhole cover') I'm told by locals, and I do, as does Scharlette. From that angle, it looks like the duke is holding something more personal, and Scharlette cackles appreciatively. In the evenings, seemingly half of Odessa turns out to promenade along the boulevard, while during the day, and particularly on weekends, it's the brides' turn. Primorsky Boulevard is the hot and happening spot for wedding parties, and during our lunch we count four brides with entourages in one hour, each pausing with her beloved for her fifteen minutes of fame by the statue and the Potemkin Stairs.

Local girls and guys are not the only clients of the 'wedding palace' (the city register office) opposite the Opera House. Odessa is Ukraine's most popular destination for foreign men in search of brides. Walking around, we've seen banners in English advertising matchmaking services: 'Bring love into your heart and warmth into your home.' There are apartments for rent so that prospective husbands can 'get to know' their brides-to-be. David and Scharlette are also quick to spot the bored-looking, attractive young women who sit in our hotel lobby in the evenings, dressed to the nines and staring at their mobile phones. Working girls, or perhaps women hoping for a love connection with a foreign guest, for a way out.

Wondering what sort of Western man goes bride-hunting in Odessa, I get my answer in the shape of forty-year-old Gary, a mechanic from Cornwall, who talks at me while I photocopy documents at the hotel's business centre. Not much of a hit with the ladies back home, he's gone out on several dates here, using an interpreter, and is discovering that conversation topics like dirt-bike racing and fishing do not titillate his potential life companions. When I tell Andrei and Petro the Elder about him, they both tell me that he should aim his sights lower – at an older woman with a child. 'The young women here – they're looking to marry someone wealthy and handsome, to go live in California or New York.'

I report back on the previous night's outing. David and Scharlette had decided that I'd be the best person to bond with Anya, and so I ended up attending a Philipp Kirkorov concert with her in order to get to know her away from her family.

She and I met in the garden of our hotel. I could tell by her surreptitiously looking around, wide-eyed, that no one had ever taken her out for a cappuccino in a fancy café before, but I'm the one who looks and feels like a fish out of water. I'm wearing that same pinstripe suit and kitten heels that I'd worn to impress David, and holding a Fendi clutch that Natasha had loaned me (because every self-respecting female here owns a handbag, and Natasha is by far the most well groomed and stylish of us all). 'I can help you pick out some clothes, if you like,' Anya offered, eyeing me critically. It was my second makeover offer. 'You dress like a lesbian,' Natasha commented a few days back, referring to my usual jeans and T-shirt get-up. 'Come to San Francisco, sweetie; I'll take you shopping.' 'We can use you as bait to attract more lesbians to our cause,' Scharlette chimed in. 'We can be choosy. "We only want lesbians with PhDs!"'

Anya also offered to teach me to apply make-up. 'Don't ask your friends to do it: they'll give you bad advice because they don't want you looking better than them.' I was taken aback by her cynicism. My experience of female friendships has been a deep and supportive one rather than death-by-a-thousand-cuts hostility masquerading as kinship.

When I commented on the endless procession of brides along Primorsky Boulevard and how young they look, Anya told me she got married at the age of twenty. 'It's hard to get married when you're older. No one wants you when you're no longer beautiful.' Career prospects? Anya doesn't work. 'I did a university degree in sociology but I haven't applied to work as a sociologist because the pay is so bad. It wouldn't even cover groceries; just bus fare to and from work.' So she cooks, keeps the house, and washes her husband's clothes whenever he's home. He's a long-distance truck driver and works very hard to make ends meet. She's twenty-three, a year younger than me, but seems a lot older, with a mix of pragmatism and world-weary acceptance that lurks beneath the fragile veneer of defiance.

The Kirkorov concert was a welcome escape. The parade of colourful costumes and acrobatics of the backing dancers, the baritone and powerful stage presence of Philipp, the bad boy of Russian pop music. In an unguarded moment, Anya's face was rapt with wonder, and she looked awfully young. There was none of the heavy security that you get during gigs back home; at one point, Philipp walked right past us, and accepted bouquets of flowers from a bevy of local beauties. During the intermission, Anya whispered to me: 'Do they beat Petro in jail?' I assured her that they did not, and she seemed relieved.

When we looked for a taxi afterwards, Anya told me that we shouldn't wait by the kerb, lest we be mistaken for hookers, and expertly steered me clear of a drunk. She finally trusted me enough to invite me to the unfinished house that Andrei was helping to build 'for when Petro comes back home', where she and her husband were staying while their apartment was being renovated. It was sparsely furnished yet immaculately kept, and she fed me the best salted herring, new potatoes, sliced baby cucumbers and tomatoes of my life. I tried to convey to her, without explicitly saying so, that making the most of humble circumstances is nothing to be ashamed of, that her brother's troubles do not reflect badly on their family any more than some random act of God would, but it's clear that 'What will people think?' is a refrain that haunts this close-knit, loving family.

'We don't socialise with our friends anymore,' her aunt Olga – Shura's sister – told us. 'We can't lie to people, and we worry that our friends would turn away from us if we tell them the truth about what happened to Petro.'

Back at Boulevard, we express sympathy with the Krylovs, who've grown up within a culture of such secrecy and mistrust that they only have each other for support. Natasha contributes that the Krylovs are by no means unique in that respect: that a Soviet upbringing often meant that you didn't know whom you could confide in, and I nod.

That was my parents' and grandparents' experience too. I've never met Petro, and while at first I felt that he'd ruined his life in pursuit of a selfish, materialistic woman, by the end of our trip, my outlook is more nuanced. While I'm a sucker for grand gestures (and what could be more grand than crossing the world for someone you love?), another way of looking at it is that Petro was driven by a desperate desire to please, and that no one forced him to sacrifice his dignity in pursuit of someone who rejected him on pecuniary grounds. And I feel sympathy for Natalie as well, for her aspirations to a life less ordinary, and her desire to escape what was likely to have been a hard, thankless existence in Ukraine, dependent on her husband, just like generations of women before her.

'Time for another bride!' declares Scharlette, snapping me out of my reverie, and we all turn to watch yet another young woman in white strike a pose at the top of the Potemkin Stairs with her man.

* * * * *

When we are not actively interviewing Petro's family and friends, I'm busy filing photos and typing up legal documents, or else we are exploring the metropolis. The defence team needs to get a real feel for Odessa to be able to convey Petro's roots to the jury. And Odessa is a remarkable city, with a unique place in the Russian Empire: an eighteenth-century naval base and trading centre founded by Empress Catherine the Great on lands conquered from the Ottoman Empire; one of the main powder kegs during the Revolution of 1905; a haven for dozens of nationalities and ethnicities; a city of literature and learning; the USSR's most important trading port; and a prime beach vacation spot on the Black Sea.

Our driver, Stas, takes us all over the city – past the port, to the trendy Arkadia beach, packed cheek by jowl with sunbathing bodies, and to the Seventh Kilometre, one of the largest flea markets in Europe. One morning, we drive down to Zatoka, a small holiday resort on the Black Sea, in order to chat to the parents, grandmother and aunts Olga and Valentina in informal, relaxed surroundings. Camp Albatross is a typical holiday camp consisting of bungalows and wooden huts by the sea. While Stas builds a campfire and gets down to the serious business of grilling *shashlik* (plump cubes of spiced pork, mutton and sturgeon, speared on metal skewers), Andrei shows us around. He hasn't been here for some time. Andrei was in charge of Camp Albatross before the Soviet Union collapsed. He set it up with running water, developed it, poured years of hard work into it. He's recognised by an old man; the man's shirt is unbuttoned and great scars on his chest mark him as a survivor of a Stalinist gulag. He asks Andrei about Petro, and Andrei makes vague excuses about how his son is too busy trying to make it in America to come visit.

Andrei tells David his life story – how he'd sailed around the world while in the navy, been at the heart of Communist politics, kept state secrets, bounced back after doctors left him for dead after a serious car accident. He's proud of the athletic achievements of his youth, of being well educated and widely read. He's a survivor. Yet he lost it all when he lost his summer camp.

'Thank you for listening to me… to my life story that's of no interest to anyone,' he says, and we assure him that his story is very interesting. I really feel for this stooped, middle-aged man with bloodshot eyes, because life has dealt him some huge blows. He's a decent person. But at the same time, I wonder how many of his life's disappointments he'd taken out on his sensitive, eager-to-please son. We've already heard about Andrei's explosive temper from Shura and Maria. In response to questions about disciplining the kids, he tells us that he took on board his own father's belief that 'one beaten kid is worth ten unbeaten ones', and used corporal punishment to raise Petro to be 'a real man', to make him tough enough to survive this world. Weak men grow up to be 'faggots', 'trannies' and 'other degenerates', according to Andrei. He means well but potentially ended up scarring his child. When Scharlette asks him what, in his opinion, is Petro's greatest strength, Andrei can't think of anything to say.

* * * * *

Scharlette, Shura and I walk to Petro's old school to interview his former teachers. They confirm that he was merely an average student, typically turning in work that earned him 3s and 4s (Cs and Bs). Back at Shura and Andrei's, Andrei tells us that he was often disappointed in Petro's academic performance, he and Shura having been straight-A students in their youth. I wince in sympathy. I'd spent two years in a Soviet school before my family emigrated, and I also brought home the occasional 3. Bright but too lazy to put much effort into something I found tedious, I was equally a disappointment to my parents, both academic overachievers.

I tell the defence team how when I was eight years old, my teacher hauled me up in front of the class, my face burning, while she criticised everything about me, from the quality of my homework and handwriting to my personality and upbringing. Public shaming was believed to be a good incentive to encourage children to work harder. You know how in American movies, parents say to their kids: 'Honey, I'm so proud of you!' As adults, my childhood friend Nikolai and

I would exchange bitter conspiratorial chuckles at the very notion. You would never, ever hear anything like that from a Soviet parent. I convey as much to David, Scharlette and Natasha, and they consider that perhaps Petro grew up with such a reinforced sense of personal inadequacy, and such a strong desire to please, that he'd assisted with the murders on his own initiative.

* * * * *

Fortified by yet more borscht with the freshest sour cream, and Shura's delicious honey cake, we are interviewing Maria and Shura. We've started filming the interviews. For the trial, the testimony will be translated and relevant sections will be shown to the jury.

Maria's life story is a harsh one. She was coerced by her family to marry a man she did not care for instead of the young man she was in love with. I think about my own maternal grandmother, and how she was in love with a young Bolshevik who broke her heart by marrying an army officer's daughter instead, in order to further his own military career. The Bolshevik sought out my grandmother years later, and begged her for forgiveness, but by that time she'd already married my grandfather, a childhood friend. In the end, Grandmother Esther dodged a bullet; her former Bolshevik love was executed during Stalin's purges of senior military figures. Marrying someone low-key was the safest bet, though sometimes even that didn't save you.

Tears roll down Maria's face as she remembers years of back-breaking work on a collective farm – the Stalinist endeavour that destroyed the USSR's agriculture for generations – then washing buses in winter, in order to secure a better pension, and learning that Petro had to wash cars in NYC.

'My grandson never said a bad word against me. He would tell off Anya when she was disrespectful towards me, mouthing off.'

'Did Petro ever get into trouble?'

Maria tells us how Petro used to steal cigarettes from home, pressured by older boys at school who threatened to beat him up otherwise. So he'd smuggle them out, and covered for the boys when caught. So Andrei's fear came true: Petro was a soft boy who could not stand up for himself.

'Was Petro punished for stealing?'

'Sometimes I would discipline him,' Maria confirms. 'Other times, I'd tell Andrei. He'd get the belt.'

Shura confirms that Andrei was harder on Petro. Anya is the father's favourite, whereas Petro was a mother's boy. 'He hated being beaten. He'd hide Andrei's belts, or cut them up with scissors.' For which he found himself in even more trouble.

* * * * *

The owners of Kumanets have clearly opted for the 'Ukrainian peasant' theme and decided to run with it a few miles. It's all brightly embroidered tablecloths, painted clay jars, waitresses in national costume and solid, hearty Ukrainian cooking. The dishes arrive: borscht with accompanying *pampushki* (fluffy, garlic-topped buns); sauerkraut and pickled garlic; *vareniki* (boiled dumplings) stuffed with potato, sour cherries or mushrooms; *golubtsy* (cooked cabbage leaves stuffed with meat and rice); bliny stuffed with meat, under a blanket of mushroom sauce; sliced fresh vegetables; dense, intensely fragrant rye bread; pitchers of *kvas* (mildly fermented bread drink). For Natasha and me, this is comfort food, beloved since childhood, and an unexpected bonus of this work trip. For David and Scharlette, it's their first proper taste of the dishes that our client has grown up with, and an important glimpse into Ukraine's culture, as far as they're concerned.

I had dropped Scharlette and David in the deep end on the morning of their arrival, when I took them to the questionably hygienic produce section of Privoz, Odessa's enormous, loud market. We were jostled and brushed aside by determined housewives wielding wicker baskets like battering rams, as they prodded, sampled, pinched and handled the food to determine which was freshest. They bargained loudly with the market sellers – impassive women, clad in colourful kerchiefs, sitting behind Soviet-era metal scales. The clamour and the smells of the meat hall on a hot summer's day sent us all reeling. Even I was a little overwhelmed. The sellers were quick to spot a dithering newbie, ignored my refusals, and I emerged clutching a stick of horse salami and a large bottle of kefir that I hadn't even known I wanted. My American companions seemed enchanted by the market – its hugeness, vitality and Eastern bazaar vibe.

Ukraine's cuisine is born out of its dark, nutrient-rich soil (*chernozyom*), the ebb and flow of its borders, and the often tumultuous relationship of Kievan Rus (a loose alliance of East Slavic and Uralic people from the ninth to the mid thirteenth century, which spanned much of present-day Ukraine, Baltic States and Western Russia) with its neighbours and conquerors: Poles, Lithuanians, Crimean Tatars, Mongolia's Golden Horde, the Ottoman Empire. Root vegetables reign supreme, with borscht – red borscht, green borscht, cold borscht – going back centuries, and the humble beetroot elevated to lofty heights. *Kholodets* (meat in aspic) was traditionally made after big feasts in Kievan Rus, with meat leftovers and bones collected, boiled down and made into a nourishing, meaty jelly. All Slavic nations have a national dumpling (Poles have *pierogi*, Russians have *pelmeni*), and *vareniki* is Ukraine's centuries-old contribution, a descendant of the even more ancient Turkish *dyush-vara*, a dumpling filled with mutton, fat and garlic. Ukrainians were not keen on mutton, so they substituted pork and other meats instead. Crimea's Cossacks created an entire cult devoted to *salo* (lard), present at our table in its salted, garlicky form. Dough for dumplings (and pancakes) can be made from flour from any of the country's grains – wheat, buckwheat, rye, barley – and you can tell which part of Ukraine someone is from by what fillings they favour. Ukrainian food is solid, dependable, hearty, peasant food. Food to get you through a siege.

We discuss Maria, and her work on a collective farm. She'd survived Holodomor – Ukraine's man-made famine of 1932–33. The Soviet policy of confiscating property from Ukraine's wealthiest and most productive peasants ('dekulakisation') and nationalising the land destroyed agricultural productivity and caused the starvation of up to twelve million Ukrainians during those two years. Punishment for stealing produce from the fields was death, and people ended up eating their pets, then the bark from the trees and, towards the end, the flesh of their own dead. Aside from my paternal grandfather, who was living in Moscow by then, all my grandparents lived through it as well, and never, ever discussed the famine with their children.

David reckons that Maria may be the monster in the family, due to her tough life, more so than volatile Andrei.

'He must've been really scared of those kids at school,' I muse. 'If he was prepared to defy both his grandmother and father.'

'I bet he helped to get rid of the bodies. Out of the best possible intentions, just like he covered for those boys at school,' Scharlette hypothesises.

Maybe he did it out of fear, I think, with Mikhel and Kadamovas replacing schoolyard bullies as the bogeymen of his life.

Or maybe he did it out of courage. Perhaps they threatened his wife and child, and he tried to protect them like he protected his family in Odessa.

I eat, and eat, and eat, until I'm barely able to move. There's a reason why I, like so many of us, seek comfort in stodge and carbs when under considerable emotional stress – as opposed to, say, a bucket of celery sticks. It's not just the primal reassurance received by my limbic brain that I will not starve to death, and it's not just that I find these flavours of my childhood familiar and soothing. I eat as if by ingesting the panacea of stuffed bliny, the sharp, sour cherries enveloped in their pockets of plump dough, followed by chocolate-covered lard for dessert, I can numb both the Krylovs' pain and that of Ukraine's collective memory.

Conversation turns darker. My pre-Odessa reading list primarily involved books on trauma in family settings, with titles such as *When a Child Kills*. There seems to be less abuse in the Krylov family than in those of most of Scharlette's and David's clients.

'Usually, when we encounter serious crime, you can guarantee that there is a history of domestic violence, substance abuse, child abuse,' Scharlette tells me. 'One of my clients – when he was little, his uncle would put him in a burlap sack and smoke him over a fire, like a ham.'

'Have you ever come across a case where there is no discernible reason as to why someone's committed a horrific crime?'

'No, never. What we usually find are cycles of trauma. A child gets abused and they pay it forward – inflicting damage on their own kids, who pass it on in turn.'

Scharlette firmly believes that monsters are made, not born.

She herself is very matter-of-fact about her own turbulent upbringing. How her violent bipolar father used to beat her, her sisters and her mother, how the local Baptist priest tried to exorcise her father's alcoholism, and how she, Scharlette, left home at the age of seventeen, after her father set the house on fire to 'punish' his family. She worked for the ACLU (American Civil Liberties Union), but before that, in the 1960s, Scharlette was a Freedom Rider.

'One time, I was locked up in a jail cell with some of the black men I was protesting alongside. "You love those n-----s so much," the sheriff told me, "you can stay with them."'

Scharlette was provided with a bucket, and to give her privacy, the men she was locked up with would form a circle around her and turn their backs whenever she needed the bathroom.

She hails from Memphis, Tennessee, and speaks with a wonderful Southern drawl that puts me in mind of grits, palmetto trees and sticky, balmy summers. Her father was a slumlord who rented primarily to African American tenants, and would take his four daughters along when it was time to collect the rent.

'He'd call it "going n-----ing", and got a real kick out of throwing them out if they couldn't pay up.'

Scharlette rebelled against the injustice of it, the fact that black kids were not allowed to attend her high school, that her mum refused to let their Mexican maids use any of the five bathrooms in their house, and would tell Scharlette off for speaking Spanish to them. But not all her sisters felt guilty that the family's fortune was built off the backs of black people.

'My younger sister got pregnant through a sperm donation from a KKK Grand Dragon, and gave birth to my niece, a really mean little girl.'

Needless to say, Scharlette and some members of her family aren't close. Years later, I come to wonder whether the fuel for her intensive work over the years, besides the 'cigarettes, cheap wine and adrenalin' of her early work life, as she cheerfully informs us, is this need to bear her family's burden, to atone for what she saw as their misdeeds.

When she and I segue to *A Child Called It*, a book detailing horrific abuse suffered by a little boy at the hands of his mother, David takes off his glasses and puts his hands over his face. Scharlette pats his arm and tells him we're not going to talk about it anymore.

* * * * *

'But not all people from abusive backgrounds turn to a life of crime,' I say to Scharlette as we walk back to our hotel. Her back is playing up, and she's leaning on my shoulder. 'You didn't. Why do you suppose some people are able to take the abuse that would break another human being?'

Scharlette is pensive. 'It's a question I've been trying to answer my whole life. Trauma, or the way it affects a person, is unique to each individual, and cannot be measured in any common way.'

* * * * *

One Saturday morning, Scharlette, Natasha and I rummage around the flea market in Moldovanka, the formerly Moldovan and later the Jewish part of the Old City. You can find some weird and wonderful offerings among the bric-a-brac – Soviet war medals, paintings by local artists, gramophones, the odd portrait of Lenin. Before World War II, Odessa was predominantly a Jewish city and has produced many famous writers and poets. The city centre is awash with commemorative plaques pointing out who used to live where. Most of the Jews are gone now, murdered by the German and Romanian forces during the Nazi occupation of Odessa, but the descendants of those who escaped or survived come back to trace their family records.

We have an appointment at the Brodska Synagogue – one of only two to survive Nazi occupation. The rabbi's secretary turns out to be fluent in English, and she gives us the concise version of Jewish history in Odessa. An elderly Argentine-Jewish couple is waiting anxiously nearby. They only speak Yiddish and Spanish, and the rabbi's secretary explains that while Yiddish was her mother's tongue, she didn't pass on the language skills to her daughter, the same as with my own grandparents and parents. I chat to the Argentine Jews – husband and wife – in Spanish and learn that they are trying to find out about the husband's father and brother who came to Buenos Aires as refugees. They have to leave the following day and have been kept waiting by the rabbi's assistant. When I wish them luck, they look very grateful, and I notice Scharlette looking in my direction approvingly.

A couple of days earlier, Andrei was showing us photos of his side of the family, and I was struck by how his older brother as a boy looked like the children rescued from Auschwitz – all huge dark eyes in an overly thin face.

'My mother was Jewish,' Andrei began, haltingly. 'She was imprisoned in the ghetto during the war… beaten by the Nazis even though she was pregnant with me. Had her teeth knocked out.' Natasha gently touched his arm, and that seems to rally him.

'Her pregnancy saved her. Her mother and sister were burned alive by the Romanians. I was unregistered when I was born…' his voice trailed off and Andrei cried silently, in that unobtrusive way that men feel they have to, discreetly dabbing at his reddened eyes with the back of his hand.

Odessa was occupied by the German and Romanian troops in October 1941. On October 22, partisans hiding in Odessa's catacombs – a massive labyrinth of underground tunnels atop which the city is built – staged a successful attack on the Nazi HQ, killing sixty-seven people. In retaliation, the Nazis rounded up much of the city's Jewish population – mostly women, children and the elderly (men of working age would have been conscripted into the Soviet army), herded them into the warehouses on the outskirts of the city, and set the warehouses alight.

Later, Natasha and I talk about what it meant to be Jewish in the USSR. She is a soothing presence on our team. When she sees me jangling with anger and other people's pain, it's enough for her to put her hand on my arm, and I instantly feel calmer. She tells me that her patients sometimes call her phone just to listen to her answering machine message; they find it comforting. I can believe that.

'Well, now we know why Andrei kept getting passed over for promotion, even though he was a loyal member of the Communist Party,' she says. 'He's half-Jewish. He hit the glass ceiling.'

It's a familiar story; no matter how hard you worked, or how bright you were, there were professions you couldn't go into and professional heights you would not reach.

'I was good at languages and wanted to be an interpreter,' Natasha continues. 'And my parents had to explain to me why that was not a viable career choice.' Institutional racism meant that Jews were not accepted as interpreters because of the belief that they were not loyal to the Soviet Union and therefore could not be trusted to interact with foreigners. Natasha went into psychiatry instead.

'My parents did their best to protect me, even by giving me a common Russian first name, but their protection only stretched so far.'

A light bulb goes on in my head. My parents have told me of Jewish and Jewish-Russian couples in the USSR giving their kids Russian first names and/or the Russian parent's surname, to try and make life easier for them, but until tonight, I never made the connection with regard to myself.

I call my mother.

'Ma, you know how I was named in honour of my great-grandmother Hannah, but my name is Anna, as common a Russian name as it gets?'

'Yes?'

'Was this to minimise my Jewishness? To protect me?'

'Yes.'

* * * * *

'Would you like to come and work for me?' Scharlette asks me. 'I'll train you to be a mitigation specialist.'

Would I ever!

'I didn't want you to come at first, you know,' she continues. 'David had to bargain with me.'

When Scharlette heard that I had death row pen pals she assumed that I was some daft girl who was looking for a bit of slap and tickle with a Bad Man behind bars. But during the course of our time in Ukraine, she saw that wasn't the case, and that I was prepared to work hard and learn quickly. And the incident at the synagogue showed her that I had empathy, she said, essential for the job that she does.

Working for Scharlette would be a challenge. I've had to miss a close friend's wedding to come to Ukraine because to Scharlette, the only acceptable excuses for not turning up to work are death and grave illness. And she's already told me off twice. Once for trying to make small talk with her while filing documents, and once for sharing too many details of my own life with the Krylovs while trying to put them at ease. 'We need to hear more about them, and less about you,' Scharlette told me. 'You don't need to tell the witnesses your entire life story.' And yet, she is nicer to me than she is to most people. During subsequent trips to Ukraine on behalf of the team, I hear from one of her interns that she'd made most of them cry at one time or another. And for someone who extends considerable empathy and understanding towards some of America's biggest villains (in years to come, she'd tell me that Dzhokhar Tsarnaev, the Boston Bomber, is 'a sweet kid, a loveable stoner'), Scharlette is unforgiving when it comes to what she perceives as weakness or failure on the part of her own friends and colleagues. If you seriously disappoint her, even once, you are banished from her life for good, and there is no appeal.

* * * * *

David and I have dinner at Ukrainskaya Lazunka one evening, a classic Ukrainian joint serving satisfying cold cuts, pickled vegetable platters as big as wagon wheels, *draniki* (potato fritters) with sour cream, *vareniki* topped with more sour cream, and the ultimate of comfort foods from my early years – intensely fragrant dark rye bread, thickly smeared with butter. Unsalted butter, of course. Salted butter is an abomination that I hadn't encountered until my family moved to the West. Whoever heard of cows giving salted milk?

I fall off my chair in the process of trying to sit down, and get flustered over my own clumsiness.

'I once walked right into a closed door while staring at a pretty girl,' David tells me by way of consolation.

'Oh yeah? I've given myself a black eye once by walking into a lamp-post,' I counter.

I'm deeply touched by how David looks out for me, and tell him so. A few days ago, Natasha teased me about the amount of food I managed to put away. David took her aside and suggested to her that maybe she'd hurt my feelings, and she came to me to apologise. Now it's David's turn to get embarrassed, and he mutters something about us looking out for each other, watching each other's backs.

We talk about the challenges of family relationships. Petro and his parents, me and mine, David and his two sons. His fifteen-year-old gets embarrassed when David cries during sad scenes in movies. I get embarrassed whenever my mother and I watch TV together and anything even remotely racy comes on, and can't understand how my sister could possibly have watched Pedro Almodóvar's *Bad Education* with her.

'Scharlette wanting to take you on as an intern is a real compliment,' he tells me, and I nod fervently. It would be an amazing opportunity – to learn from the best. I tell David I have all this energy and a need to channel it, that I need a vocation that provides me with mental stimulus... 'and purpose,' he finishes for me. Exactly.

'How do you do it, though?' What I mean by that is, 'How do you carry the weight of all the trauma from your capital cases without buckling or going under?' While Scharlette seems emotionally bulletproof, taking her clients' trauma in her stride, I sometimes think that my skin is porous, and that other people's pain seeps in, and I feel it as if it were my own.

'I figured that I'd lose some of my cases, and that some of my clients would be executed. So I converted to Catholicism several years back. It helps to believe that you are serving a higher purpose.'

Which is a much better answer than the one I got from Scharlette when I cornered her with: 'How can you stand it, comforting scores of mothers, siblings, grandmas, while knowing that there's a good chance that your client may end up on death row?'

Scharlette considered my question carefully. 'I feel privileged to be able to do so, to help as many people as I can.'

Since finding solace in a higher power is not an option for me, I do the next best thing. That night, like so many other nights, I sit alone on the parapet behind the Londonskaya, with a purring stray cat in my lap and flanked by several others, like some ragtag Queen of Street Felines, and dole out food scraps in exchange for uncomplicated, furry affection.

* * * * *

Scharlette and Natasha return from interviewing Lydia and Michael (Shura's aunt and uncle) in the countryside, with tales of a rural utopia of happy kittens, dogs and big, beautiful chickens. Shura's burden had been eased by sharing the story of Petro's misfortune with relatives outside the immediate family, who've been very supportive, and David and Scharlette decide that the tranquil rural setting would be perfect for videoing the remaining testimony.

I'm thrilled at the prospect of meeting the kittens. That evening the defence team learns of my love of felines when a friendly little cat approaches me during our dinner al fresco, puts her front paws on my leg and purrs loudly to get my attention (and my fish). Not all our evenings are doom and gloom; the rest of that particular dinner is spent swapping pet stories. Scharlette's office in San Francisco is home to a cat called Baby Jesus, another cat with mental issues who tries to dig herself into the carpet, and a large mutt who serves as a foster mother for orphaned kittens. Scharlette herself is excited to reacquaint herself with the chickens. She knows her poultry, having spent her childhood in rural Tennessee, and recounts how she'd almost succeeded in calling a chicken as a witness in a murder trial.

'I was working on this case in California. Our client had spent a decade on death row in San Quentin. IQ of 58; completely parted company with reality. He thought his mother lived in a Coca-Cola can and didn't understand what being executed meant. If you asked him about it, he'd say he was going to be reupholstered.'

'Isn't it against the law to kill someone who doesn't understand why they are being executed?'

'Well, they sent a prison psychiatrist to talk to him, and the psychiatrist testified in court that because he beat her in a game of tic-tac-toe [noughts and crosses], he was clearly compos mentis. Now, I'm from the South. When I was a kid, we used to go to the state fair, and there was this farmer, who taught his prize-winning chicken to play tic-tac-toe. I thought that chicken was the bee's knees.'

So Scharlette set off to find a similar chicken, to prove to the court that you don't even have to be human to beat the prison psychiatrist in a game of tic-tac-toe, and that tic-tac-toe victory doesn't demonstrate awareness of the consequences of one's actions. She envisaged turning up in court with the big, beautiful chicken under her arm, and the look on the psychiatrist's face when she realised she'd have to play a chicken in front of the jury.

'I really thought that this chicken could save our client's life. Chickens don't lie. They have credibility.'

Having scoured various animal fairs across the United States, Scharlette and her team eventually found a tic-tac-toe-playing goose in Montana.

'But that wouldn't do,' Scharlette continues. 'Geese can be mean. I couldn't have a goose chasing the judge and the jury in circles around the courtroom, trying to bite them.'

Finally, a suitable chicken was located in Santa Cruz, California. But sadly, the judge would not allow the submission of avian testimony, stating that bringing poultry into the courtroom would degrade the dignity of the court. 'Whereas I thought that executing a mentally retarded man would degrade the dignity of the court more,' Scharlette finishes.

Luckily for her client, the United States Supreme Court later ruled that a man as mentally disabled as he could not be executed.

* * * * *

Lydia and Michael's house is wonderful. The entire extended family is there, in the fruit orchard, and we wrap up informal family interviews over a spread of stuffed peppers and homemade cherry liqueur before taking several members aside and videoing their response to 'the hard question' in private.

'How would the family feel if Petro were executed?'

They cry – Shura, Olga, Valentina, Anya. The cousins, too. And then, each of them pulls herself together and states, in her own words, that the family would be absolutely devastated by the loss. In some capital cases, the prosecution presents testimony from the family of the victim in which they say how much the deceased meant to them and how it would help bring closure if the perpetrator is executed. In this case, 'victim impact statements' from the family of the accused are also accepted.

The whole family is so kind to us; so hopeful that we can free Petro from prison and bring him back home. Their lovingly prepared homemade food, fed to us in epic quantities – Shura's borscht, Lydia's stuffed peppers, Valentina's steamed *manty* (giant meat dumplings) – embodies their trust in us. When I'm lying awake at night, the responsibility etches lines deeper into my face and presses down on my windpipe like a lead weight. In my naïveté, I genuinely believe that if all the evidence is presented, if all the truth is told, Petro will surely go free, but David and Scharlette are more pragmatic.

'The prosecutors want to try him alongside the ringleaders, which would mean that he would almost certainly be found guilty. And then the jury would get just two options: recommending either the death penalty or life imprisonment without parole.'

They don't have the heart to tell the Krylovs that the odds are stacked in a case like this. That the prosecution will do its best to play up Petro's 'otherness' for the jury – that he's Eastern European (read: Russian mafia), someone who'd broken the law by his very presence on American soil. And the seriousness of the crime greatly lessens the chances of acquittal.

David tells me a lawyer joke.

'My client was caught driving a car with two kilos of heroin in the trunk. Doesn't own the car, no criminal record, other people's fingerprints on the bag of heroin.'

'So... he should go free, right?'

'But it's *two kilos of heroin.*'

Dark humour.

The moral of the story is that the graver the charges, the less likely the jury is to let the defendant off, just in case they accidentally let a guilty person go free. 'Innocent unless proven guilty... beyond reasonable doubt' rarely applies in practice.

The harrowing part over, we gently encourage the family to record their messages to Petro. Reticent at first, they get into the spirit of things, and end up chatting quite freely to the camera, sending their messages of love and hope. Andrei's is the most sober: he tells Petro that he approves of his honourable decision to take fate's blows like a man and not to rat out the other defendants. That he should have courage and know that he, Andrei, loves Petro, his only son.

* * * * *

Petro Krylov's trial takes place in Los Angeles in the spring of 2007, almost two years after our initial trip to Ukraine. Found guilty of participation in the kidnappings and murders, even though it's acknowledged that he did so under duress, Petro avoids the death penalty. It is sheer luck that due to illness on the part of a key member of the defence team, Petro ends up being tried separately from Mikhel and Kadamovas. During the penalty phase, the defence team end their defence of Petro with testimony from Anya, who takes the stand and tells the jury: 'I love my brother and I don't want him to die.' Several members of the jury cry.

Petro Krylov is sentenced to life imprisonment. I try to take heart in what Scharlette tells me about the verdict: 'Where there is life, there's hope.' Meaning that the laws may change in time, and perhaps someday he'll be released. And I cement my decision to walk the same path that David and Scharlette do, and to dedicate my life to trying to save those of others.

CHAPTER 3

ISLAND IN THE SUN

The bass reverberates through my chest like my heartbeat, amplified a hundredfold. Giant speakers face each other in the middle of the dark street in Jones Town ghetto, with a gaggle of teenagers dancing in between. Juggler – shirtless, sweaty, shaven-headed, with a massive grin on his face – wades into the crowd. The spotlight attached to his video camera illuminates each dancer in turn. Everyone is dressed in their best clothes: guys in jeans and their newest T-shirts and do-rags, girls in skintight tops and 'batty riders'. Each is trying to outdo the others with the slickest dance moves. The dancing is raw and sexual. The guys grind against the girls from behind. The women writhe and gyrate in time to the pulsating beat. Several hands grab me and pull me into the melee. It's sink or swim time. The spotlight blinds me. I attempt the 'dutty wine' – a mad gyrating of the hips accompanied with equally mad spinning of the head. The girls next to me fall about laughing and offer to teach me to dance properly.

It becomes apparent that there's an order to things. There are some songs that only the guys dance to, and they are *serious*! Favourite tunes are greeted with shouts of 'Bullet! Bullet!', two fingers of each hand pointing high in a mock-gun salute. Little kids join in, 'wining' on a par with the adults, each vying for Juggler's attention.

Later, I'm sitting on a plastic chair with his five-year-old son Sponge in my lap. Juju, Juggler's youngest, is asleep in James's lap, having worn himself out. It's May 2006, and I'd arrived in Jamaica a couple of days ago to volunteer at an NGO as a legal intern. James, a freckled, laid-back, 24-year-old intern from San Francisco, is here for an indefinite period of time, like me, and has assumed the role of my guide. Juggler is one of his friends – someone who gets invited to all the best street parties. By association, so do we. While Damian 'Jr Gong' Marley raps in the background about the limitations of a ghetto education and how 'di yout' dem' turn to guns when they squander it, I talk to Dale, Juggler's friend, in his forties, who wants to move his kids out of Jones Town to somewhere they'd have a better shot at life.

Abruptly, the street dance is over. The sky is beginning to lighten. As we walk down the pungent-smelling street, Juggler proclaims with irrepressible enthusiasm: 'I love my life.' As well he might, since up till now, prior to his babymother's incarceration for stabbing another woman (over Juggler, we suspect, but he keeps quiet on the subject), his job has consisted entirely of videoing and photographing people's weddings, birthdays, street parties… Now that he is the sole provider for his six children, we suggest that he may have to give up partying, and he looks mock-wistful.

Juggler's house consists of two small rooms, a cracked ceiling and peeling paint on the walls. Yet it's been made as homey as possible. Like many residents of Kingston's most deprived neighbourhoods, Juggler is very house-proud. The back wall of the bedroom he shares with his babymother is covered in a collage of family photographs. The front room, which doubles as a living room and bedroom for the kids, has framed photographs of the children as babies.

We can't stay long. We're due at work, back here in Downtown, in three hours' time. Our taxi hurtles through Kingston's waking streets to Uptown, and up the hill to Mrs Ritgard's house where we are staying. We sneak in through the back gate. I shower, put on my suit, and cast a glance down at the sea of greenery below my balcony towards the skyscrapers of Downtown. Breakfast is mackerel rundown – mackerel cooked in coconut sauce, with Scotch bonnet peppers, tomatoes and garlic. Miss Rose – our landlady's maid and cook – has outdone herself. Then James and I amble back down Beverly Drive, past the goats munching on garbage beneath a 'Don't Throw Garbage' sign, and catch our bus. We've been up since 2am. Much of my life in Jamaica is nocturnal.

* * * * *

The bus deposits us at Parade, Downtown's main square. The contrast between Beverly Hills, the lofty, affluent Uptown neighbourhood where we live, and bustling Downtown, where we work, is jarring. With its potholed streets packed with human and motor traffic; its mix of historic colonial buildings and dilapidated concrete constructions; Coronation Market, heaving with higglers and scavenging dogs and goats; schoolchildren in khaki uniforms scurrying across the street; loud dancehall music blasting from shops; hustlers on street corners; coconut sellers splitting their wares with machetes – Downtown has a raw vitality to it.

Three young men sitting on a nearby fence shout and wave, trying to get my attention. Remembering my boss Nancy's advice to newbies, I introduce myself.

'Gentlemen,' I tell them with a small bow, 'my name is Anna.'

After that, every day, they greet me by name. I'd never been to any country where I was a visible minority and for the first time ever, I appreciate how my black friends back home might feel every day. There are few pale faces Downtown, so you have to be prepared for boisterousness. People stare at you, shout things out, and it's a shock to the system to someone who's grown up in the UK, where everyone ignores one another. Few things irritate Jamaicans more than perceived standoffishness, so no matter how shy you are, you learn to formally greet people and exchange lively banter with complete strangers.

The IJCHR (Independent Jamaica Council for Human Rights) office on Tower Street is two blocks south of Parade. In emails prior to my arrival, Nancy filled me in on what the NGO does. 'We take on legal cases, pro bono, of anyone who cannot afford a lawyer. Which is pretty much all of Downtown Kingston,' she said.

* * * * *

My first day at the office, Nancy – a bespectacled lawyer in her fifties with a blonde bob and efficient manner – shows me around. IJCHR headquarters consist of a couple of sparsely furnished rooms, staffed by volunteer interns like myself and James, plus Lindsey (Nancy's middle-aged friend from Bermuda, a motherly figure) and local girl Julie on clerical duty. My work duties are broad: answering inmate mail, chasing up legal cases at the Court of Appeals, visiting prisons to interview clients. Or, as Nancy puts it, 'Anything that needs doing.'

It's still my plan to train as a mitigation specialist under Scharlette Holdman in San Francisco. But due to my being prevented from entering the United States the previous year, I've been advised to give it time before applying for a visa. So I put my San Francisco dreams on hold for two years and, with Scharlette's approval, am using that time to further my knowledge of the death penalty and prison-related work elsewhere. And what better place than the Murder Capital of the Western hemisphere?

'This is me' – Nancy points to her own office. Tiny flags of countries she's been to decorate her desk. Her bookshelves are lined with legal tomes; she teaches law part-time at the University of the West Indies.

Next door to Nancy is Wayne, a cheerful, dreadlocked lawyer from Barbados. On the phone, he waves hello while leafing through papers littering his desk.

And so I settle into the daily routine of life at the IJCHR.

Lunch is typically gobbled while working, with Denton, the short, wiry errands guy of indeterminate age, picking up an order of patties at Juici Patties for the entire office. The Jamaican patty – golden pastry with a spicy meat or fish filling – is the love child of the Cornish pasty and Indian curry, with some uniquely Jamaican flavours. Some days, I dash to a nearby hole-in-the-wall, and come back with curry goat and rice and peas (rice cooked with coconut milk, thyme and pinto beans), or else oxtail and beans. What with these lunches, and the hearty breakfasts and dinners cooked by Miss Rose, with the exception of callaloo (Jamaica's answer to spinach), not a single green vegetable passes my lips during my time in Jamaica. At Mrs Ritgard's we are fed solid Jamaican standards such as sardines on toast and ackee (a vegetable that tastes like egg) and saltfish (salted cod) for breakfast; sometimes curry goat or brown stew fish for dinner – all wonderful. On the off days, it's cow foot and beans – all bone and gelatine – and even I find it difficult to stomach it.

Jamaica offers the ultimate in nose-to-tail cuisine. During the days of slavery, slaves were given the inferior cuts of meat from the master's table – oxtail, tripe, hooves and ears – or else fed salted cod, which wouldn't spoil for months. All these staples now underpin traditional Jamaican cooking, alongside various tubers brought over from Africa – cassava, sweet potato, green banana, plantain. Occasionally, I worry that I'm on the verge of getting scurvy, which results in a guilt purchase of fruit.

Nancy takes us somewhere most evenings, and I piece together her background from the titbits that she drops. She came to Jamaica as a Peace Corps volunteer, several decades back, fell in love with the island and stayed. Wednesday night is Pegasus night, when she takes us to graze on the free buffet at the posh hotel overlooking Emancipation Park in Uptown. Some nights we hobnob with British Airways crew; other nights, it might be local politicians, lawyers and judges. By virtue of our skin colour and our work, we automatically fall into the 'elite' category of Jamaica's residents.

On Friday evenings, James and I join Nancy and Lindsey in Rae Town, a fishing village in the shadow of Tower Street prison, where we sit outside a rum shack, drink 'fish tea', knock back Red Stripes and slam down our domino pieces. As dusk falls, the air fills with the smell of jerk pork from the oil drum grills. Everyone has their own jerk recipe, and the jerk pork here is almost as good as the version at Sweetwood Jerk, across the street from the Pegasus. I sometimes sidle up there to the little window, place my usual order for a quarter pork (1/4lb pork), fried breadfruit, two festival (deep-fried cornmeal dumplings), and one Ting (Jamaica's grapefruity answer to Sprite or 7 Up), and then watch the chef precision-chop the slab of darkly smoked meat with his massive cleaver, before drizzling homemade hot sauce on top.

* * * * *

'Any new mail?'

Lindsey nods towards my in-tray. It's overflowing with inmate letters from Tower Street prison down the street, and St Catherine prison in Spanish Town, home to Jamaica's death row. Degrees of literacy and coherence vary. Many letters detail allegations of abuse by police. One is from a guy who wants asylum in the UK because his neighbours are jealous of his upcoming reggae record and call him a battyman and paedophile. On one hand, the scenario is plausible, given Jamaica's rampant homophobia; DJs always make nasty remarks about 'battymen', and angry Kingstonians boycotted the cinema that screened *Brokeback Mountain*. On the other hand, the man's wild handwriting suggests that he could also be one of those failed by Jamaica's woeful mental health services.

It seems inconceivable that some of the legal cases that inmates ask for our help with resulted in convictions in the first place. Cases in point: a young man grabbed by police because one of the original suspects fled the scene, who was charged with rape and robbery with zero evidence. Someone whose lawyer slept through his trial. But Nancy quickly disabuses me of any delusions. Since the majority of inmates lack legal representation, legal know-how and even basic literacy, how on earth can they challenge an unfair verdict?

Complaints regarding prison conditions and wanton beatings by guards are commonplace. On my last visit to Tower Street prison, one inmate presented me with a bottle of murky liquid with an object suspended inside it. It was his finger, pickled in vinegar. A guard slammed a heavy metal grille on it on purpose, and the inmate kept it as evidence. Few complaints reach the ears of the superintendents, and it takes so much time for a complaint to be heard that broken bones heal (badly, crookedly), bruises from beatings disappear, and serious ailments reach critical condition.

Prison correspondence aside, I'm working on improving the complaints procedure within prisons, and trying to convince the Department of Correctional Services to allow final-year medical students from the University of the West Indies to attend the prisons.

'It won't cost you a thing,' I tell the rep on the phone. 'The students will get extra practice, and the inmates will get the medical attention they need.'

On top of that, there are the dispossessed who haunt our hallway: walk-in clients with psychosis. There seems to be a subculture of complainants who are bounced between Kingston's NGOs, and no one seems to be able to help them.

There is always more work than we can handle.

* * * * *

While Jamaica punches far above its weight when it comes to its global contribution to music, it keeps its famous children humble at home. There is no harsher critic than a Jamaican audience. During an all-night dancehall fest that James and I attend, Lady Saw gets booed offstage for forgetting her own lyrics. Reggae greats like John Holt are happy to hang out with fans after a gig. It also seems that everyone is one step removed from the Marleys. Lindsey's son, Tariq, went to school with Damian 'Jr Gong' Marley, Bob Marley's youngest son. Jr Gong calls Lindsey 'auntie Lindsey'. Through James, I meet Jr Gong's stepfather, Tom Tavares-Finson. Tactile, courteous, extremely articulate, very much the alpha male, Tom has me and James over for dinner at his handsome mansion in Stony Hill, one of Uptown's most exclusive 'burbs. His wife cooks great Italian food – a welcome change from cow foot and the other odds and ends that Miss Rose has taken to cooking for us lately.

Tom's considered to be one of the best defence attorneys in Jamaica, yet has little sympathy for his clients.

'Why did you choose to defend murderers and drug barons?' I ask. He explains that for him it's an intellectual exercise.

'I see myself as a purveyor of doubt. I could've been a prosecutor, but that would've been like shooting fish in a barrel.'

Tavares-Finson is the personal lawyer of Christopher Michael Coke, aka Dudus – the fearsome don of Tivoli Gardens, and the leader of the Shower Posse, responsible for exporting vast quantities of drugs to the United States. Dudus grew up in luxury and attended Jamaica's elite schools before taking over as the don when his father died under mysterious circumstances in Tower Street prison. Dudus, Zekes, Willie Haggart and their peers are notoriously brutal men who command immense loyalty. They look after their own, feed struggling families in their respective fiefdoms, pay to send the children of single mothers to school. They step in where the government falls short.

Violent crime in Kingston is largely confined to the downtown ghettos. It stems from turf wars between rival gangs, going back decades. Outsiders are not deliberately targeted, but it's possible to get caught in the crossfire. In the 1970s, the leaders of Jamaica's two rival political parties, the Jamaica Labour Party (JLP) and the People's National Party (PNP), doled out guns and money to residents of Kingston's poorest neighbourhoods in exchange for their intimidating and killing rival party supporters. Affiliation either to the JLP or the PNP camp still defines whether or not you may walk down a particular street or cross borders between ghettos. But now, according to my liaison at Kingston Victim Support, 'the politicians no longer control the monsters they've created.' Since the United States cracked down on the cocaine that once travelled from Colombia through Mexico,

Colombian drug barons have made a deal with the Jamaican ghetto dons instead, who spend profits on guns and thus no longer have to rely on politicians for power and influence.

* * * * *

Weeks into our stay in Jamaica, James and I are joined by Paddy, Paul and Sarah from London. Paddy – a bespectacled, lightning-brained, zany Irishman up for any adventure – and Sarah – a great dancer whose 'wining' is viewed with hostility by local girls at street parties since they see her as a potential poacher of their men – are barristers-in-training. Paul – muscled, tattooed, cerebral – spent three years in prison for stabbing someone in a drunken incident when he was a teenager. While incarcerated, he developed a taste for classic Russian literature, and decided to dedicate his life to making sure other young people don't follow his example. With these new arrivals, Mrs Ritgard's house is now full of randy twenty-somethings (and a randy fifteen-year-old if you count young Alex, the grandchild of her friends in Brown's Town, who goes to school in Kingston). Before long, most of us are in and out of each other's rooms. With the exception of Paddy, who's literally charmed the pants off Natalie, a glamorous older woman who lives further up the hill.

'Where've you been?' Mrs Ritgard's visiting grandchildren inquire when Paddy turns up at breakfast after a night of passion.

'Erm… running?'

Miss Rose, who doesn't miss a trick, looks pointedly at Paddy's formal shoes. She also gives Sarah the evils after seeing her emerge from Paul's room one morning, since Paul is a married man. And while I acknowledge that young Alex is very mature and intelligent for his age, and can see him growing into a really handsome man, I'm not willing to add statutory rape to my list of sins.

We end up corrupting the minor in other ways. When they first arrive, James, Alex and I take the newbies to a rooftop dance club, to test their nerve and see whether the guys can handle local girls throwing themselves at them. Another night, we end up at a dance club/strip bar, where Alex is mesmerised by the pole dancers. It's not as seedy as it sounds: an outdoor dance space, where when the 'professional' dancers take a break, local girls take a spin around the pole. One of the girls chats to me very frankly about what it's like, being a lady of negotiable affection, before bluntly propositioning Paddy.

* * * * *

We continue to straddle two worlds. Our nights are spent in the ghettos; our diurnal life among lawyers, judges, journalists, politicians, diplomats. One day, the British High Commissioner and Baroness Scotland come by to learn about IJCHR's work in promoting human rights in Jamaica. Another day, we're talking with veteran Jamaican journalist John Maxwell about the plight of Haitian refugees. Paul and I get packed off to the British embassy for the Queen's birthday festivities, where the Deputy High Commissioner jokes to me that Fort Augusta – Jamaica's only prison for women – is his second home, due to the sheer number of incarcerated British women. Though the police tend to turn a blind eye to personal use of 'di herb' by tourists, if you try to export it, you find your 'holiday' extended by twenty-four months.

'The worst thing is boredom,' one of the inmates tells me when James and I accompany Juggler to Fort Augusta. The prison is clean and quiet, compared to the men's facilities in Tower Street and St Catherine, and the guards don't carry wooden batons, battered from overuse. Juggler is visiting the mother of SpongeBob and Juju, a short, quiet woman who doesn't look like a street brawler. Deferential to the guards, Juggler seems subdued compared to his usual exuberant self. The couple are allowed ten minutes together – merely a chance to exchange a few words and for Juggler to hand over some food and hygiene products.

Jamaican women seem more loyal to their men than vice versa. You don't see long lines of men waiting patiently outside Fort Augusta the way the women do outside Tower Street and St Catherine prisons, bringing provisions. Though bags are searched thoroughly by the guards, Andrew, my sometime domino opponent in Rae Town, tells me that it's all for appearances' sake: 'If you have the money, you can get anyt'ing' – drugs, food, even sex.

* * * * *

St Catherine prison in Spanish Town is a fortress, built by the British in 1714, its stone walls crowned with barbed wire, and heavy metal gates creaking in protest as they let us in. It's a very informal set-up, compared to the US prisons. Inmates walk around freely, some doing their laundry in the tub in the yard. Around the corner from the cells are the gallows.

The biblical idea of 'an eye for an eye' gets a lot of traction in Jamaica, and there's a lot of support for capital punishment because the murder rate is one of the highest in the world. No one has been hanged since 1988 – death sentences are automatically commuted to life imprisonment after five years – but there are six people on death row when Nancy arrives with us interns in tow.

The superintendent lets us chat to the death row guys – all men in their twenties. Paul, my formerly incarcerated friend, exchanges thumb flicks with one of them through the bars of his cell – an abbreviated version of the elaborate Jamaican handshake.

The living quarters are very basic. Small stone cells, bare mattresses, toilet buckets in the corner, nudie pics of women, cut out of magazines, on the walls as the only decoration.

* * * * *

In what little spare time we have, we explore Jamaica. Sometimes, we hop on the bus to Port Royal, former pirate capital of the Caribbean and now a sleepy fishing village. We haggle with local fishermen over speedboat rides to tiny Lime Cay, with its pristine white beach and crystal-clear blue waters. If we want something livelier, we take a minibus to Hellshire Beach, Kingstonians' favourite weekend haunt – a buzzing stretch of sand with music pumping from dozens of brightly painted wooden huts serving fried fish, jerk chicken and beer.

Other times, Natalie, Paddy's up-the-hill lover, drives us up to Ocho Rios, the popular beach resort on the north coast, or to Winnifred Beach – the only undeveloped, pristine white sand beach in Jamaica that is open to locals. Or we pile into overcrowded minibuses that careen around blind corners of mountain roads at breakneck speed, heading for the furthest corners of the island.

We hit Negril – postcard-pretty west coast Jamaica, with its wide crescent of white sand – live off curried conch and festival from a roadside shack, and jump off the cliff at Rick's Cafe, where local daredevils perform complicated dives for tourist dollars. On the north coast, we stay near Frenchman's Cove and eat lobster by candlelight in a tiny cliffside hut called Dickie's. In the bohemian, spread-out village of Treasure Beach on the south coast, we crash in some shack belonging to an old man called Chicken Charlie, wash out of a bucket, and attend poetry slams at the Calabash Literary Festival. At the nearby fishing village of Alligator Pond, we consume such prodigious quantities of curried lobster and brown stew fish at the rickety, legendary eatery Little Ochie, that in the end we're all covered in scales and fishbones like extras from *Lord of the Flies*.

'The idea came to the owner in a dream,' Captain Teddy tells us, when he takes us in his boat to Pelican Bar, a hut on stilts built on an underwater sandbar. We dangle our feet in the water and drink Red Stripes before leaving payment in the honour kitty. Fishermen often stop there for a beer on the way home. 'When Hurricane Ivan come, it nuh fall.' Since Ivan wreaked havoc in much of Jamaica, the survival of this ramshackle crow's nest of a bar seems like a small miracle. Salty with sea spray, sunburned, cheerful and exhausted, we return to Chicken Charlie's, where we wolf down curry goat and rice at his brother's tiny cookshop, and dance to the point of exhaustion at some party on the beach.

One weekend, Paddy and I ditch the others, and hit Reach Falls on the unpeopled east coast, via the town of Morant Bay (the historical site of the Morant Bay slave rebellion, brutally suppressed by the British). We find the waterfalls closed for 'improvement', but Niha, a local guide, takes us up the river regardless. Paddy and I swim in deep sinkholes of turquoise water, and pretend to be a honeymooning couple for Niha's benefit, hamming it up for the camera and giving each other doe-eyed looks while being pummelled by the relentless white spray. 'This is the life,' I think to myself.

It rains heavily on the way back, and we smell downtown Kingston long before we arrive. If Kingston were a bottled scent, it would be a potent, complex fragrance of jerk pork and chicken cooking on oil drum grills, with high notes of rotting garbage, marijuana smoke, urine and ripe mango. Once it reaches your nostrils, you truly feel like you've come home.

* * * * *

In spite of incessant work and very little sleep, I run out of neither curiosity nor energy. In my memory, those months spent in Jamaica are rendered in full Technicolor, the bold aquamarines, lime greens and startling pinks of the tropics contrasting with my muted, low-key life in the UK. And yet, the more oppressive aspects of Jamaican life begin to grate.

Kingston sometimes feels like a city under siege – bristling with barbed wire, dotted with the all-seeing eyes of security cameras, its buildings ringed with concrete fencing. In some ways, it's quite remarkable that we hardly ever find ourselves in trouble. Especially given the amount of time we spend in sketchy parts of Downtown. There are some near misses, though.

When Paddy and I get back from Reach Falls, Parade after dark is ominously quiet. A few higglers are wearily packing up their produce, and two edgy-looking men eye Paddy with undisguised hostility. Another time, Paul, Paddy, James and I hitch a ride back to Kingston from Hellshire Beach in the back of someone's pick-up truck. Three men in their twenties are sitting there already. One of them openly eyes me up, and then orders me: 'Buy me a beer.' I carefully tell him that where I come from, it's usually the gentleman who offers to buy the lady a drink. A guy wearing a do-rag starts saying that we should pay the pick-up truck driver for the ride, and offers to pass our fare on to him. We tell him that we'll reimburse the driver directly, at which point the do-rag guy loudly speculates whether our blood would be a regular red if he were to cut us. This attempt at intimidation is a jarring contrast with the friendliness and kindness we've experienced from most Jamaicans.

During one of our nocturnal excursions to Jones Town, James and I are eyeballed by a gaggle of young men, and one of them, Kabuki – Juggler's obnoxious older son – yells out some pretend Chinese gibberish at me. It's a reference to my skin tone. Jamaicans are very sensitive to gradations in skin colour – this harks back to the centuries of plantation slavery – and they distinguish between my 'yellow' skin, and pink-skinned 'whiteys'. Coupled with my Asian eyes, it means that I often get mistaken either for a member of Kingston's Chinese community, who run Downtown's corner shops, or else for one of the stoned Japanese tourists who occasionally turn up to Rae Town's oldies' night.

In contrast to plantation slavery in the Deep South, in the Caribbean, the lines were much more blurred. While in the States, the merest hint of black blood was enough to demote a person to a 'lower' class, in Jamaica, white planters occasionally married their slave mistresses, emancipated their mixed-race children and even sent them to be educated in Britain, and you could improve your social status by marrying someone with lighter skin than yourself. It genuinely surprises me that categorising people in this way is still very much the norm in present-day Jamaica. When James tries to set up Julie from our office with Kerron, a shy, twenty-something Jamaican student living with us at Mrs Ritgard's, Julie dismisses him as 'too dark'. Darker than her own, café-au-lait countenance, that is, and therefore not up for consideration as a romantic prospect.

Being female carries its own perils. On one hand, being in Jamaica can do wonders for a woman's self-esteem (if you measure it by how often men hit on you). I can honestly say that I've never received as many approving and/or outright lascivious glances and frank propositions as I have in Jamaica, including – memorably – from an old Rasta who had one of each: teeth, hands, eyes. Another time, as I was walking along the beach in Negril, a friendly guy my age joined me and introduced himself as Dr Feelgood. He was sporting twelve inches of 'big bamboo', he informed me, and it was my lucky day. Negril is a bit of an extreme case. Ever since the fictional Stella 'got her groove back' by hooking up with a younger man in Montego Bay, Jamaica – and Negril in particular – has been a destination for older American and European women. They come here for a bit of fun in the sun with 'rastitutes' – young men who make a living out of being wined and dined by the women while attending to their physical needs. All non-Jamaican women are considered to be fair game.

'Sorry, I'm married,' I told him. 'But I'll look you up if I come back as a single woman.'

That way, he got to save face and I could retreat with my womanly virtue intact. I was getting better at banter with local men, and didn't feel intimidated by Dr Feelgood's frank approach, but still, I rather resented the fact that he was much more likely to respect my being the 'property' of a fictional husband than an honest, 'I'm flattered, but just not interested.'

'At least a quarter of all Jamaican women experience some form of sexual assault before they are eighteen,' a doctor at Kingston's Victim Support clinic tells me. 'And those are just the cases we know about.'

Domestic violence is endemic, and in the worst cases he and his staff find themselves counselling teenage victims of incestual rape, only to have to send them back to their home to continue living with their abuser. There are no government-funded refuges for these women.

I'm appalled but not hugely surprised, given the prevailing culture of hyper-macho masculinity. Listen to a bunch of ghetto lads brag about their sexual exploits, and you get the impression that the objective of a sexual encounter is to bang a woman like a barn door. The concept of tenderness, of giving your partner pleasure, is non-existent. Women are told that they're 'nuh real 'ooman' unless they've given birth, and in the majority of ghetto families, households are headed by women. Men prove their virility by fathering as many children as possible, often with multiple women, but rarely stick around to provide for them, so the economic burden falls on the mothers and the extended family. Juggler is an exception to the rule. A sociologist I talk to puts forward the theory that this is rooted in plantation slavery: there was no point in male and female slaves getting too attached to one another, because they'd be split up, with no consideration for family units. And even in well-to-do families in Jamaica, it's almost expected that the man will stray and that the woman will just put up with it. And the womanising is of course the fault of the women he strays with, and never his own.

* * * * *

No account of my time in Jamaica would be complete without mentioning the mind-altering substances. 'Di herb' is everywhere. Joints are cheaper than cigarettes, Rastas sell massive branches of their produce at the Coronation Market, and our nocturnal street parties are wreathed in fragrant smoke. On Sunday nights in Rae Town, I find myself swaying to old-school reggae with a joint in one hand and a Red Stripe in the other. It seems to have little effect on me, except to make me more talkative than normal.

Weed also almost gets us into serious trouble. During my travels with James on the west side of the island, along with his two friends from San Francisco – Bob and Sandie, a bookish, arty couple – we are offered a tour of a ganja plantation near Orange Hill, a village near Negril. James, always up for an adventure, convinces Bob to come with him. Sandie and I stay in the car. A youngish Rasta with an air of palpable menace about him is friendly enough towards us, but an hour later, the guys still aren't back and Sandie and I joke about having to pay a ransom for them. James and Bob finally emerge and get a large sum of money out. They are paying for their lives. There was a hefty and unexpected fee for the 'tour' when they were up in the hills, and their guides made it quite clear that if they didn't pay up, they would not make it out of Orange Hill intact.

Our sampling of Miss Brown's otherworldly wares is more benign. Miss Brown's is a locally legendary, nondescript-looking cookshop across the road from the Negril police station, from which James emerges triumphantly, clutching a bottle full of mud-brown liquid. It's mushroom 'tea'. We have no idea how strong the hallucinogenic brew is, and to my disappointment, I don't see unicorns or anything that's not actually there, but while my companions become giggly and silly and splash in the evening surf, I lie back in the sand beneath the night sky and feel this tremendous feeling of peace and well-being. The stars seem to be yielding their secrets to me, and I keep thinking that if you join them up, like a connect-the-dots puzzle, they make up the outline of a spaceship. 'Beam me up,' I think to myself, ready to leave Earth on a bigger adventure. 'I'm ready.'

Later, I try to continue star-gazing by climbing on to the roof of our guesthouse, but my travelling companions hold me back, fearing that I might do a Superman impression. I then spend the longest time looking at my own reflection in the mirror, fascinated by my own face, thinking, 'I've never quite seen it from *this* angle before.'

* * * * *

Towards the end of my stay in Kingston, I'm flagging. Sometimes, I find myself thinking glumly that even if we worked around the clock, all our lives, we would never be able to assist all the people so desperately in need of our help. That we can pick at the very edges of the system, but there is little hope of effecting meaningful, lasting change.

One day, James waves a rather desperate-sounding letter at me, written in Spanish, and as the sole Spanish speakers at the office, we're dispatched to the notorious Hunts Bay lockup. Nine Honduran fishermen have drifted off course and been rounded up by the coastguard in Jamaican waters. But because they have no papers, apparently Immigration can't ascertain where they are from and send them back to their country. Which is asinine, since why else would they ask to be sent back to Honduras? Their families have no idea what's happened to them. James and I try to contact the Honduran ambassador, but he's gone AWOL, so two 24-year-old legal interns are the Hondurans' last hope.

'Jamaican fishermen come into our waters too,' one of the fishermen comments bitterly when we visit them, 'but we welcome foreigners with open arms rather than throw them in prison.'

We're granted an audience with Superintendent Clunis – Hunts Bay's head honcho – and he assures us that he will help the fishermen, but since we leave Jamaica soon after, we have no way of knowing whether this has come to pass.

* * * * *

Sometimes – all too rarely – there are bright flashes of victory.

'Come with me.' Nancy is rushing out the door. 'Ricky's getting out today.'

I fall into step beside her.

'Remind me, what did he do?'

'He didn't.'

Nancy has been fighting Ricardo Williams's case for over a decade. Ricky has spent twelve years in prison for a murder he didn't commit. In 1994, one of his older neighbours shot and killed another guy in a dispute, then ran off. The police grabbed the boy nearest to the crime scene: Ricky, who at the time was just twelve years old. He was subsequently convicted of murder after being beaten, denied food and drink, and coerced into signing a written statement which he couldn't read. No attempt was made to contact his parents, nor was he advised of his right to speak to a lawyer. Ricky would've disappeared forever into Jamaica's labyrinthine legal system if it hadn't been for Nancy, and once his case reached the Privy Council in London – still Jamaica's highest court of appeal due to Jamaica being a former Crown colony and the Privy Council's role being entrenched in Jamaica's Constitution – they ordered his immediate release.

Ricky's father, a tall, thin, bearded man, waits outside the gates of Tower Street prison. Nancy presents the release order, signed by the Queen of England, to the superintendent. The wardens shake hands with Ricky. No hard feelings, apparently. The three of us walk out, and then it's like a scene out of a movie. Ricky looks up at the sky and says: 'Thank you, Jesus!' His father walks towards him, kneels down and kisses the ground by Ricky's feet before embracing his son tightly. Nancy cries.

'So what happens now?' I ask Nancy, nodding in Ricky's direction when he joins us for a dominoes session at Rae Town.

She shrugs. 'Nothing.' No police officer is ever charged over their misconduct towards Ricky. He gets no compensation from the Jamaican government, since it is impossible to prove 'malicious intent' on the part of the judiciary, even though anyone with any scruples, legal acumen and a pair of eyes should've been aware that trying a twelve-year-old child as an adult was beyond the pale. Ricky walks out illiterate, with no trade or skills. But IJCHR helps him enrol in literacy classes and he is optimistic about his future.

* * * * *

The Land Rover pick-up climbs the mountain road from Stony Hill, with the lights of Kingston spreading out beneath us. Paddy, James, Natalie and I stand on the metal benches at the back of the truck, with the night breeze whipping back our hair. At the blink-and-you'll-miss-it village of Hagley Gap, the paved road and the street lights disappear. We pass farmers walking home in the dark, their way lit solely by the stars peeping through the forest canopy. Eventually, we pull up by Whitfield Hall, the base for our hike. Our digs are a very basic dormitory – not that we'll be doing much sleeping. The ascent must be done at night if we want to see the sunrise from Jamaica's tallest peak.

It's not just Kingston that never sleeps. Lured by the faint pounding bass and the scent of jerk chicken, we stumble upon an impromptu party in a clearing framed by tall eucalyptus trees, where several dozen locals are dancing along to a mix of the latest dancehall tunes and rock'n'roll. Cups of Ting and rum and 'fish tea' get passed around, and Paddy and Natalie dance exuberantly to 'Rock Around The Clock'.

Awoken at 2am, we stagger sleepily in single file along a narrow path. The moon is high and sparks fly all around us. They are fireflies, known locally as kittyboo or peenie-wallies. Paddy tells us the Irish legend of the will-o'-the-wisp, which lures you into the swamp, but these are benevolent sprites. The higher we get, the colder it is, and as the sky lightens, tropical vegetation gives way to an abundance of ferns, evergreens, pine trees, wild strawberries, white wisps of old man's beard, lichen-covered rocks. We summit the peak just as the sun slowly rises above the mist-shrouded Blue Mountains. Way out to sea is the shimmering, faint outline of Cuba.

Upon our return to the lodge, the breakfast of champions awaits: heaped plates of ackee, saltfish, callaloo, fried dumpling, fresh bread and coffee. Blue Mountain coffee, of course; we saw the plants during our descent. One of my earliest childhood memories is that of my father, walking up and down our kitchen in Chernogolovka, grinding beans using a steel coffee-grinder that's now older than I am. I come to appreciate coffee quite late in life, but it's apt that my first proper taste of good brew takes place right here.

Gazing out at the impenetrable vegetation, we discuss the runaway slaves that once hid out here. Natalie tells us that Jamaica would get the wild, untamed warrior people, such as the Ashanti, whereas the smaller Caribbean islands would get the slaves less inclined towards insurrection, hence Jamaica's numerous slave rebellions.

* * * * *

Back in Jamaica a decade after my initial stay in Kingston, I find myself attending the Maroon New Year in Accompong, a remote settlement on the edge of Cockpit Country – Jamaica's no man's land of impenetrable vegetation, limestone caves, cliffs and sinkholes. The festivities are in full swing. Accompanied by the beating of traditional *goombeh* drums and the blowing of *abeng* cow horns (like those once blown as a call to arms, to mark the beginning of the slave rebellion), the procession slowly makes its way up the main street. It's led by Colonel Williams, the elected leader of the Accompong Maroons, dressed in a red robe and garlanded with greenery – a nod to the runaway slaves' ancient camouflage. There is chanting in Coromantee – a language brought over from West Africa during the slave trade, which is still spoken here, at least by the elders.

Accompong's status in the Jamaican imagination and its place in Jamaican history is second to none. Its residents – the Maroons – are descendants of Jamaica's runaway slaves, originally from Ghana, who escaped from the plantations into the island's interior, from where they waged a guerrilla war against the British. Successfully, too: January 6 marks the signing of the 1739 Peace Treaty in which the British essentially committed to leaving the Maroons alone. Cudjoe, his brother Accompong, and Nanny are all legendary Maroon leaders, attributed almost supernatural powers. When the treaty was signed in the Peace Cave, an hour's hike through the jungle, Cudjoe and his British counterpart allegedly slashed their wrists, mixing the blood in a calabash dish with rum and drinking it to cement the agreement.

The procession ends at the Kindah Tree at the top of the village – a centuries-old mango tree beneath which Cudjoe once met with the other village elders. I make my way through the crowd, past the sellers carrying boxes filled with marijuana branches and Pringles, to the smoking oil drum grills that line the street. I'm drawn by one barbecue grill in particular, crowned with a pig's head. It's wearing sunglasses and someone's stuck a joint in its mouth. Below it, slabs of jerk pork are slowly being smoked over a pimento (allspice) wood fire. For old times' sake, I order 'a quarter pork' and am not disappointed. Jerk pork is one of the most wonderful things on earth, redolent with the punch of Scotch bonnet chillies, with back notes of thyme, spring onion, garlic and allspice, sometimes with a sweet hint of brown sugar. Done the traditional way, the Maroon way, it's smoky, quite dry, and with a fire and a sweetness that makes me ache with nostalgia. It takes me back to those vivid months in Kingston in 2006, and tastes like my restless Jamaican days and my sleepless Jamaican nights.

* * * * *

In May 2007, I submit my apprenticeship visa application at the US Embassy in London, with supporting papers from Scharlette, and letters of recommendation from numerous friends – all respected professionals – willing to vouch for the fact that I'm an upstanding citizen. But my application is rejected for petty bureaucratic reasons, reinforcing my darker thoughts from my time in Jamaica: that no matter how much I try to help others, I will ultimately fail. Not unkindly, the immigration official tells me that there is little point in me reapplying for a US visa unless my circumstances change or a substantial amount of time passes since my original infraction. My hopes of being trained by Scharlette and becoming a mitigation specialist are over.

But exactly a week later, an email arrives. The title reads: 'Your Dream Job'.

CHAPTER 4
WANDERING JEW

Turn the corner in the heart of Jerusalem's Old City, and you may stumble upon Abu Shukri, an unprepossessing hole-in-the-wall that serves the best hummus I've ever tasted. It's a thick, creamy swirl of chickpea, tahini, garlic and lemon juice puree, sitting in a deep pool of fruity olive oil, generously topped with pine nuts and a handful of chickpeas, and sprinkled with parsley and tiny mounds of zaatar and paprika. It's pretty much the only thing on the menu, with flatbread to mop it up with.

'No self-respecting Israeli eats flavoured hummus,' my cousin Guy told me days earlier, when went in search of the best hummus in Tel Aviv and discussed the beetroot and spinach hummus favoured by some Brits. Guy's favourite hummus joint is Abu Hassan, a thimble-sized establishment a short walk south of the Clock Tower in Jaffa. Disappointingly, it turned out to be closed that evening, so we grabbed a *sabikh* (pita stuffed with grilled aubergine, potato, spicy mango sauce and salad) from a street food stall instead.

'Everyone has their own favourite hummus spot and will argue to the death that their place is the best,' Guy informed me. 'In fact, if you get two Israelis is a room, you get five different opinions.' That may be true, but many Jerusalem residents agree that even if Abu Shukri is not the absolute pinnacle of hummus making, it's definitely up there with the very best.

I find Abu Shukri by chance, thrilled to lose myself in the Old City's labyrinthine narrow lanes, among millennia-old sandstone buildings and the fragrant spice stalls of the covered market. Eventually, I make my way to the Western Wall where, some twenty years earlier, my mother got told off for bringing me into the women's section because the faithful mistook me for a boy. This time, no one pays attention to me, and though I have no written message for the Almighty to stuff into one of the cracks, I place my hand on the warm stone and stand there for a while.

This is the land of my ancestors, too. I'm a Cohen on my father's side – a direct descendant of Aaron, Moses' brother, the First Priest of the First Temple, as the legend goes. If you're religious, being a Cohen entails certain extra duties and responsibilities. For someone like me, my lineage makes little difference, though I'm supposed to steer clear of cemeteries and hospitals. Can't remember why, and it's too late, anyway. I've worked in a hospital and enjoy haunting necropolises.

For my immediate family, Israel was the road not taken. After we'd left the Soviet Union, my father was offered permanent positions in three different places: Cambridge, UK; Gainesville, Florida; and Rehovot, Israel. I ponder how different my life would have been, had I grown up Israeli instead.

My family is Jewish. Or Jew-ish, depending on whom you ask. Ethnic Jews rather than practitioners of the Jewish faith. Until my paternal uncle and his family moved to Israel after the collapse of the Soviet Union, and his younger son became a proper Haredi, much to the surprise of his secular parents, the last person to regularly attend a synagogue was my great-grandfather Aron, before the 1917 Revolution. In the atheist Soviet Union, most synagogues were converted into warehouses or gyms. After my parents became part of the brain drain to the West, we'd half-heartedly observe Passover and Hanukkah. Yet I've been made aware of my Jewish roots from a young age, with all the attendant blessings and curses. If you peel back the layers of my identity, I'm a Jew first, then a Brit, then someone born in a country that no longer exists. And my Israeli cousins – two brothers – embody the contradiction that is Israel perfectly: one is a ham-eating, laid-back, secular world traveller like myself, and the other is an ultra-Orthodox Haredi, dedicated to studying the Torah his entire life.

* * * * *

To me, the taste of certain foods is forever linked with memorials to humanity's worst acts.

Hummus tastes like Yad Vashem.

Before exploring the Old City, I pay a visit to Jerusalem's Holocaust museum – deeply sobering and uplifting by turns. There's the solitary cattle car on the edge of rails, symbolising the death trains that deposited Jews at Auschwitz. The tree sculpture that reminds me of the Holocaust Tree of Life memorial behind Budapest's Great Synagogue, its metal leaves inscribed with the names of hundreds of thousands of murdered Jews. Digitised accounts of victims' lives. There are so many of them.

Then a hopeful note: the Avenue of the Righteous Among the Nations, flanked by trees planted in the 1960s in honour of non-Jews who risked their own lives during the Shoah to save Jews, simply because that was the decent human thing to do. Had I been in their shoes, would I have risked everything in order to help desperate, persecuted people who weren't my kin, but who would otherwise have been killed? It's a question I ask myself often, particularly in recent times, with the far right on the rise around the globe, the increased 'othering' of the vulnerable and the stateless, and the propensity to excuse the inexcusable.

When I was fourteen years old, my school organised a trip to Poland. My mentor Jolyon – an anthropologist and adventurer with a particular interest in the history of Nazi Germany – encouraged me to go, as did my parents. I wasn't keen on going without my close friends, but my parents insisted. Having both visited the death camps, they felt that I, too, should witness that aspect of my heritage.

That was the first trip I took without my family. I remember my embarrassment when my teachers had to wait for me, since I was travelling on a Russian passport, with a letter from my school translated into Polish, and took forever to clear customs. The cobbled streets of Warsaw and Kraków. Drinking cheap vodka of questionable origin that Chloe and Sarah bought in some corner shop where they had no issue with serving fourteen-year-old foreigners, and then sleeping in a chair in Chloe's room. Being dared to lick the wall of the underground salt cathedral, and a claustrophobia-inducing ride in a subterranean lift. Spotting bison in the Bialowieza Forest, and an epic snowball fight.

And then there were the death camps. It wasn't Auschwitz that made the biggest impression on me. Its displays of horror were too brash, too 'in your face' – the mountains of prosthetic limbs, the lamps made with flayed human skin, the piles of spectacles and of suitcases, mounds of wedding rings, of gold teeth.

It was the mountain of battered luggage that did it for one of my friends: 'They wrote their addresses on the suitcases, because they believed they'd be coming home.'

For me, it was Treblinka – the sheer desolation of it. There was nothing there, just a snowy expanse surrounded by trees, and a stone monument to the victims. I found a tiny flag of Israel on a toothpick in the snow, and kept it as a ghoulish memento.

My extended family didn't perish in the death camps in Poland, as far as we know. Most likely, those who remained in Ukraine during World War II were massacred by the advancing Germans where they lived at the time. This almost happened to my maternal great-grandfather, who originally resisted his children's entreaties to relocate to Moscow. 'I know the Germans,' he'd tell them, referring to the Nazis' World War I counterparts, who romanced Ukrainian girls and generally treated civilians well.

It was this early trip to Poland, and my subsequent interactions with my mentor over the years, that cemented in my mind the importance of bearing witness. Like many teenagers from troubled homes, subconsciously aware of the limitations that were always going to be part of my relationships with my immediate family, I sought out role models elsewhere. I was extremely lucky: my mentor, Jolyon, encouraged my intellectual development – lending me books, instilling in me the basics of critical thinking, and dispensing thoughtful advice whenever I was in a quandary; while Maureen, one of my school teachers, provided me with the nurturing that I lacked at home. One of my mentor's core convictions – that I subsequently adopted as my own – was that the Holocaust was not just a Jewish tragedy, but a human one, and that it was incumbent on any decent person to pay homage to victims of atrocities, to not avert one's gaze from the worst things that human beings do to one another.

Not to sound glib, but from that Poland trip onwards, I've been subconsciously pairing memorials to atrocities with food. What I mean is this: every small detail of those sombre visits is etched with crystal clarity into my memory, with the flavours and textures of the meals consumed on those days suspended within the amber of my recollections alongside them. Beef goulash served in a bowl made of rye bread, and Auschwitz.

Slivers of teppanyaki beef, and the dark stain left in stone by a vaporised human being at the Hiroshima Peace Memorial Museum. Graphic photos of Agent Orange victims at the War Remnants Museum, Ho Chi Minh City, and bowlfuls of *bun cha* – barbecued pork served in sweet and salty broth, fragrant with fresh herbs.

But I only became conscious of this during my very first travel writing gig, in the Baltics, courtesy of Rough Guides, who were recruiting young, experienced travellers in May 2007 to research Europe on a shoestring for their new On a Budget series. The 'dream job' email that came from my university friend Steve turned out to be an ad from Rough Guides, looking for fresh young writers. I applied and got in.

* * * * *

An ancient red behemoth of a train drops me at Lithuania's Paneriai train station, a concrete booth in the middle of nowhere. From there, I follow a dirt track into the forest. There's no one around. It's a hot and sunny day, and the tall pines around me are fragrant with that wonderful, heady scent that forever puts me in mind of childhood summers. There are wild strawberries and blueberries ripening in the undergrowth by the road, and I stop to graze.

In a clearing near me stands a stone obelisk, topped with a star, dedicated to 'Victims of Fascist terror.' Nearby is another memorial, decorated with a Star of David, inscribed in Hebrew, Yiddish, Lithuanian and Russian. One of the paths radiating from the central clearing ends in a pit. The plaque reads: 'Here Hitler's occupying forces burned the dead bodies.'

For centuries, Vilnius had been a centre of Jewish learning and innovation, and before World War II, had a population of seventy thousand Jews. *After the war, there were none.* This is where most of them perished. Around seven thousand survived the war, but didn't necessarily return to Vilnius. Couldn't face returning.

The fireball building in my stomach is compounded by what I've learned about Lithuania's recent history in Vilnius's House of Terror, the former KGB headquarters. When the Russians occupied the Baltic States at the end of World War II and forcibly incorporated them into the USSR, this is where decisions were made regarding mass deportations of Lithuanians to Siberia, and the forced repatriation of Poles to Poland, and where political prisoners were interrogated in padded cells. Later on in the trip, I'd visit similar museums of occupation in Riga and Tallinn, detailing Soviet atrocities in other occupied Baltic States – thousands of families rounded up in the middle of the night and deported to Siberia, scrawling letters on pieces of toilet paper and throwing them out of the windows of the trains, hoping against hope that their loved ones would find them.

My sympathy for Lithuanian victims of Soviet repressions is tempered somewhat by the graphic displays in Green House, one of the branches of the Vilna Gaon Jewish State Museum. It's a small wooden hut. Nothing high-tech. But there are photos of Lithuanian pogroms against the Jews. Jewish businesses trashed and looted. Bodies piled up in the street after a local mob beat them to death. Public rape of Jewish women. Graphic eyewitness accounts of Nazis raping Jewish girls and having their mothers watch, then killing the mothers in front of the children. I learn all of this on the very first day of my very first travel writing gig, and since I'm yet to cultivate a protective numbness against the worst of the human condition, these are the museums I find the most traumatic.

* * * * *

A medieval cellar off cobbled Stikliu street, Lokys is an underground cavern with low stone ceilings, torches flickering in sconces, atmospheric nooks and crannies, and a menu specialising in game dishes – wild boar sausages, beaver stew, venison steak – as well as unusual fare such as bilberry dumplings.

When I'd revisit Vilnius on behalf of both Rough Guides and Lonely Planet in later years, my research would be considerably more streamlined. My messenger bag would be packed with my camera (or smartphone), notebook, pens, the chapter I'm updating, unceremoniously torn out of the guidebook, photocopied maps with everything I need to visit on any given day marked up in red, any new and exciting recommendations dotted about in green. I'd know exactly what I'd be researching on any given day, with the city divided into sections to maximise efficiency, and attraction/restaurant/bar opening hours googled in advance so that I wouldn't be caught out by unorthodox schedules. And I'd have my own room, in order to be able to write up my research in the evenings, rather than crash in the cheapest fleapit imaginable.

But as a complete rookie, I'm still figuring all this out. I've yet to cross the line of defacing guidebooks or even annotating them (harming a book, *any* book, is a sacrilege to someone brought up by bibliophiles), and my first research trip is a bit haphazard. I find myself retracing my steps, pounding the streets for hours longer than I should, chasing up hostels and hotels (because no one wants you visiting during the morning checkout rush or while rooms are being made up), picking the worst possible accommodation and, of course, paying the clueless foreigner surcharge.

When I land in Vilnius in July 2007, I promptly get ripped off by a Russian taxi driver who takes advantage of my late evening arrival. And while Old Town Youth Hostel has a terrific location, just up from the Gate of Dawn – a chapel built into a stone archway, leading into Old Town – I find myself sharing a mixed dorm with five lads and stumble upon a fresh puddle of vomit in our shared bathroom. The responsible party had also thoughtfully vomited in the sink. Ah, the glamorous side of travel writing.

And yet, in spite of that inauspicious start, Vilnius beguiles me. I love the chiaroscuro of the cobbled streets in the city's medieval heart; the very Eastern European bustle and clamour at the Hales Turgus produce market; the irreverence of the Užupis 'republic' – the arty, somewhat rundown neighbourhood just across the Vilnia river from Old Town, with its abstract sculptures, and even its own constitution that gives its citizens the rights 'to love and take care of a cat' and 'to make mistakes'. I love how characterful Vilnius's deserted main square is at night, with the eerily lit up cathedral and bell tower. Alone there in the dark, and feeling a rush of affection for the city as if it were my own, I close my eyes and pivot clockwise on one foot on the *stebuklus*. It's the tile that marks one end of the giant human chain that spanned the Baltics in 1991, when two million people across Lithuania, Latvia and Estonia joined hands to protest against Soviet rule. Allegedly, this tile grants wishes.

And while Vilnius isn't yet the gastronomic powerhouse it would be by 2019, when I return for my penultimate pre-pandemic gig to peruse the city's craft beer bars, Michelin-starred restaurants and speciality coffee shops, its dining scene is unexpectedly diverse. There's the authentic Indian place, frequented by the Indian embassy staff, a Mexican joint, run by a family from Oaxaca, and even a 'raw food' café, well ahead of its time. I correctly predict that in a country where a meal is deemed incomplete without a grilled slab of meat, this restaurant's ambitions far outstrip its chances of survival, but I give the owners points for sheer gumption and review it for the guide. I work in a line from that *Sex and the City* episode where Samantha pulls the hot blonde waiter in a raw food restaurant, and tells him: 'I've eaten a fucking cactus!' and am gratified when my editor doesn't cut it. Sixty-word reviews don't give you much room to flex your literary muscle, so I learn to be playful within those parameters, throwing in puns, innuendo, double entendres and deliberately obscure words, seeing what I can get away with.

In a corner nook in Lokys, I hum happily as I wolf down some palate-pleasing sweetness and stodge in the form of bilberry *koldunai* (dumplings) and *bulviniai blynai* (potato pancakes), noting down the flavours and the nouns and adjectives that the décor brings to mind in my little notebook in order to write it up while it's fresh in my head.

By contrast, *cepelinai* (zeppelins) – Lithuania's national dish that I tried upon my return from the Paneriai mass graves – were a crime against the potato. Imagine something the size of a small rugby ball, made of sticky, dense potato dough that threatens to keep your fork hostage like a glue trap. Dig deeper. No, deeper than that. Encased inside the gluey exterior is your grand prize in the form of a lump of minced meat. Or Spam. But by the time you've unearthed it, you've stopped caring.

* * * * *

The most insightful piece of advice I was given as a newbie writer was this: 'You don't need to be an expert in everything. That's impossible. But you need to be able to find the experts.' So during my first gig and beyond, I made extensive use of Couchsurfing – either staying for free with open-minded, usually well-travelled locals who threw their doors open to like-minded souls on trust, or meeting up with them to get to know places new to me through discerning local eyes.

In Kaunas – Lithuania's second city – I end up staying with twenty-year-old Gintaras, a slender, serious, beetle-browed computer programmer. During the day, I pace the cobbled streets of Old Town and the tree-lined boulevard leading up to the onion-domed Church of the Archangel, checking out museums, churches, Kaunas's remaining synagogue, hostels and places to eat at breakneck speed. I slow down only for the wonderful Museum of Devils – which started as a private collection of Lucifer images and morphed into a delightfully macabre display of devil masks and figures from around the world.

In the evenings, Gintaras shows me around, from the best views of the Old Town from the hilltop Christ's Resurrection Basilica, to a medieval cellar bar off the pedestrianised Vilniaus gatve, where we clink bottles of Vilniaus beer and tuck into traditional Lithuanian beer snacks: *kepta duona* (strips of rye bread, fried in caraway oil and rubbed with salt and garlic) and smoked pig's ears, cut into thin slivers. The pig's ear is a duel between rapture and revulsion: the smoky taste and the soft, jelly-like parts are a delight, juxtaposed with the unpleasantly crunchy texture of the cartilage.

On my last day in Kaunas, Gintaras takes me to the Ninth Fort – an out-of-town memorial where local teens on mopeds gather for piss-ups. Two huge jagged blocks of stone mark the spot where up to fifty thousand Jews, including most of Kaunas's Jewish population, were murdered by the Nazis and their Lithuanian collaborators, along with prisoners of war who were imprisoned in the adjacent nineteenth-century fort.

Maybe because my Russian is less fluent than my English, or maybe because Gintaras is shy, I keep trying to find mutually interesting conversation topics and getting monosyllabic answers. Until we find ourselves driving through farmland and forest, that is, and he becomes animated.

'Me and my friends, we sometimes rent a house in the countryside. In the middle of nowhere, with a lake or river nearby.'

'What do you do out here?'

'Just chill out. Swim, drink, steam in the sauna.' (Because every self-respecting house in the countryside has one.)

'Sounds great.'

'It is. But' – he points to a scar across his forehead – 'one time I came out of the sauna drunk. Dived into the lake. Didn't check to see how deep it was, and cut my head open on a rock.'

'So did you go to the hospital?'

'Nah. Went back in the sauna, had more vodka.'

'What else do you do for fun around here?'

'I jump with a parachute. But my girl doesn't like it.'

I laugh. After that, the conversation flows easily.

For my farewell dinner, Gintaras takes me to Etno Dvaras, one part of a Lithuanian restaurant chain where they push the cutesy Lithuanian peasant theme and celebrate the humble potato prepared several dozen different ways, including in the wretched zeppelin form. Gintaras urges me to sample another classic dish: animal intestines stuffed with baked spud and topped with the generic creamy sauce they seem to smother everything with around here. It smells exactly like the sausages in fish and chip shops back home.

* * * * *

I pump the forestock, and brace the pump-action shotgun against my shoulder. Aim. Squint. Squeeze the trigger. The powerful kick jars me, but there's a massive hole in the shadowy bad guy. There are deafening gun blasts all around. I'm in an underground bunker in Riga, partaking in the nightly group outing organised by the hostel I'm staying in, the presence of guns a residue of the violence that shaped the Baltic States during the Soviet era. Somehow, I've ended up as the translator, since the bunker is run by middle-aged Russian guys who don't speak English, although the expressive hand gestures on how to hold a firearm are pretty clear. We shoot AK-47s, Uzis, handguns. Turns out I'm not a bad marksman, and the gun handler firmly shakes my hand at the end. 'Well done,' he tells me. 'You shot well.'

We move on to another type of shot. On arrival at Riga's top party hostel I've been presented with a complimentary pint of beer by Caspar – a zany Swedish guy who looks like a happy Kurt Cobain – and roped into a nocturnal excursion. A diminutive lightweight with a general aversion to crowds, nightclubs and noise, I'm well outside my comfort zone, but feel I should experience it all in order to write about it accurately. And Caspar is very persuasive. He's funny, approachable, and easy to talk to. Tells me that he's twenty-three, used to be in a punk band, that he sold all his stuff on a whim and moved from Sweden to Riga.

'Now I'm trying to beat Sean's record,' Caspar confesses. The Aussie hostel owner's been drunk 405 nights in a row, whereas Caspar is barely halfway there. Several of us – Caspar as the hostel rep, plus three guests – go around the corner to a local nightclub. After 1am, things are in full swing. There's a really friendly vibe and I end up having a good time in spite of myself. I was expecting something akin to Russia's 'face control', with clubbers being turned away for not being pretty enough, well dressed enough, or cool enough. But no one's overdressed and the dancing errs heavily on the side of enthusiasm rather than skill.

'This is real Latvia!' Caspar shouts to me as he and I bounce around on the dance floor to hip-hop and funk. Then the other two guests from the hostel grab me and I get pulled into knocking back B52s – something I've never done in my entire young life. During my university years, I avoided serious inebriation. Loss of control was unpalatable. Several shots later, Caspar pours some unidentified liquid into my open mouth and hands me a lighted match. Sticking it in my mouth and then watching the flames dancing on my tongue goes against my every instinct of self-preservation, but I do it, and it feels like some rite of passage.

In the wee hours of the morning, I find myself in Caspar's attic room along with one of the other girls, listening to him play melancholy songs of his own creation on the guitar, in the most clichéd, angsty-student-movie way ever. We dangle our feet out of the window with the sheer drop below, while Caspar recounts a story of his roommate crawling out on to the roof while drunk to get it on with an adventurous girl: 'One wrong move, and it would've been two naked dead bodies on the pavement.'

Bone-tired, in a haze of alcohol-induced contentment, the three of us fall silent and cuddle, watching the sky lighten over the rooftops of Art Deco buildings, the gentle human contact an antidote to the brash violence of the bunker outing. I see what Caspar means about Riga. 'It just sucks you in.'

* * * * *

My prison cell is meant to be shared by at least two people. I have it all to myself. The dark corridor that leads to it smells seriously musty, as does the cell itself. Around the corner are Soviet-style squatter latrines. There is no furniture besides some wooden slats with a thin mattress on top.

Unlike the former inmates, I get perks, such as clean sheets, as well as access to the staff headquarters with its abundant collection of Soviet kitsch – old banners, Lenin busts, revolutionary books – and, most importantly, the freedom to wander the premises.

Karosta Prison, in Liepaja, Latvia, is a two-storey, forbidding-looking red brick building. It was a military prison up until 1997; now, foreign visitors are actively encouraged to stay overnight. Juris, the paunchy, middle-aged guard with conspicuous sweat stains under his arms, brings me a better supper than the prison's inmates would've received: *piragi* (small, crescent-shaped buns filled with bacon and sautéed onion) and a typical summer salad – sliced cucumbers, tomatoes and onions.

'You're on your own now,' he tells me, before locking me up until morning.

I lie back on my wooden slats and try to imagine what it would've been like to spend a lifetime here, looking up at the narrow window near the ceiling, breathing in the smells of decades-old sewage, and perhaps having your life brutally cut short. When Juris gave me a tour in heavily accented Russian, he'd pointed out a small plaque that marked the spot where political prisoners were shot.

'Maybe it's a bit simplistic and sentimental,' I told one of my friends later, 'but I think that it's important to deprive yourself of creature comforts to appreciate what other people go through.'

My friend told me that he didn't need to stay in a prison to understand what it's like, or to sympathise with the incarcerated, but I disagreed: 'If we don't experience something on our own skin, if only for a bit, we can only imagine the experience, and our imagination isn't necessarily accurate.'

But I draw the line at the group activities that Karosta Prison offers. Across the Baltics, nostalgia for the bygone Soviet era is milked like a prize cow for the benefit of foreign tourists. In Kuressaare, on the Estonian island of Saaremaa, you can stay in an old-fashioned sanatorium and undergo Soviet-style treatments such as Charcot's Shower. This involves stripping naked, standing against the wall and having your cellulite pummelled with high-pressure jets of cold water – supposedly excellent for improving circulation – by a gruff-looking, middle-aged matron. Karosta, meanwhile, offers role-playing activities, with 'prisoners' dressing up and being subjected to regular bed checks at night, as well as mock interrogation and verbal abuse from the 'guards', to make the experience more 'authentic'.

This would fill my parents' generation with horror, because they'd have known people – or of people – who'd been interrogated, tortured and imprisoned for real. The play-acting is too close to the bone. Seriously bad taste.

Speaking of bad taste… picture the scene: Soviet martial music blares from the speakers in the trees. Barbed wire surrounds you. Beyond the barbed wire are guard towers. In clearing after clearing, there are monuments to bygone Communist greats: Lenin, Stalin, Marx, Engels. Bigwigs of Lithuania's Communist Party. Heroic sculptures of Soviet soldiers, about to take on the Fascist enemy, and statues of Lithuanian snipers, killed in their prime. Huts brimming over with Lenin imagery – on banners, badges, even Turkish-style rugs.

This is Gruto Parkas, a quasi-reconstruction of a gulag in the south of Lithuania, near the spa town of Druskininkai. When the Soviet Union fell apart, its monuments consigned to the dustbin of history, Lithuania's mushroom magnate Viliumas Malinauskas rounded up the statuary and founded this sculpture garden and museum. At the entrance to Grutas Parkas is a cattle train carriage, of the kind used to transport Lithuanians to exile in Siberia. Originally, Malinauskas intended for visitors to be brought into the park inside such cattle cars, to simulate the deportation experience. For me, all this Soviet memorabilia doesn't have the same negative connotations or carry the oppressive weight that it would for older generations of my family. I like the woven Lenin rugs. I like the sombre martial music, too. It makes me nostalgic for a past that never existed.

* * * * *

My sister Genie joins me for a few days in Tallinn as my research assistant – a role she would reprise in other countries over the years. During the course of my writing life, I learn to choose my travelling companions carefully, aiming for the company of those who actively assist with sightseeing and dining out, as opposed to those who believe that my work is all a bit of a lark and expect to be entertained at all times. Together, sis and I discover a cool photography exhibition in the basement of one of Tallinn's medieval defence towers, climb uneven spiral staircases until our thigh muscles spasm from the exertion, learn about the suffering of the local population under the Nazis and the Soviets in the interactive Museum of Occupations, and commune with murmuring heads of historical figures in the Kumu contemporary art gallery. By night, we exchange salty banter with cheeky wenches in period costume at Olde Hansa, while tucking into elk and boar sausages with onion jam, home-dried elk meat strips, and homemade bread – allegedly the fare of medieval noblemen and merchants – in a centuries-old cellar lit by flaming torches.

Prior to Genie's arrival, one lunchtime found me at DaDa, a kitsch restaurant in Riga, Latvia, allegedly inspired by the Dadaist art movement, with mismatched chairs dangling from the ceiling. It was a semi-self-serve place, and the trick to getting your money's worth was to load up your bowl with as much noodles, vegetables, seafood, various toppings as possible, and then getting one of the cooks to flash-fry it for you with a sauce of your choice. While performing a delicate balancing act with my Jenga tower of ingredients, I noticed a curly-haired, bearded young man – obviously a foreigner – who was also by himself, and impulsively invited him to join me. For the next couple of days, Jacob the Kiwi shadowed me while I checked out Latvia's beach resort of Jurmala and some castle ruins in forested Sigulda.

It was the start of another pattern. On the road, I flit between extremes. I go through spells during which I avoid human company like the plague (beyond the necessary interactions required to do my job), but after a while, the need for proper conversation and genuine human interaction outweighs my need for solitude. I discover then that it's possible for a really shy person to reinvent herself by wearing the mask of someone considerably more sociable and outgoing.

Sometimes, companions find me. Towards the end of my stay in Lithuania, I find myself in Nida, a former fishing village located on the Curonian Spit – a thin sliver of land jutting into the Baltic Sea, covered in sand dunes and dense pine forest. According to the local museum, during hard times, Nida's fishing folk used to trap crows and bite off the heads, washing away the taste with slugs of vodka. But by the time I get there, it's a popular holiday spot, spread out along the Curonian Lagoon, its waters pearlescent during the long summer evenings and its air scented with the aroma of smoked fish.

At my guesthouse I'm befriended by 59-year-old Barbara from Hamburg, Germany, who is cycling around the Baltics for fun. When I tell her about my death row pen pals, my work in Ukraine, my travels, she tells me that I'm the most remarkable young person she's ever met – that 25-year-old Germans only seem to care about parties and what clothes to buy. I end up hanging out with Barbara for several days. I like her sense of humour and have always gravitated towards people with more life experience than me: older, well-travelled individuals or, more recently, fellow travel writers. She and I climb Pardinis Dune – a sand mountain in the 'Lithuanian Sahara', admire *krikštai* (pagan grave markers) in Nida's tiny cemetery, and cycle through pine forest to Juodkrante, a smaller village further along the Spit, known for its macabre sculpture trail of carved wooden devils, witches and other mythological figures. Barbara is decidedly unsympathetic about my saddle sores, inflicted by my sit-up-and-beg rental bike. To make it back to Nida, I improvise padding by stripping down to my bikini top and sticking my T-shirt down my shorts, like my travel writing/cycling heroine, Josie Dew. And yes, as she says, it feels like sitting on a dead cat. On the way back, Barbara and I stop to splash in the freezing cold sea, and follow our noses to the fish smokery in the little village of Preila. We buy an entire two-foot-long smoked eel, and dine out on it on the picnic table in the garden, smearing the rich, fishy, smoky eel fat on crackers and sipping cold lager. In the morning, I find a note from Barbara under my door, with an open-ended invitation to come and stay with her if I ever happen to pass through Hamburg.

* * * * *

On our last night in Estonia, my sister and I join a free nightlife tour run by local students who enjoy showing visitors what they consider to be the true highlights of Tallinn. It's right up my readers' street. Lisa and Lina – both tall, with curly dark hair, in their late teens – take us up the 'drinking hill', where we sit, clutching our illicit whisky-and-cokes, and watch the sun set over the pointed spires of churches and the medieval wall.

'We and our friends come up here because you can see the police coming and hide the booze,' Lina grins.

'But you can't buy alcohol in stores anymore after 8pm,' Lisa chimes in. 'Earlier this year, in April, we had two nights of rioting when the city authorities moved the Bronze Soldier.' Erected in 1947 and dedicated to the 'Soviet liberators of Tallinn' (adding insult to injury, since Estonia didn't get a say in whether it wished to be occupied by Russia), the statue was moved to a nearby military cemetery. But some Russian nationalists went on the rampage and looted some shops.

'I don't think they particularly cared about politics,' Lina adds. 'They just wanted to make trouble.' The one thing that wasn't trashed was a 24-hour Hesburger (Finland's answer to McDonald's) outlet, 'because both Russians and Estonians eat there.'

Earlier, my sister and I took a boat to the small forested island of Aegna. On the boat, a Russian guy, Sergei, heard us talking in English and came over to practise his own. I chose not to reveal that we were actually fluent in Russian and elbowed my sister when she was about to say something. I wanted his perspective on the animosity between Russians and Estonians, while remaining neutral. Sergei told us that he was twenty-eight, born in Estonia, but speaks little Estonian, has no Estonian friends, feels a great affinity for Mother Russia (he comes from a noble family that fled the country before the 1917 Revolution) and isn't bothered about getting an Estonian passport.

I've read about Estonia's 'stateless' Russians, caught between two worlds. They don't have a home in Russia, and they don't have Estonian citizenship, because they have to pass the language test to get it and many seem reluctant to learn Estonian. The older Russians don't identify with the country they've found themselves in after the collapse of the USSR. They are resentful of having become second-class citizens, when for much of their lives they were first among equals. I didn't think that this was true of the younger generation, but Sergei's bitter attitude changes my mind.

'Why did you shush me?' My sister snapped at me when we caught the tram back to the city centre. 'Why didn't you tell him that we're Russian?'

'Because we aren't, are we,' I retorted. 'We're from Russia, but not Russian.'

Genie felt that concealing our fluency in Russian was fundamentally dishonest. But I didn't feel like volunteering our origins to a stranger, because that would've led to a deeper discussion of our roots, our Jewishness, my conflicted relationship with the country of my birth. It's like the tiresome constant refrains of 'Where are you from?' that I've grown up with in the UK, marked by my surname, my accent. 'Cambridge,' I'd tell them curtly. 'But where are you *really* from…?' they'd say, with the unspoken second half of that question being: 'And when are you leaving?'

Given that my sister and I have spent precisely zero time living in post-Soviet Russia, it's curious how she'd always put 'Moscow, Russia' on forms when asked for place of origin, whereas I'd write 'Cambridge, UK'. I was born in Moscow, too, but felt no need to identify with a country that treated my parents badly, and their parents before that. I also struggle with pigeonholing myself when forms ask for my ethnicity. I don't fall under 'Asian', 'Black' or 'Mixed' categories, which leaves 'White', the only subcategories being 'White British', 'White Irish' and 'White Other'. Am I white? Depends on whom you ask. Certainly not, according to Russians, Asians or Jamaicans. Absolutely, according to some of my friends. Not sure, is my own response. Am I British? I'm a naturalised Brit rather than British by birth, so… Typically, I get a migraine and tick 'Other'.

Critical in my own head of immigrants who don't try to assimilate, or learn the language of their host country, I'm unpleasantly jolted by the realisation that I empathise with part of Sergei's outlook. He's not an immigrant. He feels – or is made to feel – that he doesn't belong in the country of his birth, which isn't too dissimilar from my parents. They did their best to fit in, however, and wanted a better lot for their daughters, so they emigrated.

Lina and Lisa both have Russian friends (with whom they speak English), perhaps because their friends are also in their late teens and don't have one foot in a country that no longer exists. They take me and Genie to several more bars, and then our evening ends on an introspective note, at a late-night café specialising in hot chocolate, continuing our conversation about race relations in Estonia. Lisa is half-Estonian, half-Yemeni, and because of her dark complexion, she's been given grief by some kids at school.

'It's not just Russians who face discrimination here, for not wanting to assimilate,' she tells us. 'I'm Estonian, Estonian is my mother tongue, but some people have difficulty accepting me as a local. It's a problem. But it's my country too, and to solve the problem, first we need to acknowledge that it's there.'

And perhaps because I'm still mulling over Sergei's story, I find myself thinking that it's time I returned to Mother Russia to explore my love–hate relationship with the country of my birth.

CHAPTER 5
RIDING THE RAILS

'After days of taiga and cynical grey Soviet towns, Komsomolsk-na-Amure hits the BAM adventurer like a mini St Petersburg' crows my guidebook. Have they ever been to St Petersburg? Since I've just come up from the main Trans-Siberian railway (Moscow to Vladivostok) to join the BAM (Baikalo-Amurskaya Magistral) – the railway line connecting Russia's Pacific coast to the north end of Lake Baikal – I'm momentarily filled with horror at the thought of grimmer towns to come.

Trudging into town beneath a leaden sky, I'm attacked by vicious Siberian mosquitoes. Komsomolsk feels like a depressing 80s time warp: identical grey apartment buildings, broken paving, men with red faces and glazed eyes sitting around on park benches, swigging from two-litre cans of Baltika beer. 'A sober Russia is the will of the people!' a notice on the wall proclaims, engaging in some not-too-subtle trolling of the town's visible residents.

* * * * *

Earlier in the year, I'd met one of the original Lonely Planet authors, Bryn Thomas, at a travel show in London. He founded his own guidebook series, Trailblazer, and asked me if I would be interested in updating his iconic Trailblazer Trans-Siberian Handbook. I was. And so I became the first (and only) native Russian speaker to take on an entire guidebook by myself, and committed myself to spending months riding the rails in Russia, Mongolia and China. Three months prior, when I began my slow train journey across Russia from Moscow – in order to explore the country of my birth for the very first time while simultaneously updating the guidebook – I was accompanied for the first leg by my sister Genie and Steve, a snarky Yorkshireman with puppy-dog eyes, whom I've been friends with since university. The last bunk-bed in our four-person *kupe* (second-class carriage compartment) was briefly occupied by a 'lodger', Igor from Usolye-Sibirskoye, the salt capital of Siberia. Overweight, in his forties and accompanied by a strong odour of stale sweat and cigarette smoke, he was a self-proclaimed 'historian' who tried to educate us about modern-day Russia.

'Things are different in Siberia. People are kinder here. It's a different mindset from Western Russia.' He complained that the government was funnelling all of Siberia's vast mineral wealth to the capital and openly complained about the president: 'Putin is a very hard man, not popular here.'

Comparing 2010 to how things were before 1991, Igor said: 'The quality of life is somewhat better now. We have freedom of speech, but under the Communists, people knew that on the first of the month, they'd get paid, and the pension went so much further.'

I did wonder who could actually afford to shop in Moscow's posh supermarkets, expensive even by British standards. 'Most people live on the poverty line,' Igor confirmed. His solution was to bring back absolute monarchy: 'Russia's always had a tsar. People are investing abroad because they don't trust the temporary stability. I think that without a tsar, we'll never have that stability.' I refrained from pointing out that Russia's tsars were not exactly known for their equitable treatment of the population and ranged from the mildly odd and woefully incompetent to the dangerously bizarre and despotic.

*　*　*　*　*

I eventually find myself on the banks of the mighty Amur river. Compared to Khabarovsk, the port city further south, Komsomolsk's river port seems utterly dead. The only people around are three fishermen standing motionlessly on the litter-strewn sandy beach. There are some dented bumper cars there, and maybe the place comes alive at night. At the Regional Museum, I peruse the collection of arrowheads, bark-covered canoes and hide-covered skis, as well as the obligatory stuffed, pickled and pinned wildlife. The staff outnumber the visitors (me) five to one, and one of the ladies attaches herself to me like a limpet. I find this intensely irritating, and am tempted to tiptoe theatrically around the corner, as if I'm about to graffiti a taxidermied moose.

Then the sun comes out and the city is transformed. Not so you'd mistake it for St Petersburg, but enough to light up the heroic Communist mosaics on walls and the broad boulevards. It still feels like the city is trying too hard, though, the attempts to spruce it up too desperate. The shopping centre might be called 'Singapore', taking a stab at being delightfully exotic, but it fails to 'make all my dreams come true', as the sign outside promises. Inside it's the same collection of overpriced goods that few can afford. The U-City Pizza Parlour – seemingly the only place to eat around here – is a stab at an American diner, where local trendies pay over the odds for lukewarm, microwaved pizza slices and non-functioning wi-fi.

There are other breaks with the past – notices on walls offering to find you a romantic partner and to help you fix your marital problems. In Communist times, the idea of going to a psychiatrist was unthinkable. Who would trust a complete stranger with the innermost workings of their mind, given how political dissidents were locked up indefinitely in insane asylums?

In another advert, a self-styled shaman called Vladimir invites readers to 'training' sessions which will teach them to be 'on the same wavelength with nature'. He also promises to make you 'Healthier! Stronger! Richer!' I didn't think that shamans cared about worldly stuff like money.

On the way back to the train station, a sinister piece of graffiti asks:

'Когда у тебя кончится терпение, моя Русь?' ('When will you run out of patience, my Russia?')

What's more ominous is the swastika scribbled above that sentence.

I get out of town on the evening train.

* * * * *

Living on board long-distance trains is second nature by now. I grab my oversized rucksack from train station storage, am first in the queue to board the train, present the *provodnitsa* (female carriage attendant) with my passport and ticket, rush on board, claim my favourite bunk #51, stow my luggage, lay out my bedding, change into my pyjamas, and make myself a cup of tea while others are still boarding.

While most foreign travellers opt to be crammed into a four-person *kupe* compartment, complete with lockable door, I vastly prefer the open-plan *platzkart* (third-class) carriage: a dormitory consisting of fifty-four bunks, divided into lots of six. The main carriage entrance, the train attendant's cubicle, a toilet and the samovar are located at one end, with another toilet and smoking area at the far end of the carriage. You have two lots of two bunks facing each other and sharing a table, and another two across the aisle, stretching along the wall. *Platzkart* carriages are the most sociable places on the train, where fellow travellers engage in that age-old ritual of trading life stories and food.

So why bunk #51? It's a bottom side bunk, near the train carriage attendant, more compact than the other bottom bunks and therefore perfect for those under the height of 5ft 5. It's a choice window berth that turns into two seats and a table during the day, but when you convert it to a bunk at night, your luggage goes underneath. You're across the aisle from the majority of the bunks, so it's (marginally) easier to avoid your companions if you're not gregariously inclined. Its polar opposite is the dreaded berth #38 at the smoking end of the carriage: expect stale cigarette smoke to filter through and to be disturbed by everyone and their grandmother on their way to the bathroom.

I've come to really enjoy sleeping on board these long-distance Russian trundlers. Being constantly in motion appeals to my restless nature, and the chugging rhythm of the train lulls me to sleep.

Neighbours, however, are always a bit of a wild card. Having ended up with a top bunk for the Komsomolsk to Tynda stretch, I groan inwardly when it turns out that my neighbours for part of the 37-hour journey are an obnoxious thirty-something woman and her stroppy ten-year-old son. The woman is joined by her boyfriend in his early twenties. Full-on canoodling commences on the bottom bunk, and while I generally don't have a problem with open displays of affection, I can't help but compare the way she treats her son (snapping at him constantly, hitting him) and the way she coos over her boyfriend. The boy kicks the wall in frustration over being ignored.

I feel for him, figuring that she must've had him when she was very young, and probably blames the kid for standing in the way of her fun. The mum and the boyfriend continue yakking into the night. Their mobiles periodically go off at top volume, and then they complain of a draught and get me out of bed so that they can close the window (the top bunk gets in the way) without asking me if that's okay with me or saying thank you.

This obsession with draughts drives me bonkers. Broadly speaking, Russians can be divided into two groups: fresh-air fiends like me who sleep with their windows open, year round, and those who shy away from fresh air at all costs, believing that it causes illness. Much of my time aboard the train is spent battling my fellow travellers and the *provodnitsa* for access to fresh air. I go around opening all windows within sight. The *provodnitsa* then comes round, closing them again. I open them again. She closes them. And on and on, ad nauseam, until her patience runs out and she locks them for good. Then the only way for me to get fresh air is to lurk by the one half-open window above the samovar.

* * * * *

Luckily, the woman, the boyfriend and the stroppy son get off in the middle of the night. By the time I'm awake the following morning, they've been replaced by two men, Yura and Andrei. When Andrei looks up at me, I think: 'It's George Clooney!' Well, a heavyset, Russian George Clooney who's really let himself go and is drinking beer at 9am. They're both travelling for work, they tell me. Andrei is a miner, while Yura (blonde, with a weathered face and bloodshot blue eyes) is returning to Tynda, his home town, because the mining company he's worked for hasn't paid him in four months. He's forty-nine, has two children and has worked in mines along the BAM his whole adult life. When he finds out that I'm travelling around Russia to encourage foreign visitors to come here, he starts reciting the names of all the tiny stations, and what there is to see and where.

'We'll go into business together, you and me,' he tells me. 'We'll bring ecotourism to the BAM. The fishing here is out of this world!' He starts talking enthusiastically about some fish which is the tastiest in the world. I fail to point out that while fly-fishing can indeed bring in big money, really wealthy people tend to go to Patagonia where you get amazing rivers and great accommodation, and where everything works like clockwork. Getting to the BAM is a headache and a half, fishing in nature reserves is forbidden by Russian law, and the anachronistic visa system needs scrapping.

'Do you like caviar?' asks Valera, joining us. He's a blonde guy my age with a nose that looks like it's been broken more than once and a scar on his cheek, travelling north of the BAM to work in a gold mine. He's from Vanino, in Russia's extreme far east, but work is scarce there, and his sister has given him a bucket of red caviar for the road. We all sit and dig into the communal pot with spoons, washing down the salty bubbles with hot, sweet black tea with lemon.

Everyone wants to know what British life is like and I want to know about the Siberian equivalent in return. What's the cost of monthly rent? What's the price of bread? Is the weather similar to Russia's? How much do you earn? How much does it cost to raise a family? Some of the questions stump a city slicker like me, just like when the cleaning ladies at the Komsomolsk train station asked me what types of soil we have in the UK – a natural question to ask if you're used to growing your own vegetables.

Partaking in this merry caviar feast and barrage of questions forces me, with some internal shame, to confront both my own preconceptions about working-class Russians and the intellectual snobbery that I've been inadvertently raised with. My parents, who value education above all else, faced with a bunch of miners who swear and drink, would have assumed that they have no common ground, nothing to talk about. But to me, it's a fascinating insight into the lives of ordinary Russians, affected in a major way by the changes brought about by the collapse of the Soviet Union some twenty years back. My *platzkart* companions are surprisingly (and here again I'm embarrassed at having assumed otherwise) well informed about the actions of their own government, take a keen interest in the world beyond Russia's borders, and can name the British prime minister. How many of their British counterparts would be able to name Russia's president, or comment in an informed and articulate manner on the politics of other countries?

Tanya, a dark-haired 21-year-old who expertly fends off Andrei's drunken advances, comes from the village of Fevralskoye and tells me that she enjoys learning English. I overhear her talking to a friend on the phone: 'I've just been talking to someone from England! Cool!'

I have a curious double status here: I'm both of Russia and not, so everyone treats me as a guest of honour.

Yura tells me that in the winter the temperature in Tynda drops to -47°C, and in the summer it can be in the mid 30s. 'When we lived in Khabarovsk, where the winters are mild, nothing below −30, my son asked me in March: "Dad, when is winter coming?"' My companions find it hysterical that in the UK the coldest winter in decades was −12°C. and that everything comes to a standstill when we get two inches of snow. Yura then enthusiastically describes England's climate to Tanya, despite having never been there.

My bunkmates keep drinking all day and both pass out around sundown. The train stops at Marevya, a tiny stop in the middle of the taiga, and I hop out in search of fresh provisions. My months-long journey has taught me the importance of a) boarding a long-distance train with adequate supplies of food and b) topping up whenever possible.

* * * * *

When Genie, Steve and I originally boarded the Trans-Siberian train in Moscow, our attempt to have dinner in the so-called 'dining car' played out like a comedy sketch.

An oversized matron with a bad hair dye job handed us bilingual menus, so that we could browse such delights as 'meat a la French' and 'peasant meal'. I opted for *solyanka*.

'We don't have *solyanka*.'

'Okay, I'll have the pizza.'

'We don't have pizza.'

'Okay, I'll have the pancakes.'

'We don't have pancakes.'

After we'd gone through pretty much the entire menu in that manner, I finally got annoyed and asked her to tell me exactly what was available. The attendant heaved a heavy sigh, as if my request were a huge imposition. 'Seafood salad, chicken salad and beef tongue with horseradish.' I was astounded. They just hadn't bothered to stock up. The last item was the vilest thing I'd eaten in a very, very long time, and that includes guinea pig tripe in Peru.

When I told another temporary 'lodger' of ours– Sergei, a young mechanic on his way home to Novosibirsk – about our misadventures in the dining car, he laughed. 'Rookie mistake. Everyone knows that you get the best food on the platforms.'

And so it proved. The longer stops became a source of great excitement, with grannies selling everything from homemade booze and baked goods to ice cream, bundles of smoked fish, and cups of pine nuts. We stocked up on fresh berries, salted cucumbers, dumplings, pancakes. One old lady patted Genie on the shoulder: 'You look like you could use some vitamins. Have some blackcurrants, for yourself, for your son.' It was unclear whether she thought my sister was pregnant. Half-affronted, half-amused, Genie ended up buying the berries.

* * * * *

There are a couple of babushkas on the platform at Marevya, shouldering baskets of *pirozhki* stuffed with meat and mushrooms. That'll do. The smell of pine is intense, intoxicating. If in Komsomolsk I'd reached my nadir, utterly fed up with being on the road, here I perk up again, looking out over Siberia's vast forest that stretches as far as the eye can see. The sun is setting, and the sky is a seething mass of oranges, reds and purples.

I end up talking late into the night with Nikita from Khabarovsk, a sandy-haired, stooped man in his mid-thirties. Although he has finished university, he is travelling to work in a mine. Both he and his wife, also a graduate, have been forced to take on any employment they can find to feed their son. He tells me how he'd like to move abroad, ideally to Japan: 'All I want is a stable job, enough to provide for my family, go on holiday sometimes, and to live and work with dignity.' Of course, if that were possible in Russia, he'd prefer to stay here, but life is too stressful, too hard. He's tired of what he considers to be a lack of patriotism, of everyone taking bribes, of general discourtesy towards others, the stultifying bureaucracy: 'And it's all about connections. If you don't know the right people, it's difficult to get anything done.'

'Surely it would be in everyone's interests if everything worked efficiently, if ordinary lives were better and the country were richer?' I ask.

'Yes, but I don't think that the mentality will change. Decent people eventually get fed up with fighting the system and go abroad if they can. So all you have left are these bureaucrats who bend the rules to suit themselves and who don't care about Russia's future: only about their own. I think Putin is trying to change things, and he did get around ten percent done of what he'd promised – which is a lot! – but there are too many vested interests standing in his way.'

It seems that the Communist ideals of self-sacrifice and working for the common good have been replaced with incredible selfishness. So when my travelling companions ask me if I want to move back to Russia, I tell them that I'm happy to visit, but that I prefer to live somewhere where life is stable. Where people are law-abiding, where you don't encounter irrational bureaucracy and mindless opposition whenever you try to get anything done, I add silently.

'I don't know the rules here,' I explain. 'I don't know whom to bribe, how to bribe, how much to bribe. I don't think I'd fit in here.'

* * * * *

Yura had promised to show me around Tynda, the biggest town on the BAM – a veritable metropolis compared to the tiny, forlorn villages that we'd passed. But when we get off the train in the morning, I decide not to wait for him; he's so hungover he can barely speak.

EYEBALL TACOS AND KANGAROO STEW

Tynda's train station is a vast, airy space, with gigantic posters celebrating the thirty-fifth anniversary of the BAM (a year earlier, in 2009) and praising 'the road built with love'. Nice try. I happen to know that the railway was built on the blood and bones of at least half a million people – from political dissidents to Japanese prisoners of war – starting from the 1930s onwards, and although its official completion date was 1974, it actually continued right up until 1984. Admittedly, in the later stages, the work was done by young Komsomol (Soviet political youth organisation) members, some of whom were enticed with triple wages and other perks, while others were driven by genuinely patriotic feelings. The railway that runs north of and parallel to the eastern half of the Trans-Siberian railway was conceived in the 1930s as a hugely ambitious engineering project that would make Siberia's vast mineral wealth more accessible. Rails were laid across boggy tundra and tunnels blasted through sheer rock with great accuracy. Failure was not an option, as it would've been punished by execution.

I happen to be in Tynda at the same time as I finish reading Dervla Murphy's *Through Siberia By Accident*. She recuperated here after injuring her leg while planning to cycle across Siberia – a venture considered to be bordering on insanity by the locals. I recognise Hotel Yunost, where she stayed – it seems to be the only hotel in town. Try as I might, however, I can't find the heroic statue of the BAM worker, a muscled man brandishing a sledgehammer, mentioned in the book, or the *banya* (Russian sauna) next to it. The market, though, is exactly as Murphy described, filled with cheap Chinese tat, sold by traditionally attired Tajik women.

Locals walking around are dressed in Siberia's idea of high fashion: Adidas tracksuits and loud patterned shirts and tops. Mullets abound. I can't help but think that had we stayed in Russia, both I and my childhood friend Nikolai would now be bad dressers with questionable haircuts, a couple of kids apiece, stressful jobs and a major nicotine habit.

Crossing the bridge back towards the train station, I spot a piece of graffiti which asks for a 'мир, где нет чужих'. That can be interpreted either as 'a world where no one is a stranger' or 'Russia without foreigners'. I choose to think that it's the former.

Having calculated that in the next two and a half weeks I will spend exactly five nights in a bed, as opposed to on an overnight train, I nab a twin occupancy 'rest room' at the very basic train station hotel and tell the *dezhurnaya* (middle-aged woman on duty, a zealous guardian of the keys) to warn anyone who may wish to room with me that I snore like a pirate.

In the morning, I'm woken up by the piano riff that precedes railway announcements, stolen from Gloria Gaynor's 'I Will Survive'. I keep waiting for the woman making the announcements to burst into: '*First I was afraid, I was petrified…*' But she never does.

* * * * *

When we board the train in Tynda, pandemonium ensues. It turns out that the train arrived an hour ago and the carriages are not in order, so what was originally carriage #5 becomes carriage #3 once we've all boarded and are settled. When the *provodnitsas* tell us to swap carriages, the middle-aged ladies express exactly how they feel about this cock-up. Our *provodnitsa* tries to placate a particularly furious matron: 'My dear, I totally understand why you're upset…' but said matron continues loudly cursing everything under the sun.

My neighbours are Galya, a retired BAM worker who moved from the Urals to Siberia to work on the BAM because of the concessions on offer and stayed there because she liked Tynda, and Valera and Nastya – a couple of *provodniks* in their early thirties who normally work this route, but who are off home to Severobaikalsk on leave.

Galya states that life in Communist times was 'like paradise'. You don't say, I think to myself. I do appreciate that she misses the relative stability of the bygone days, though. She's done all right, she tells me; managed to save up to buy flats for her offspring. Galya generously shares her food with me, refusing my own offerings – but she asks too many personal questions, leading me to retreat to my bunk.

* * * * *

'What would you say are the main differences between Russians and Brits?' I was asked by a young Couchsurfing couple, Misha and Zhenya, on whose floor I slept while in Krasnoyarsk – the Siberian city bisected by the Lena river, from which Lenin took his *nom de guerre*. I babbled something about Russians being more hospitable, but also more prone to asking direct questions that Brits would consider rude, and to giving unsolicited advice. Not just Russians: I've found this to be the case across Central Asia as well. Former Soviets. Perhaps it's a generational thing, too.

A few years after my original Trans-Siberian journey, while travelling between Astana and Almaty, I found myself sharing an SV (first-class private compartment, with two sleeping bunks and private bathroom) with Baglan, a middle-aged Kazakh. He treated me to tea and meat pie, and enlightened me about daily life and politics of present-day Kazakhstan, but eventually, and wearingly, conversation drifted towards my private life.

'How old are you?'

'Thirty-six.'

'Do you have any children?'

'No, not yet.'

'You really ought to have children while you're young, you know', he informed me, making me sound like a dried-up old prune. Travelling in Russia over the years, and being given similar advice on multiple occasions, at first I found it quaint, then exhausting, then tear-out-my-hair infuriating. Suppose they pose this question to someone who desperately wants kids but suffers from infertility? Or someone who's suffered a bereavement?

Unwilling to discuss the fruitfulness (or otherwise) of my loins, I'd slunk upstairs to my bunk bed and pointedly got my book out to signal the end of our interaction.

* * * * *

In *Through Siberia by Accident*, Dervla Murphy wrote of the incredible hospitality she received in Tynda where, after her injury, complete strangers put her up, looked after her, and made her feel extremely welcome. Do Brits go out of their way to be kind to strangers, especially foreigners? Maybe in small remote villages somewhere.

I've also been the beneficiary of exceptional kindness from strangers, on numerous occasions, across the former Soviet Union. While taking the train across the border from Shymkent, Kazakhstan, to Tashkent, Uzbekistan, I was exceptionally fretful about being in possession of a stack of Uzbek *som* (local currency). I knew that all currency had to be declared before entering Uzbekistan. I also knew that *som* wasn't supposed to be exported outside the country's borders, and that I could potentially get into serious trouble for having it on me. Tatyana, one of the middle-aged Uzbek ladies sitting near me – who'd already served me some herbal tea to soothe my tubercular-sounding asthmatic cough – noticed my nervousness, asked me about it and, when I confided in her, taught me what to do: 'Just hide it in your bra; it'll be fine.'

I did, patting my cups into place so that they wouldn't look too lopsided and lumpy. This caused much merriment among the ladies – Tatyana and her two companions, Irina and Alina – and further broke the ice. Before we arrived in Tashkent, they'd told me their life stories (they all worked in Yekaterinburg in Russia for ten months a year, then came home to be with their families); Alina invited me to an Uzbek wedding; Tatyana told me that I was welcome to stay with her and her family anytime and, proving to be a real firecracker, gave me unsolicited tips on how to please a man. She even demonstrated a sexy little dance – no mean feat for a woman as wide as she was tall.

* * * * *

Valera returns from socialising in another carriage, covered in blood. He got inebriated, and then got beaten up by one of his co-drinkers who didn't take kindly to being accused of stealing Valera's mobile phone. I produce my first aid kit and offer to clean the gash on his chin, but his girlfriend waves me away.

'If they throw him off the train, it's fine by me,' Nastya tells me bitterly.

'It can't be easy, living with a man like that,' I convey my assessment of the Nastya–Valera relationship to Galya. Galya is unsympathetic:

'She ditched her husband and two kids to be with him, so she deserves what's coming to her.'

Nastya keeps swigging beer from a two-litre bottle, but at least she's not rowdy. Valera is talking loudly about the state of Russia today, addressing no one in particular. Everything is going to hell, according to him, and he wouldn't vote for Putin or Medvedev because 'none of them care what's happening to the country. Our population is decreasing; in a decade or two we'll all die out or else become farmland for the EU or China.'

The scenery we're passing through becomes more and more dramatic. First it's dense forest, with the odd little BAM town every now and then. Then there are pine-covered cliffs rising to the right of us; we cross several wide rivers, and the land becomes more rugged. The birches are turning gold and red and freshly fallen snow covers the tops of the mountains. Glacial streams criss-cross the land and a low-hanging mist obscures the foothills. It's more Patagonia than Russia. I haven't seen a proper autumn in many years and stare out of the window, enthralled.

* * * * *

At first glance, Severobaikalsk is a pretty grim place: a row of shabby multi-storey buildings.

But the local museum turns out to be the town's saving grace. There's a temporary art exhibit by Valery Kondakov, a local artist from Nizhneangarsk. The woman in charge gives me a tour, explaining the significance of his sculptures and artwork which employs sewing and weaving techniques to great effect.

'His work has been inspired by, and dedicated to, the native Evenk [indigenous Siberian people] culture, and its purpose is to make people think.' She speaks of the balance between humans and nature. There's something very attractive about his wooden sculptures. I'm particularly taken with the 'Matrix', made of a block of polished wood, dotted with tiny copper pipes, with several white blocks on top, representing modern-day buildings. A weaving incorporates a round Evenk rug; visually it's both balanced and striking. I'd love to speak to the artist, and Nizhneangarsk is on my way back to Moscow, but I'm too shy to just turn up on his doorstep.

Staying at the Baikal Trail Hostel, run by the energetic Anya, I meet Jennifer and Joy, both from the Lake Tahoe area, California, and both taking part in the Great Baikal Trail project. Every year, improving the existing hiking trails is done by local and international volunteers.

'The original idea was to have a continuous trail that runs along the entire lakeshore, but we've come to realise that it's impractical and are focusing on existing ancient trails, such as those used by the Evenk reindeer herders for centuries,' I'm told by the Severobaikalsk coordinator of the project. Earlier in my trip, in the village of Listvyanka at Lake Baikal's southern end, I'd spoken with Yevgeniy 'Jack' Sheremetoff, a tourism operator who organises dog sledding, ice hiking and ice cycling on Lake Baikal during the colder months. He laughed at the idea of the Great Baikal Trail, since the locals had long known it as just a handy footpath between villages before it somehow acquired the 'great' sobriquet.

Jennifer and Joy are part of an exchange programme for Russian and American students who spend time at each other's lakes, learning about conservation and ecology. Jennifer speaks fluent Russian. I tag along with them and Anya to the Goudzhekit hot springs on a blustery, cold and rainy night. To someone who hasn't had a bath for months, the soak is marvellous, and I float around with a daft grin on my face. 'During the colder months, when the temperature drops to −40° Celsius, this is hard to beat,' Anya smiles.

Some middle-aged Russian guy floats up to me and Joy. First he asks if she's Native American. 'No, I'm Japanese-American, but the Native Americans also mistake me for one of them.' Then he starts telling us about some trendy cult before Anya shoos him away. Joy's family hails from Hawaii and her uncle was interned in a camp during World War II. 'He was given a choice: either he signs a document, pledging his allegiance to the government, or he gets sent back to Japan. What "back to Japan"? He was born in the States. He refused to sign it and was sent to the bad boys' camp.'

The next day, I take a walk to Lake Baikal's northern shores. There's no one about to spoil my appreciation of the steep, pine-covered slopes, the rocky beach and Russia's vast inland sea – the world's deepest lake. I dip my feet in the clear water. Within seconds, they lose all feeling.

They say that a swim in Lake Baikal adds five years to your life. Weeks earlier, while staying at Nikita's Homestead – a motley collection of 'gingerbread' cottages and yurts on Olkhon Island, a crooked finger of land that juts into the lake some 125 miles south of Severobaikalsk – my sister, Steve and I tried to figure out how much extra time I'd get for having dived into the 9-degrees water, flailing and shrieking for around ten seconds and then rushing back out.

We warmed up in the homestead's *banya*, something that my sister and I were completely unfamiliar with, having never been to rural Russia. It consisted of a changing room, a small antechamber, and the *banya* itself – an incredibly hot sauna. Weaklings compared to 'proper' Russians, not only were we not drinking vodka and carousing, but we couldn't handle more than a couple minutes in the *banya* at a time, and kept rushing out for improvised cold showers from barrels of cold water provided. Strangers in a strange land, indeed!

But the lake itself is a wonder – a vast expanse of glass-still waters, fringed by tall cliffs, with nerpas (freshwater seals) dwelling somewhere in its epic depths. From Nikita's, located practically on a clifftop, it was an easy walk to Shamanka (Shaman's Rock) – a great crag sticking out into the lake and one of the holiest local places for shamanists. Shamanism has enjoyed a revival in Russia since the fall of Communism, Nikita, the Homestead's owner, told me.

'I know a shaman; he's a level four. There are nine levels in all, but all the top-level shamans were killed during Communist times. Today's shamans still perform various rites, but don't expect them to levitate!'

At the insistence of 'Jack' Sheremetoff, Genie, Steve and I signed up for a day trip to the Khoboy peninsula, Olkhon Island's northernmost tip. Our Soviet-era minibus trundled across the island's hilly, grass-covered interior. To one side lay a string of wild, white-sand beaches. We passed hikers with enormous rucksacks; the island is still remote enough for people to camp on deserted beaches at night and cook on campfires.

Peschanaya, a small village beside an attractive pebbly beach, was our first stop. 'There used to be a gulag here,' our driver told us. 'Political prisoners were sent here to work at the fish processing factory.' The factory was long gone, the pier rotted away. An elderly Buryat woman smiled and waved from her porch. 'That's the oldest grandmother on the island. She married a "political" back in the day.' All things considered, this must've been one of the nicer gulags, what with Siberia being dotted with forced labour/prison camps from which few people returned alive.

At another stop, we clambered along three precipitous cliffs known as the 'Three Brothers'. Colourful ribbons were tied to surrounding trees, marking this as a shamanist site as well. Offerings of coins and cigarettes lay all around a tree stump festooned with ribbons.

Khoboy – twin rocky crests bookending a narrow hillock that ended in a sheer cliff – was our final stop. There were Soviet-style minibuses parked all over the hill, the drivers staying behind to cook *ukha* (fish soup) on an open fire for our picnic lunch. On one side of the cliff, a natural window in the rock face permitted us to look down some 1,642m into Baikal's dizzying blue depths. On top of the hill there was an *obo*, a holy spot marked with a tree trunk wrapped in colourful ribbons.

'The ribbons are prayers,' our driver explained earlier. 'This is where you communicate with the gods; the only colour ribbon you wouldn't use is black, the colour of death.'

On the way back, I peppered him with questions about the island, shamanism, the resident Buryat people. Chain-smoking out of the window, he was happy to share his knowledge.

'Olkhon has been inhabited for the past two thousand years. The earlier people built great walls facing east; we think it was for sun worship rather than defence. Were the Buryats here before the Russians? Just about; they came as part of the Golden Horde [a Mongol force that conquered a large chunk of present-day Russia in the thirteenth century] and stayed. In Mongolian, "Buryat" means "traitor". The island's a mixed bag; here you have Russians, Ukrainians, Belarusians… yep, the descendants of exiles. Are the shamans mostly Buryat? No, others also. They're medicine men and perform certain rites – for luck, or if you want to have children. You're heading to Mongolia next? No problem, they all speak Russian there. The problem's the food: they don't eat fish at all. Hope you like mutton!'

Prophetic words, as it turned out.

* * * * *

During my last long stretch on the BAM train – thirty-four hours to Krasnoyarsk – I doze on and off, and at one point wake up to find the piercing sapphire gaze of a handsome stranger upon me. I'd like to talk to him, but can't think of any opening lines beyond 'Hi. What's your name?' Lame, Anna K, really lame. In the end, I'm content with the extended eye contact. Then the stranger winks at me and alights at Gidrostroitel, one of the stops near Russia's biggest dam. Dozing off again, and waking up later in the middle of the night, I wonder if I'd dreamt the entire encounter.

CHAPTER 6
AMONG THE TSAATAN

'What's the worst meal you've ever had?' I get asked. Because, having reviewed thousands of eating establishments over nearly fifteen years, I must've had a few bad experiences. And I have. There were also places, prior to my becoming a travel writer, that made me physically sick. When taking a summer Spanish course in Santander as a nineteen-year-old, I caught salmonella, as did everyone who had eggs that day at the university canteen. This happened on 9/11, and when we watched the footage of the planes flying into the Twin Towers on an endless loop that afternoon, I thought that the fever and vomiting was triggered by the emotional shock. My friend Magda – the only person who didn't have eggs that day – took me to see a young Spanish doctor, whose attractiveness and great bedside manner led Magda to wish she were in need of TLC as well. Another time, bad scallops at a mediocre Thai place in San Diego knocked me flat for days and prevented me from partaking in the San Francisco Crab Festival.

Then, during one of my Lonely Planet gigs, there was the eight-course fiasco at the Rock and Sea Bubble Ecolodge in Watamu, on the Kenyan coast, where the chef laboured under the misapprehension that if you threw together the most exotic ingredients you can think of – including no less than six types of salt – you get gastronomic masterpieces. Alas. The 'lobster in her corals sauce' was the saddest crustacean I'd ever seen. The poor thing had clearly died of old age and then lay there, preserved in ice, awaiting some luckless diner. It was also bright blue. A bill that threatened to bankrupt me added insult to injury.

But if we are talking countries with consistently bad food, then the grand prize must go to the homeland of Chinggis Khan. Mongolian food is more often horrible than not. During my first visit to Mongolia, while researching the Trailblazer Trans-Siberian Handbook, I discovered that being omnivorous and open-minded didn't save me there. Some things – such as gristly, elderly mutton that's unavoidable outside the capital – I just cannot and will not eat. When I returned three years later to cover half the country for Lonely Planet, I came bearing my weight in camping food rather than chance the horrors of roadside dining.

* * * * *

'I want you to come to Chechnya with us.'

The email from Scharlette comes out of the blue in December 2013. She's been assigned to the Boston Bomber's all-star defence team and, since some of Tsarnaev's family members live in Chechnya, wants me to put my life on hold for a year and join them as an interpreter. I'm reluctant. I worry that my burgeoning career in travel writing may suffer because Rough Guides and Lonely Planet may not tolerate a year-long hiatus. Also, while Scharlette fearlessly goes wherever her work requires her to, Chechnya is one of most troubled parts of the Russian Caucasus, marred by many years of atrocities against civilians, Islamic terrorism, and being ruled by a Kremlin-friendly despot. But I acquiesce. Scharlette is really difficult to say no to.

Then, due to unforeseen circumstances, the trip falls through. By the time the defence team gets on the road, I'd already accepted travel assignments and cannot join them. I'm both disappointed and relieved. Disappointed – because working with Scharlette in Ukraine had been one of the most intense experiences of my life. Relieved, because it feels as if I've dodged a bullet. Perhaps quite literally. When the defence team – all of them Americans – get into some trouble with the Russian authorities over their stated reasons for visiting Dagestan and Chechnya, it occurs to me how vulnerable I would have been, travelling on a Russian passport. I would've been completely at the mercy of the local authorities. My being detained and 'disappeared' would not have been out of the realm of possibility, and the defence team would not have been able to help me.

But since I've now committed myself to a different career path, there's this undercurrent of exhilaration – the hurtling headlong into the unknown and the glee of tackling a new and formidable destination. Instead of Chechnya, I find myself in Mongolia.

* * * * *

Another question I get asked sometimes is: 'Is there any country that you wouldn't go back to?' And I answer: 'Mongolia'. At least, not for work. Mongolia is one of the toughest (due to logistics and language barriers) and most expensive destinations I've ever covered. To get anywhere off the beaten track outside Ulaanbaatar you really need a driver and guide, and travel around Mongolia is often an exercise in endurance. And yet, when the Lonely Planet guide to Mongolia was being commissioned, I jumped at the chance. When my colleague Leonid once interviewed me for a piece he was writing, 'Why Do People Travel?', I responded that I like to see remote places and witness things that few others get to see. That's like knowing a secret, and secrets, as we all know, are delicious. That, and the desire to experience humanity in all its diversity. One of the most rewarding parts of my work has been my interaction with remote indigenous cultures, the opportunity to experience fragile and unique ways of life. And Mongolia's Tsaatan, the nomadic reindeer herders who live along the border between Mongolia and Russia, are remote even by Mongolian standards and as unique as they come.

Then there's the question of my own heritage. For years, I've been using the pan-Asian genetic imprint of my almond-shaped eyes to claim various ethnic heritages (tongue-in-cheek). But if I'm honest, I strongly suspect that my Asian ancestors hail from these very steppes. After all, in the thirteenth century, the Mongol Empire spread as far as Western Europe, conquering Russia en route, and eyes like mine are a dime a dozen in the former Soviet Union.

I relish the challenge, too. During my many years of work for Lonely Planet and Rough Guides, I've been one of the few women writers who's taken on 'machete' gigs in remoter and more challenging parts of the world – Papua New Guinea, Borneo, Arctic Russia, Suriname, the Amazon Basin. I like the idea of being a trailblazer of sorts – the first woman writer to cover Mongolia for LP. And even a prior brief stint in Mongolia in 2010 isn't enough to deter me.

* * * * *

Mishig – my short, middle-aged, surly guide, with grey hair dyed jet black – and I have been driving all day. First we follow the road from Murun – the last town of any size in Mongolia's north – to Hatgal, a village at the south end of Khovsgol Lake, Mongolia's inland sea and Lake Baikal's little brother. Here the road ends and rolling grassland gives way to alpine scenery of snow-tipped mountains. Mishig is from this part of the country, so I trust him implicitly when he cuts across the countryside and makes for an isolated ger. Parking the jeep, we venture inside. Our hostess, a wrinkle-faced, middle-aged lady wearing a headscarf, pours us cups of milky salted tea. The head of the family, an elderly chap with a scraggly goatee, wanders in wearing a combination of pyjama bottoms and riding boots, and offers Mishig a pinch of snuff from his snuff bottle, while younger family members assemble on the rug opposite ours. I feel the familiar nausea of nervous anticipation building up in my stomach, and distract myself by checking out our surroundings.

Our hosts' ger has orange roof supports with colourful designs, a stove in the middle, its exhaust pipe disappearing into a hole in the roof, linoleum on the floor, and a wall rug decorated with the face of Chinggis Khan. Most of the family's belongings are stored neatly in large wooden chests. Beds with brightly embroidered cushions are arranged around the perimeter. There is no privacy: guests are expected to sleep on the rugs next to the family beds. The family's prized possessions include a clock covered with stickers of horses and Tweety Pie, and a prehistoric-looking, staticky TV set, powered by the solar panels. Everyone quietens down and stares at me expectantly. I stand up, trying to ignore my legs turning to jelly, take a deep breath, and prepare, once more, to sing for my supper.

The first time I came to Mongolia, three years back, in 2010, I made friends with two young women from Norway in our Trans-Mongolian train carriage when I, as the sole Russian speaker in the carriage, acted as an interpreter on their behalf and placated the *provodnitsa* after someone managed to piss her off. It's never a good idea to get on the wrong side of the woman in charge of the samovar and other carriage conveniences. When we discussed our plans for our four days in Ulaanbaatar and around, Laila and

Maja-Stina were particularly excited about their traditional homestay out in the countryside, and the custom of singing before the evening meal. The guests provide entertainment in exchange for the hospitality, and both Norwegians belonged to a choir and were keen to show off their vocal range. Me – not so much. I'd spent the best part of my teenage years and my early twenties trying to overcome my painful shyness by forcing myself to volunteer at school and university events, knocking back a can of Lilt as carbonated courage before stints of public speaking. But performing in front of others is always an ordeal.

Mongolia is not the only culture that requires guests to be the floor show. When I covered Suriname for Rough Guides in 2012, I spent several days in a Saramaccan village in the middle of impenetrable rainforest, reachable either via tiny Cessna or a month-long canoe journey from Paramaribo, the capital. West African slaves were brought to Suriname by the Dutch in the seventeenth and eighteenth centuries to work on the sugar and coffee plantations and the Saramaccans are the descendants of the runaways who escaped into the jungle and staged armed rebellions.

We – myself and two Dutch couples, all about two feet taller than me – were taken one day from our rustic lodge to a nearby Saramaccan village with palm fronds above the entrance ('to keep evil spirits from getting in,' according to Elton, our guide; most Saramaccans hold on to West African spiritual traditions and practise something akin to Vodou). In the evening, Elton brought us to the communal area. The women of the village lined up, and began clapping in unison. One of them began to sing, and the others picked it up – a cheerful call-and-response chant. Then, one by one, they began to dance, their movements graceful. The expectation on the part of the women was palpable: it seemed that we were supposed to try and imitate this sinuous swaying of the hips. We did our best. Then one of the few male inhabitants of the village (most of the men work in the capital or in the gold mines) showed us a more exuberant dance for men only. The two Dutch guys followed his cue and flew at each other like fighting roosters. Then there was strength in numbers, whereas now, I must take to the stage alone.

I manage. Sending a silent thanks to my primary school teacher, Miss Heywood, I belt out such classics as 'She'll Be Coming Round the Mountain', 'My Old Man Said Follow The Van', 'I Do Like To Be Beside The Seaside' and 'All The Nice Girls Love a Sailor' that she taught me, and finish off with a spirited recitation of Alfred Lord Tennyson's 'The Lady of Shalott', a poem I'd learned off by heart in secondary school.

'Out flew the web and floated wide,' I intone menacingly, spreading my arms on 'wide'. 'The mirror crack'd' – I punch the air with an open hand on the last word – 'from side to side.' Now in falsetto: '"A curse has come upon me!" cried the Lady of Shalott.'

I've never had such an attentive and forgiving audience as this Mongolian family. They stare at me, wide-eyed, throughout the entire performance and applaud afterwards. Then it's their turn. One of the younger women stands up and sings. I'm clearly a philistine, because Mongolian throat singing sounds to me like a decidedly unmelodious series of warbles and screeches. The young man accompanying her on a horse-head fiddle is infinitely better, his two-string instrument sounding both like a bass and a violin.

Finally, the entertainment portion of the evening over and done with, it's time for the 'reward'. A large pot is placed in the centre of the ger. My heart sinks. I know exactly what's inside, and I'm dreading it.

EYEBALL TACOS AND KANGAROO STEW

* * * * *

When you're fresh off the train after days of gentle trundling across half of Russia, Ulaanbaatar is a shock to the system. Rule of thumb when crossing the road in Mongolia's capital: the pedestrian *never, ever* has the right of way. My first impression of Ulaanbaatar, in 2010, was that of uncontrolled and haphazard development: cranes everywhere; fugly Soviet-style multi-storey buildings mingling with wooden huts and ger encampments on the outskirts of town; the elegant marble of the Parliament building in Sukhbaatar Square, flanked by statues of Chinggis Khan and his sons; a mishmash of ancient Buddhist temples against a backdrop of sail-like glass skyscrapers. The city was also one of the most traffic-choked and chaotic I'd ever seen. Signalling? What's that? Lane? What's a lane? Drivers would overtake and undertake, and the racket from car horns was incredible.

Most travellers riding the Trans-Mongolian railway from Moscow to Beijing via Ulaanbaatar overnight in UB, get out into the countryside for a couple of days, then hop back on the train for the final leg to China's neon and bright lights. My friend Steve and I followed suit, visiting a Buddhist temple up a mountain, with stupendous views of the valley below, riding camels over sand dunes, getting chewed on by a baby camel (that was just me), making friends with Rottweiler crossbreeds, sleeping on the floor of a ger next to our hosts.

On the way to our first national park, we broke for lunch in the middle of nowhere. Describing that roadside establishment as a 'restaurant' would be stretching the rubber band of truth almost to the point of snapping. I discovered that I'd become the protagonist in the classic 'Waiter, waiter: there's a fly in my soup' joke. Except that there were two flies: one paddling quite merrily to shore, the other floating motionlessly, having given up the fight. Moving on to the second park, we stopped beside a ger in the middle of some valley. Horses were saddled up outside it, tossing their heads. 'I'll have a calm horse, please,' I told Oogli, the guide, having ridden only two horses in my life. (The first was a docile beast in San Martín de Los Andes, Argentina, while the second – a wilful steed near Paraty, Brazil – took off at high speed and left me clinging to its neck for dear life.) Oogli laughed. There is no such thing as a 'calm' horse in Mongolia. We started off with gentle trotting through the hills and pastures, but then the guide let the horses run free, and once again, I experienced exhilarated terror as we cantered through the meadows.

* * * * *

When I return to Mongolia for Lonely Planet, my experience is as different as it could be. There are the weeks spent in the endless flatlands of eastern Mongolia with Pikheh the driver, Mazdakh the eighteen-year-old interpreter and Kurt, a middle-aged American teacher who tags along and nicknames me 'Boss Lady'. There are the fourteen-hour days spent trundling across grassland, with me periodically leaping out to take the GPS coordinates of the odd *ovoo* (sacred stone heap or tree, bedecked with prayer flags and tied with blue ceremonial silk scarves) – the only landmarks for miles around – while my Mongolian companions make an offering – a coin, a cigarette. There's the massive lightning storm that catches us in the middle of nowhere, on the shores of Buir Lake, and we break into someone's disused ger to spend the night rather than remain the tallest objects on the steppe. We pay our respects to the Russian and Mongolian dead near the Soviet-style military monuments marking the forgotten eastern front of World War II near Khalkhgol, where their joined forces pushed back a Japanese invasion in 1939. We visit the supposed location of Chinggis Khan's birth, and drink from a sacred spring. I climb Shiliin Bogd Uul, an extinct volcano sacred to shamanists – one of the few sacred mountains in Mongolia that women are allowed to summit. We gatecrash a clandestine hunting lodge in the Eastern Mongolia Nature Reserve, catering to Chinese hunters determined to make Mongolia's endangered gazelle extinct. And then, finally, I find myself in Murun, northern Mongolia, having spent a purgatorial night in an overcrowded minibus from Ulaanbaatar, wedged between an old man with one leg and a jagged piece of metal machinery. I'm met by Mishig, and we set off in search of the Tsaatan.

In the morning, I catch Mishig beckoning someone through the open ger door. There are two Tsaatan riders out there who've come to lead us to their summer encampment. It's my fourth time on a horse. Surely I've inherited some equestrian skills from my Mongolian ancestors. But I am disabused of that notion very quickly. While the other three ride as if born in the saddle (Mongolian kids learn to ride at the age of three and compete in races aged five), my horse senses an inexperienced rider and flatly refuses to cooperate.

'What are the commands?' I ask Mishig with some desperation. He rolls his eyes. 'Tchoo,' he calls, and my horse speeds up.

'How do I make it go slower?' I yell. He shrugs. Tugging at the reins to make it go either left or right seems to have little effect. Mishig finally takes pity on me and ropes my horse to his, but that doesn't stop my steed from occasionally stumbling and jolting me. I'm also having trouble with my stirrups. My legs cramp up very quickly when I ride in the same position as the other riders, and when Mishig loosens them for me, they end up being too long, meaning that for the rest of the journey, as our horses alternate between finding their way through dense spruce forest and galloping through meadows, all my weight is on my backside. If you can imagine what it feels like to be relentlessly spanked for hours on end, you get some sense of my ordeal. Thank goodness it's not a traditional wooden saddle, is all I can think.

The weather turns as we ride non-stop for five hours. The sky turns leaden and the landscape looks increasingly rocky and barren. On the final approach to the Tsaatan camp, we dismount to lead the horses down the steep, muddy slope. I am so stiff that I literally fall off my steed. I'm not cut out for this, I think with unexpected bitterness. Why am I here, and not in some restaurant in Grozny, comparing notes with Scharlette about Tsarnaev's relatives?

A broad valley flanked by spruce-covered hills, and snow-tipped mountains beyond, opens up in front of us. The valley floor is dotted with a couple dozen nomad dwellings that look like tepees (locally known as *ortz*) arranged in two clusters. I feel as though I've walked into a childhood dream of cowboys and Indians. Human presence is indicated by smoke rising from the tents. A chorus of barks and howls from husky-like hunting dogs greets our arrival. An ancient-looking woman dressed in a traditional Mongolian *deel* (kaftan) ushers Mishig and me inside the nearest tepee. I judge her to be around seventy, going by her weathered face and a handful of remaining teeth, but when a teenage girl serves us the ubiquitous, milky tea from a boiling cauldron, Mishig tells me that she's the woman's daughter. This is what a lifetime of hard living does to a forty-year-old. Inside, the wooden skeleton of the *ortz* is strung with bits of string, from which pieces of smoked meat dangle freely. I hope it's not dinner, and then remember that I have several packs of camping food left. 'Please thank our hosts for their hospitality, but tell them that I'll be sleeping by myself,' I tell Mishig, and stagger outside to put up my tent. Setting up separate sleeping quarters is all I've got energy for, besides tipping boiling water into the food pouch to rehydrate my mash and peas.

A begrimed little face belonging to a very young girl peeks around the side of my tent. At her age, I was very wary of strangers, but this child has no fear. She toddles over in her rubber boots and oversized pink coat, plonks herself down on the grass beside me and looks at me expectantly. Do I feed an infant who is clearly hungry? What if she's allergic to potato, or chokes on the rehydrated peas?? Is it the done thing here to feed a child that's not your own?? Where are her parents??? I look around frantically, but no one seems to be coming to collect her. Finally, I relent and root around for a spare spoon. I know how cranky I get if not fed at regular intervals. She opens her mouth, and I carefully spoon-feed her, feeling oddly protective, and rather discombobulated by that unfamiliar feeling. I've never done this before.

Sated, she wanders off towards an *ortz* some distance away. I rehydrate more mash and peas. But no sooner have I retreated inside my tent than a young woman's face peers through the open flap.

'Anna, right?' she asks in perfect English.

I gawp at her. Outside Ulaanbaatar I hadn't encountered a single English speaker, and Mishig and I are able to communicate only because he attended the University of Karaganda in Kazakhstan in his youth and speaks fluent, heavily accented Russian.

'Mishig's mentioned that he brought a travel writer with him. He also said that you're weird,' she smiles. I suppose it's hard to argue with that assessment. Weird in what respects, though?

'Would you like to come to my tent for some *buuz*?' she continues. I don't need to be asked twice, and lurch painfully to my feet to follow her. Her being Zaya. She grew up in Colorado, she tells me when I compliment her on her English.

'This is me.' She points to a large *ortz* with a husky lying in front of it, and a small solar panel next to it.

'I wasn't really expecting canvas and solar panels,' I confess, and then immediately feel guilty. I'm very critical of travellers who seem to think that remote indigenous cultures should remain technology-free in perpetuity, for the sole viewing pleasure of those who come in search of 'primitive' peoples. Why wouldn't the Tsaatan want modern conveniences, just like everyone else?

'We used to cover our tents with animal skins, back in the day, but that's not practical,' she explains. 'So now we use waterproof canvas. And pretty much everyone in the countryside owns a solar panel. Luckily, we get a lot of sunlight.'

Inside, while Zaya busies herself with kneading dough for the *buuz*, I ask her about the Tsaatan. I know that they're nomadic reindeer herders, that they number around five hundred people split between two groups, and that they live in the mountains and the taiga, a harsh and remote corner of the country.

'Actually, we call ourselves the Dukha,' Zaya says. '"Tsaatan" is the Mongolian name for us.'

'But aren't you Mongolian?'

'Yes and no. Me – yes. My husband is Dukha.'

I mean to ask Zaya how she and her husband met, but am reluctant to interrupt her storytelling and in the end I never find out.

'The Dukha are a Mongolian people originally from Tuva, across the border in Russia, and we speak both Mongolian and Tuvan,' she continues. 'Before 1944, the Dukha were able to herd our reindeer freely into Tuva and back. But now we can't.'

Sounds familiar. As part of my work, I've spent time among the reindeer-herding Sami in Sweden and Russia's Kola Peninsula, and while Scandinavian Sami benefit from an agreement between the governments of Norway, Sweden and Finland that allows them to herd reindeer across country borders, the Sami of the Kola Peninsula are not even recognised by the Russian government as a unique ethnic group.

I tell Zaya about how a Sami herder in Storuman, Sweden, told me about his travels to Lovozero, a Sami town in Russia, where he found that he could communicate with the Russian Sami in the dialect spoken in Sweden's southern Arctic (there are ten Sami dialects).

'But while the Swedish Sami get government support these days to preserve their culture and traditional livelihood, in Arctic Russia few Sami even own reindeer because they were forced to settle down during the mass collectivisation in the 1950s.'

Zaya nods. 'It was the same with the Dukha. Decades under Communism have cost us most of our reindeer.'

In the USSR, other reindeer people, such as the Even and Evenk of Siberia, lost their livelihoods as well, and their nomadic, reindeer-herding lifestyle gave way to despair, alcoholism and mass unemployment. The Soviets didn't trust nomads, since they were hard to pin down, quantify and control.

As we talk, a reindeer pokes its head through the entrance and startles me.

'Don't mind her,' Zaya laughs. 'That's just Britney Spears. She's here for her salt lick.' Turns out that reindeer have to seek out salty mineral deposits in the soil to get the nutrients that they cannot obtain from lichen and grass, and Britney's come for a top-up.

'Here.' Zaya pours salt into my hand. 'You can feed Led Zeppelin.' She motions to five more reindeer who are making a beeline for the tent. They push their warm muzzles into my hand.

It's clear that Zaya treats her reindeer with great affection, as if they are family members, and I tell her so.

'Well, they kind of are. They look after us. We don't dress in reindeer hides anymore, but we still get most of what we need from our reindeer. Wolves killed two of our young reindeer the other week. A massive loss, since every animal is precious.'

Before collectivisation, the Dukha, like the Sami, would have had over a hundred reindeer per family, but now they are lucky if it's fifteen or twenty.

'So you never eat them?' I ask.

'Very, very rarely. Only if they are injured. We can't spare them for food, because we need them for the milk and as pack animals.'

A few weeks ago they'd had visitors who arrived on horses that had never seen reindeer.

'One of the horses freaked out, lashed out with its hooves, and crippled a reindeer, so she had to be put down.'

'That's one of the problems we have,' Zaya confesses. 'We get visitors from all over, because coming here is, you know, a Big Adventure. And we are happy to have guests as long as they are genuinely interested in learning about our way of life and interacting with us. Some turn up without an interpreter – and I'm not an interpreter,' she hastens to add. 'I can translate if necessary, but I'm a member of the community. There's a lot of work to be done every day. So they camp over there' – she points beyond the furthest group of tents – 'don't talk to us, take photos of us from a distance as if we are animals at the zoo, shower in our drinking water and drop litter.'

Having finished kneading the dough, Zaya swiftly closes the dough circles around lumps of meat filling – 'Our hunters shot an elk a few days ago' – and sets them to steam while she grabs a tin pail and beckons for me to follow her.

'So what do you guys eat?'

'We fish, we hunt, we gather wild berries in the summer. Sometimes we pick up extra supplies from Murun, but not often.'

'It sounds like a rather precarious existence.'

Zaya agrees.

'We have to watch out for wolves and bears, all the time. We have a shaman – a healer – but if someone is seriously ill or hurt, medical help is really far away. And it's not as if they can get to us easily, either… we have to move every few weeks, to find fresh grazing for the reindeer…'

She points to a large cloth bundle hanging in the back of the tent and explains that it's a sacred sack, used in shamanist rituals that play an important part in their lives.

'Juniper branches are burned under it as an offering in the mornings,' she says. Shamans assume the twin roles of healer and spiritual leader.

'Do you actually ride the reindeer?' I interrupt. 'That's what the Tsaatan are supposedly known for, compared to the other reindeer people.'

'Most adults don't. Reindeer can only carry about 130 pounds, tops. But the kids, and some of the older people, yes.'

Zaya ties Britney's front legs together with a length of rope, to stop her from bolting. She then squats down, milking the animal with quick, practised squeezes.

'Reindeer produce only around half a pint per session. We milk them twice a day.'

The Tsaatan don't drink the milk; they make crumbly, salty cheese out of it.

'I don't remember the Sami milking their reindeer,' I tell her.

'They don't,' Zaya responds. 'When some Sami visitors from Finland came to stay with us, they took photos of us milking our reindeer to show their families back home, since they don't milk their own reindeer anymore; there's no need.' Which is true. Modern-day Sami in Scandinavia often hold other jobs and herd reindeer on the side.

By the time we get back to Zaya's *ortz* the *buuz* are ready, and she encourages me to dig in. I make an utter mess of myself, trying to manoeuvre a giant dumpling into my mouth. The meat juices go all over my jacket. Zaya sees me struggling and teaches me how to eat the *buuz* properly:

'Here – bite a tiny hole in the dough, drink the hot meat juice, and then eat the rest.'

I do it her way. Yes, I'm ravenous from the day's riding, but it's utterly remarkable what you can do with limited ingredients. The broth inside the dumpling sings with wild herbs and the elk meat is juicy and salty and gamey-tasting. I'm not exaggerating when I say that it's not just the best meal I've had in Mongolia (because that's really not much of a horse race), but also one of the best things I've had on the road, anywhere.

From the *pelmeni* of my childhood, my love affair with dumplings progressed to encompass Chinese dim sum, Japanese gyoza, Korean mandu, Nepalese momo, Central Asian *manty*, and now, *buuz*. 'If you think about it,' Zaya tells me, 'it's the ideal food for nomads. It's easy to make – all you need is flour, water, salt and meat – and it's two dishes in one: soup and entrée.'

'But sometimes we don't have much to eat,' she continues. 'Particularly between January and March. Tsaagan Sar (White Moon) festival in February is traditionally celebrated by making dumplings, which we can only do if our men have been successful during their hunting expeditions.'

Outsiders are not always put off by the challenges of the Tsaatan way of life. 'I'm not the only one who's not from here originally,' Zaya tells me. 'There's this Frenchwoman who comes here every summer to visit her sons. One of our men is the father, and she felt that the boys should live with their dad.'

Zaya's been here six years, but intends to live as a nomad for the rest of her life.

'What keeps you here?' I ask.

'Love,' Zaya responds, taking in with a glance her beloved reindeer, her and her husband's simple home, the darkening taiga outside.

As I trudge back to my tent, past the silhouettes of *ortz* aglow from the inside with fires from their hearths, with the shadows of their inhabitants moving within, my throat tightens with a familiar bittersweetness. It's as if I'm a child, my face pressed against the window, always on the outside and looking in. But at the same time, this wistfulness is underpinned by the thrill of exhilaration at being right here, right now, under these very stars.

Through the mesh skylight in my tent, I try to spot Orion – the constellation that my mother first pointed out to me in the night sky when I was little, and one that I always look for, wherever I happen to be in the world. I think back to the Saramaccans, and of our boatman, paddling us upstream in almost total darkness, guided by his intimate knowledge of the river's every rock and every bend, the stars his only source of light. I found myself contemplating the twists and turns of my strange life that brought a small-town Soviet kid to the Surinamese jungle. I ponder the same thing now. As I drift off, I wonder also whether my ancestors, thousands of years ago, also found themselves looking up at the night sky, feeling profoundly moved, and not knowing why.

CHAPTER 7
JUNGLE DEEP, MOUNTAIN HIGH

As I round the crest of the hill en route from the Torres del Paine National Park visitor centre to the Serón campsite, and begin my descent towards Río Paine, I catch sight of movement below me.

It's a tawny-coloured feline form, around one hundred yards downhill from me. A large, beautiful puma. I freeze. All the other hikers have already gone on ahead. There is no one for miles around. I feel horribly exposed.

The brochure on the park's wildlife recommends 'making yourself look bigger,' and shouting, but that's not terribly helpful in my case. The puma is so much larger than me. Do I have any weapon on me? Why, why didn't I bring my emergency whistle?

In the end, I decide that trying to remain unnoticed would be my best move. There hasn't been a puma attack on humans in Torres del Paine since 1987, but I don't want to buck that trend. I remain rooted to the spot, blood pounding in my temples. Clutching my hiking poles, I prepare to sell my life dearly, if it comes to that.

But the puma pads purposefully along the slope and disappears around the side of the hill. After waiting for interminable minutes, I leg it downhill, aggravating an old knee injury, and limp to the campsite as fast as I can. On the banks of Río Paine, I find a disembowelled carcass of a wild horse. It's possible that the puma wasn't hungry. But I can't stop looking over my shoulder, convinced that it's stalking me across the field of daisies. It's not until I've collapsed inside my tent that the adrenalin seeps out of me.

I miss Nikolai.

* * * * *

The last time I came this way was in 2008, a decade earlier, with my oldest childhood friend. Then, my travel writing assignment involved tackling southern Chile's most iconic trek, the Circuit: a week-long loop which circles the bell-like Los Cuernos peaks and the sharp trident points of Las Torres, crosses glacial torrents, traverses a high mountain pass, and leads past five glacial lakes in varying shades of aquamarine and teal, as well as the vast ice field of Glacier Grey.

Nikolai and I have known each other since he was two years old and I was five. We hail from the same home town in the former USSR, but while I'd grown up in the UK, his family settled in the States. We'd reconnected when I was in my early twenties, and I had stayed with his family in Maryland during one of my backpacking ventures. But we'd never hiked together, and several days into the trek, our differing paces were making themselves known. An early riser, I'd be packed within minutes, happy to eat during the hike, and chafing at the bit to get going. Nikolai eased into his morning, and preferred to have breakfast first thing. On our toughest hiking day (nineteen miles, ten hours' hike), since Nikolai was the faster hiker, I offered to go on ahead and have him catch up, but he proposed sticking together in case of injury/accident. I acquiesced, grudgingly.

Once we were on our way, we kept up a steady pace, crossing swampy ground, climbing grassy hills and skirting the side of Lake Paine to arrive at Refugio Dickson, a bunk hut and park ranger post. Our arrival coincided with that of a *huaso*, the Chilean equivalent of an Argentinian gaucho, a cowboy from the pampas. Clad in a heavy woollen poncho, black beret and knee-high leather boots, he leapt down from his sheepskin saddle and exchanged greetings with the park ranger. He then reached for the beaver-skin bag strapped to his belt and produced a *guampa* (hollow calabash gourd cup) before filling it to the brim with yerba-maté from a small hot-water flask.

Observing the *huaso* sipping the herbal brew through a *bombilla* (silver straw), I was reminded of my very first trip to the south of Chile and Argentina with my friend Mike, and my first ever horse ride in San Martín de los Andes, in Argentina's Lake District. When our gaucho guide offered us yerba-maté at the end and asked me if I wanted sugar in mine, I said no. The gaucho looked at me approvingly and said, 'Porque la vida ya es muy dulce!' ('Because life is already sweet enough!')

I turned to Nikolai, who, like me, was watching the *huaso* with considerable interest. 'These guys live in the middle of nowhere and are fiercely self-sufficient,' I told him. 'There's long-standing rivalry between the two countries, but the *huasos* in Chile and the gauchos in Argentina think of themselves as Patagonian first, and Chilean or Argentinian second.'

When we pressed on towards our day's final destination, the Los Perros campsite, the weather turned. Our seemingly endless slog through the dripping forest of southern beeches and ferns and across glacial streams became an ordeal. By the time we'd arrived, I was frozen, with barely enough energy to erect my tent. I left Nikolai on his own to try and fry potatoes in a tin pot on our little portable gas stove, feeling completely inadequate as a hiking companion and as a friend. He'd envisioned us reliving our Soviet childhood pastime – roasting potatoes in the hot coals of a campfire – and I didn't have the heart to tell him that fires are forbidden in Torres del Paine, since the place is a tinderbox, with the fierce Patagonian wind – 'la escoba de dios' ('God's broom') fanning the flames of forest fires. And on top of that, I didn't even have the energy to be sociable.

But Nikolai seemed undaunted by my dark mood. Lying in my tent, too exhausted to move, I reflected on the things I'd come to appreciate about him after spending a couple of weeks at close quarters. That while he criticised my packing and organisational skills, he never, ever complained about the physical exertion or roughing it in tents, with rocks digging into our backs at night. That he gallantly carried the extra luggage that I'd foolishly brought with me, with good humour and just a couple of wry remarks. How he'd resolutely swing his rucksack on to his shoulders over his head in the morning and then do his best to motivate me for the hike ahead by telling me in Russian: 'Onwards! Sing as we march!'

When I finally crawled out of my tent to partake of the just-add-boiling-water chilli con carne and fried potatoes, I realised with a rush of affection that while our respective lives on different sides of the Atlantic had taken us in different directions, and that as adults, we were half-strangers to one another, I trusted this broad-shouldered, occasionally taciturn man implicitly. I knew that if I was injured, he'd carry me to safety. I didn't say anything, because an exuberant display of sentimentality would've embarrassed him, but permitted myself a grateful smile in his direction.

Since Nikolai had a flight to catch, he and I had pushed ourselves to reach Los Perros with two days to spare before attempting to cross the John Gardner pass (1,200m) – the highest point of the trek and the most treacherous. In inclement weather, hikers have been blown off the top to their deaths. But we were in luck. The day after we camped at Los Perros, the rain and wind abated, and our final day dawned cold and clear. Trudging across the snow higher up on the slopes, we easily made the top of the pass, the vast ice field of Glacier Grey spread out beneath us. I whooped with glee. The hard part behind us, the rest was downhill all the way to Lake Grey, where car-sized chunks of ice bobbed by the shore. I'd been overly optimistic in bringing my bikini with me. 'Patagonian summer' is a relative thing.

* * * * *

Over the years, I've had ample occasion to consider what makes a good travelling companion. If I had to put out an advert, I'd mention the following. 'Steadfastness. Reliability. Good humour. Enthusiasm for sightseeing. Similar interests. Schedules that gel.' The last was a bit of a sticking point with my mother and my sister, my sometime research assistants over the years. My mother would go to bed early and be up at the crack of dawn. In the mornings, I'd find our toiletries lined up in order of height in our shared bathroom. With my sister, our squabble-free travel limit is three days. Whenever we'd shared a room, I got accused of typing 'aggressively' and muttering to myself while she was trying to rest.

I ought to mention 'multiple travelling companions'. On the one hand, travelling with a group takes the pressure off me to be constantly congenial towards one person, but it also presents its own challenges. Interesting group dynamics. Conflicting hiking schedules.

The two times I participated in group treks, it was unavoidable. The first was when I hiked the classic Inca Trail on behalf of Rough Guides. This was circa 2009–2010, when advance bookings and guided tours were already mandatory. I was introduced to the pleasure of hiking with nothing but a daypack, while donkeys carried the rest of my gear, porters put up my tent and the chef cooked gourmet three-course meals for our group. The inadequate hygiene of my fellow hikers for the three-day duration was less glamorous. It was icy bucket showers or nothing. My trekking companions chose the latter. Also – and there were a dozen or so in our group – most made no attempt to get to know other members and made no impression on me whatsoever. Except for the woman who ignored instructions to acclimatise in Cusco before attempting the high-altitude trek, got altitude sickness on the first day, and had to be dispatched back down the valley on a donkey.

The ruins did make an impression, though. It was one of two times I threw my weight around as a guidebook writer in order to get my way. In this case, to obtain permission to go on ahead to Machu Picchu with one of the porters at sunset, rather than camp overnight and proceed to the ruins at daybreak. (The other time was while trying to gain access to the remarkable Textile Museum in Ahmedabad, India. It was by prior arrangement only, which I didn't know. Feeling like a total cliché, I'd started saying 'Don't you know who I am?' – while the heavy wooden door slammed in my face.) Machu Picchu, glowing golden through a stone gateway, lit by the setting sun, really was all that.

The second time I hiked with a group was during a multi-day trek to the Ciudad Perdida ruins in the middle of the jungle in Colombia. The ruins themselves – a collection of lofty stone platforms that predate Machu Picchu by some seven hundred years – were less memorable than the company. Mark (a drummer from Florida), his wife Alejandra (a doula), Daniel, Felipe and Diana (a trio of cousins from Bogotá), Manfred (a German mercilessly eaten by mosquitoes), Katrina and Olga (old friends from the States) and I formed a lively multinational family of twenty- and thirty-somethings. A decade later, many of us are still in touch. We encouraged and cajoled each other across rough spots and up the endless steps to the ruins, upstaged by the cook, who, in his shorts and flip-flops, would whizz past us in our full hiking gear. We bathed in the river together; spotted snakes and toucans; and interacted with the shy indigenous Kogi people near one of our overnight camps. In the evenings, surrounded by the never-silent jungle, we ate together in gratitude – everything from the ubiquitous spaghetti and fresh coffee during the trek to grilled fish and *patacones* (fried plantains) to mark its successful culmination. At night, we slept next to one another under bug netting on rickety wooden pallet beds at rustic camps, the fragrant night lit by faint flashes of fireflies, and shared extra-vivid dreams.

* * * * *

But there's a world of difference between entrusting your life and well-being to an old friend, or a group of new friends, and doing the same with a complete stranger. And yet, that's what I've opted to do in Nepal.

My tiny plane manoeuvres its way between the massive Himalayan peaks and begins its wobbly descent into Lukla. Dubbed 'the world's most dangerous airport', Lukla airstrip leaves no room for error, since it ends abruptly in a mountainside. We make it.

Bishal, my 24-year-old porter-guide, is waiting there to lead me to Everest Base Camp. It's 2016, the year after Nepal suffered a devastating earthquake, and I'm killing two birds with one stone: checking up on the rebuilding efforts in the Everest region on behalf of Lonely Planet, and fulfilling my lifelong dream of paying homage to the world's highest mountain.

It's impossible to get lost along the way, but it helps local communities when you hire guides and porters. Also, you feel every extra ounce of your gear at altitude. But there is a more vital reason for having an experienced companion. Hikers at high altitude can be inexplicably struck down by either pulmonary or cerebral oedema, become muddled and need someone who understands what's happening to get them down to a lower altitude, fast, or else they die. I need Bishal to do that for me, if it comes to that.

* * * * *

At first, the trail meanders between huge boulders inscribed with Tibetan mantras and passes along fields of ripening wheat. The second day's ascent to Namche Bazaar – an amphitheatre of houses overlooked by some of the Himalayas' giant peaks – is interminable. The relentless, serpentine climb through woodlands after crossing a precipitous bridge high above the Dhudh Kosi river saps every last bit of my energy.

Bishal and I bump heads for the first time when I discover with dismay that my lodgings for the night consist of a broom-cupboard-sized room with bare slats for me to lay my sleeping bag on. Up the main street, I find Khumbu Lodge, complete with hot running water and electric blankets. Luxury! On my way back down to my guesthouse, I wonder how I'm going to break the news that I'll be staying elsewhere to Bishal without hurting his feelings. I manage to communicate that, in days to come, if given the choice between a basic hovel for $5 or the likes of the Khumbu Lodge for $20, I'd prefer the latter. I don't mind roughing it if I must, but frankly, I've done my time – sleeping on airport floors, in grim hovels, in crowded overnight minibuses. I have nothing to prove.

Bishal doesn't seem offended. But in order for him to save face, I keep up the pretence that I'm staying at the guesthouse by taking my evening meal there, then surreptitiously scurry to Khumbu Lodge to sleep.

My guide has a bone to pick with me, as well.

'You need to leave some things here,' Bishal informs me bluntly, shouldering my heavy backpack with his own small one strapped to the top. My friend and fellow Lonely Planet author Celeste would've laughed at that. When I road-tripped with her and her aunt Kem in French Guiana, the two women who were travelling for a month had bags the size of day sacks while I sported an enormous rucksack. They made me empty it and do a show-and-tell, and discovered that I was carrying a mini-library consisting of fourteen books. Embarrassed, I go through my stuff, and end up discarding several pounds of clothing and all my 'just in case' spare batteries.

Since we've gained around 600m between Lukla and Namche Bazaar (3,440m), to aid my acclimatisation Bishal takes me for a day's side trek to the village of Thame (3,800m), the jumping-off point for the Three Passes trek. We hike a gentle trail that meanders through pine and rhododendron forest before crossing the Theshyo Khola river, narrowly avoiding being bumped into the frigid waters by a yak train making its slow, plodding way to the Saturday market. Out of all the adventurers who've summited Everest, it's the foreigners who tend to get most of the accolades; few people know that this small scattering of houses in the shadow of Numbur, Khumbu Yui Lha, Kongde Ri and other peaks is home to some of the world's most accomplished mountaineers, such as Apa Sherpa and Kami Rita Sherpa, who, at the time of writing, have summited Everest twenty-one and twenty-five times respectively.

JUNGLE DEEP, MOUNTAIN HIGH

* * * * *

My days with Bishal settle into a rhythm: early morning start, steady pace, frequent stops at teahouses en route. Our hike is accompanied by the melodious jingling of yak bells, the smell of pine and yak dung, spectacular mountain vistas opening up after each bend in the trail. After we hike uphill from Namche Bazaar, the tip of Everest comes into view for the first time, peeking from behind Cholatse, Nuptse and Khumbutse peaks like some coquettish ingénue. I've spent time in the mountains – the Alps, the Rockies, the Andes – for much of my life, but the Himalayas are on an entirely different scale. It's ironic that I'm a communicator for a living, because I find myself struggling to find words to adequately convey their sheer size. 'I'm normally dwarfed by mountains, and now I'm even more dwarfed than usual,' is the best I can do.

Bishal and I climb up steep switchbacks towards the eerie ghost village of Tengboche, the cold, swirling mist obscuring the pines. We carry on further down to tiny Deboche instead, where we are welcomed by the cheery proprietress at the wonderfully named Rivendell Lodge, which duly feels like a place of sanctuary (minus the Elves of Middle-earth), with its electric blankets, hot water and ambitious menu that extends beyond the Nepalese staple of vegetable curry, rice, lentils and *achar* (a pungent pickle) that Bishal and I eat twice a day. Here there are momos (steamed dumplings) and a Nepalese version of the hash brown. But no fresh fruit. When I see another hiker eating a pomegranate that his guide has thoughtfully brought with him, I feel intense envy and a wave of irritation that Bishal hasn't done the same for me.

Fruit procurement fail aside, Bishal proves to be good, unobtrusive company, in spite of my reservations about trekking with a stranger. He's irrepressibly cheerful, very strong for a man marginally taller than me, and a steady hiker. In the evenings, sometimes he tells me about his family ('Two brothers, a sister. My mother died when I was young, and my father is a farmer') and his professional ambitions ('I want to lead my own trekking company'), but also picks up on my mood if I'm particularly tired and grumpy and leaves me alone.

The closer to Everest, the more basic the accommodation. From Dingboche onwards, there are no showers. Not that I care. The last thing I want to do in the evening cold is peel off my multiple layers of clothing and thermal underwear. The rooms are frigid, so Bishal and I linger around the yak-dung stove fires in the guesthouse dining rooms to stay warm for as long as possible in the evenings. In *Where the Indus is Young*, Dervla Murphy recounts her travels in the Karakorum in winter: how you learn not to wash for weeks on end and cultivate a protective layer of grime. I'm working on mine.

From tiny Gorak Shep (5,164m) – a huddle of squat brick housing, and the highest village along this route – a narrow path meanders across the moraine towards Everest Base Camp. I've asked Bishal to lead me to the camp and back that same afternoon, so that we don't overnight above 5,000m more than once. He agrees. I'm particularly breathless and lethargic during that seemingly interminable two-hour hike to the 'town' of several dozen yellow and orange tents that nestles next to a vast ice field – the Khumbu Glacier. Moving slowly, deliberately, having to concentrate on putting one foot in front of the other, I find myself getting irrationally angry at the smug hikers who've already made it to Base Camp and are on their way back down.

Finally, there she is.

I face the mountain that I'd read so much about, and whose features I know by heart. In front of me is the west shoulder, to the right of which rises Nuptse (7,861m). Between the two snakes a wide river of ice. This is the treacherous Khumbu Icefall, where avalanches have killed so many over the years. Above it are Camp 1, Camp 2, Camp 3 and Camp 4. The climbers make a summit push from Camp 4 on the most favourable of May days, up the narrow Bottleneck, where a 'traffic queue' so often forms these days, with slow climbers holding everyone else up. Whether or not you've summited is irrelevant if you can't get yourself back down, with every minute spent above 8,000m (in the 'death zone') killing your body's cells.

I understand the compulsion to climb the world's highest peaks. It's part of the endless curiosity that drives humanity, the same curiosity that's taken humans to the stars. I've been an 'armchair mountaineer' since my teens, reading climbers' accounts of Everest, K2 and other Himalayan massifs. My parents have taken me and my sister up mountains since we were small, starting with Aspen Mountain and the Maroon Bells in Colorado. And though I originally whined, I grew to appreciate the challenge and the tremendous sense of achievement upon summiting. My mother would sing 'Vershina' ('Summit') by Soviet bard Vladimir Vysotsky, by way of encouragement.

Lurking near a cairn strung with prayer flags, I stand on hallowed ground once trodden by the likes of Reinhold Messner, Tenzing Norgay, Edmund Hillary, Alison Hargreaves, Gerlinde Kaltenbrunner and other elite mountaineers whose adventures I devoured from my mid-teens onwards. I'll never be fit enough to match their achievements, and I've made my peace with that.

The climbers are back in force this year: 289 hopefuls are gunning for the summit, according to *The Himalayan Times*. As I wander around the tent city, where climbers are readying their gear in preparation for the summit push, I wonder how many of them won't make it back down alive.

All along the trail to Everest Base Camp, there are sobering reminders that the surrounding mountains have claimed many for their own. At the top of the pass between the villages of Dughla and Lobuche, there's a tangle of prayer flags and a graveyard of cairns and memorials. Up above is the memorial to Scott Fischer, a mountain guide who died on Everest in 1996. Beyond it, another to Eve Girawong, one of eighteen people who died on Everest during the 2015 earthquake.

Guided trips up Everest are nothing new. They've been going on for decades now, but more and more climbing permits are being granted each year, bringing a welcome cash injection into the Nepalese economy, and more and more inexperienced climbers are trying to reach the summit, meaning more bottlenecks on crucial stretches of the climb, and more fatalities.

Into Thin Air by Jon Krakauer is a brilliant, tense account of the 1996 Everest disaster that resulted in eight deaths. He describes in painstaking detail what exactly went wrong, and how and why various members of the expeditions perished that year. Most years bring more casualties. Given that Everest is littered with empty oxygen canisters and the frozen bodies of the luckless, there's a raging debate about whether wealthy but inexperienced climbers paying $30,000–130,000 for the privilege of being shepherded up the mountain should be allowed on Everest at all, or whether the ascent should be only for those few who can summit without outside help. A part of me agrees with the elite climbers, but Bishal had already explained that the villages of Dughla, Lobuche and Gorak Shep rely exclusively on tourism. Sherpa mountain guides and porters are dependent on income from climbing expeditions for survival, while also being deeply uncomfortable with the trashing of the mountain that they, Sherpas, reverently call Chomolungma, 'Goddess Mother of the World', and honour as a deity.

At the Yak Resort in Gorak Shep, I'm introduced to a Sherpa guide who's summited Everest three times.

'Do you worry about getting up and down the mountain safely?' I ask.

'I trust that Chomolungma will look after me and let me come back to my family,' he tells me.

Amazed to see a deep-fried Mars Bar on the menu – something I'd never tried outside of Glasgow – I order one as a treat. But my palate, having grown used to mild vegetable curry, vehemently rejects this violent intrusion of sugar and fat.

Overnighting in Gorak Shep is terrible. I can't shake my headache and I can't get warm. Wearing all the clothes I've brought with me, including my winter hat and down jacket, I shiver in my (allegedly) four-season sleeping bag with a pile of heavy blankets on top until exhaustion overwhelms me. Hiking back down from Everest to Lukla is pure joy and takes us four days – half the ascent time. We lose 900m in five hours between Gorak Shep and Pheriche, passing the climbers' tent camp at the base of the pyramid-like Pumori and yet more trains of yaks plodding uphill. The lower we get, the lighter and more energised I feel, practically skipping down the valley.

In Pheriche, a cheery village at the foot of the twin-peaked Ama Dablam, I swing by the non-profit Himalayan Rescue Centre (HRC) to donate my supply of Diamox altitude sickness pills. Staffed by three international volunteer doctors, HRC is a seasonal clinic that mostly deals with hikers who succumb to altitude sickness.

'While we are here, locals come from villages all over the region and we treat any medical issues they may have as well,' one of the doctors explains. Access to medical care in rural Nepal is practically non-existent, so the HRC fulfils a vital role.

'We had dozens of patients here when the earthquake hit,' the receptionist tells me. 'Locals, climbers from Base Camp. We were working around the clock. Luckily the clinic survived.'

The last three days – Pheriche to Deboche, Deboche to Namche Bazaar and Namche Bazaar to Lukla – go by in a blur. After almost two weeks of rice, curry and lentils, I make a beeline for Everest Burger – Lukla's answer to Burger King – and claim my reward: a yak burger.

Crocodile skin markings, Kanganaman village (Middle Sepik, Papua New Guinea).

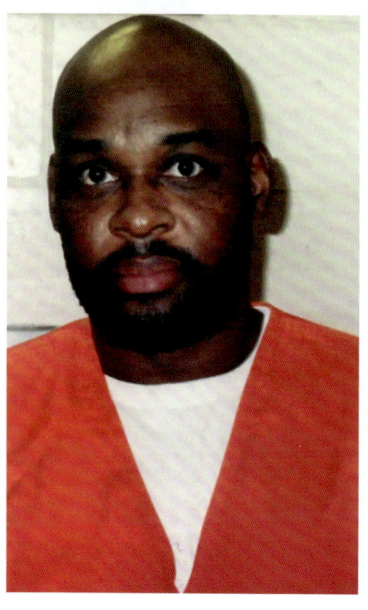 

above left Marvin Jones (1965–2020), one of my death row pen pals (Florida, USA).

above right My grandparents, Peter and Esther, in their early twenties. My grandmother crossed the Soviet Union in 1943 in order to prove my grandfather's innocence and save him from certain death in a gulag.

below San Quentin State Prison (California, USA).

above left James jumping off a cliff at Rick's Cafe in Negril (Jamaica).

above right The Krylov case defence team in Odessa (Ukraine) (**left to right** David Evans, me, Natasha Khazanov, Scharlette Holdman).

below Hellshire Beach – a weekend escape for Kingstonians (Jamaica).

above Dominoes night at Rae Town, Kingston (Jamaica) (**left to right** Paddy, me, Paul, Nancy).

below Two dance crews facing off against each other in Arnett Gardens, Kingston (Jamaica).

above left Krikštai – pagan grave markers in Nida (Lithuania).

above right The Marxist pantheon at the Gruto Parkas sculpture garden (Lithuania) (*left to right* Marx, Engels, Lenin, Stalin).

below Elaborate weathervanes in Nida (Lithuania).

above left My sister Genie with her edible acquisitions, somewhere along the Trans-Siberian railway.

above right An obo – holy shamanist spot – on the Khoboy peninsula, Olkhon Island, Lake Baikal (Russia).

below Tea and caviar with fellow BAM (Baikalo–Amurskaya Magistral) railway travellers in Siberia (*left to right* Yura, Valera, Andrei, Tanya).

above left Tsaatan girl (Mongolia).

above right Zaya giving Britney Spears her salt lick.

below Tsaatan camp near the Russia–Mongolia border.

above left Crossing a glacial stream in Torres del Paine National Park (Patagonia, Chile).

above right Me and Nikolai at the Las Torres lookout in Torres del Paine (Patagonia, Chile).

below At the Ciudad Perdida in Colombia (*left to right* Olga, Katrina, the three cousins from Bogotá, me, Mark, Alejandra, Manfred).

above left Yam house in the Trobriand Islands (Papua New Guinea).

above right In a dugout canoe on the Sepik river (Papua New Guinea).

below Cassowary dance in front of a *haus tambaran* in Kanganaman village (Middle Sepik, Papua New Guinea).

above left Artist André Eugène with one of his sculptures in Port-au-Prince (Haiti).

above right Painted human skull – a symbol of Baron Samedi, Port-au-Prince (Haiti).

below Dinner at the Leongs' home, Bangkok (Thailand).

above left Linden showing me how to throw a boomerang on the shores of Lake Ballard in the Australian outback.

above right 'Jazz hands' and emu prints in Carnarvon Gorge (Queensland, Australia).

below Trevor stirring the kangaroo stew, cooked over a campfire.

above With my laden scooter, halfway between Kasi and Luang Prabang (Laos).

below Dinner in Kasi with Tom Jones and his mechanic friend (Laos).

above left Pootoogook with his bear rifle, Kinngait (Nunavut, Canada).

above right *Inukshuk* (tundra marker) on Mallik Island near Kinngait (Nunavut, Canada).

below Inuit getting ready to go camping during the brief Arctic summer in Kinggait (Nunavut, Canada).

above left Shrine to Santa Muerte (Mexico City).

above right Celeste enthusiastically mopping up the chocolate from our *chocolate con churros*, on one of my many trips to Tijuana (Mexico).

below Miscellaneous meat and eyeball tacos at the Flechita Roja (Zihuatanejo, Mexico).

above left A Strollers outing – this time up Rio Higuerón (Frigiliana, Spain).

above right Sichuan-style battered squid – one of the dishes cooked for my first dinner guests in Cómpeta.

below The Strollers summit yet another Andalusian peak.

The view from my balcony in Cómpeta.

CHAPTER 8
RAINMAKERS AND CROCODILE SKIN

Recently, over dinner, I was asked: 'Who's been your biggest source of inspiration as a traveller?'

I was evasive. 'Oh... too many to name.'

Which is partly accurate. I have a great deal of respect for my older travel writer colleagues, many of whom have either a greater depth or breadth of travel experience than I do, and whose writing inspired me to roam. But few individuals have had a greater impact on me than my mentor.

When I was in my early teens, my mentor showed me photographs from his trip to Irian Jaya (West Papua). He'd stayed with a remote tribe where the men still hunted the way human beings have done for millennia, and killed a feral pig in his honour, cooking it in a pit for his welcome feast. My sheltered, solidly Western middle-class upbringing – skiing holidays in the Alps in the winter, summers spent touring Europe's museums – hadn't prepared me for the wonderment of seeing these fearsome, dark-skinned men, brandishing spears and bows and arrows, their faces streaked with white ritual paint, and wearing nothing but penis gourds – hollowed-out branches of the acacia tree, secured with rattan string around the waist.

'They do not consider themselves to be properly dressed unless they are wearing these,' he explained, which prompted predictable sniggering from a twelve-year-old.

I had no idea that such places, such remote cultures, still existed outside story books. Someday I'll get to see this too, I promised myself.

And so, the same year that I realise a long-standing ambition by making it to the base of Mount Everest, here I am, in Papua New Guinea, fulfilling another.

Papua New Guinea (PNG) is a place like no other, with immense cultural and biological diversity. A country of less than nine million people, yet with 851 languages spoken. Much of it is still covered in rainforest that's so difficult to breach that there are still uncontacted tribes out there, beyond the reach of even the most persistent Christian missionaries.

I'm winging it out here, armed only with advice from Jolyon, who'd spent time in the country, plus assorted literary material absorbed over the years about PNG's tribes. In my bag there's a dog-eared copy of *Four Corners* by Kira Salak, a disciple of Ayn Rand who traversed PNG's mountains, rainforest and rivers via dugout canoe and on foot at the age of twenty-four, stayed with cannibals, and was nearly killed on more than one occasion. It's the only PNG travelogue that I could find that was written by a woman traveller, whose experience could possibly prepare me for my own. I'm most emphatically *not* Kira Salak, though, so the odds of my being terrorised by drunk *raskols* (bandits) in some remote village are remote. However, just weeks earlier, Lindsay – my co-author of the Lonely Planet guide to Papua New Guinea – and his driver were held up on their way from Madang to Goroka in the Highlands by tribesmen at war with another tribe. They were lucky; their car was allowed to pass. The car behind them was not. As they sped off, their rear-view mirror framed the scene of the occupants of the other car being dragged out, their subsequent fate uncertain.

PNG's reputation precedes it. The promise of sudden violence is a fact of life here. A friend of a friend from Port Moresby, PNG's infamous capital, has a scar across her throat; thugs tried to decapitate her, but their knife was too blunt. News items that I've found on the internet invariably revolve around stories of foreigners attacked and raped, or of Papuan women accused of sorcery and subsequently lynched by their neighbours. I choose not to tell my parents that I appear to be heading into the land of sorcery, sexual violence and mob rule. But for the first time ever, I email copies of my itinerary to Mike and Heather, two of my friends, just in case. In case of what? In case I disappear. I don't expect anyone to come looking for me, but perhaps they could notify my next of kin.

* * * * *

In the little settlement of Alotau, spread across the hillsides and shore fringing Milne Bay, I hop on a plane to Kiriwina, one of the Trobriand Islands, best known for three things: their enormous yams, 'free love' and violent cricket games.

In the early twentieth century, Polish anthropologist Bronislaw Malinowski, who'd spent time on the islands in the 1910s and 1920s, fired up the Western imagination with *The Sexual Life of Savages in North-Western Melanesia*, which was loaned to me by Jolyon some years back and which made a big impression. Malinowski wrote about the sexual promiscuity that accompanies the Milamala (yam harvest), and how although foreigners are permitted to attend festivities, they have to shelve any amorous dreams of slap and tickle with bare-breasted Polynesian women or bare-chested Polynesian men. While yams (the longer the better), as well as being a staple food, are considered to be objects of great beauty, foreigners are not, and the so-called 'free love' comes within the framework of complex social structures.

As for the yams, they are a sign of prestige and gardening expertise, as well as a vital tie between villages and clans. During the harvest, they are dug up and displayed for admiration purposes, before being stored in the highly decorated yam houses. The chief's yam house – the largest and most elaborately painted – is the first to be filled, followed by the yam houses of each of the men. Since my timing coincides with yam season, I'm hoping to witness this celebration and to taste their prodigious yams.

A torrential deluge greets my arrival at Kiriwina 'airport', a shack by the airstrip. It's the first time I've seen rain in PNG – a source of joy for the locals, since the drought's been going on far too long this year. Butia Lodge, where I'm staying, has a soaring, conical thatched roof, and its entrance, painted in traditional white, red and black, is magnificently decorated with large cowrie shells. I'm the only guest. In fact, as Agnes the housekeeper tells me, I'm the only stranger on the entire island. A shy young man – the hotel owner's son – keeps me company while Agnes works pure magic with Spam and two-minute noodles for my lunch. I've eaten worse things in gourmet restaurants.

Goom, a short, wiry man of indeterminate age, with bloodshot eyes and betel-stained teeth, comes by to take me walking. Kiriwina is the largest of the four main Trobriand Islands, but unlike the impenetrable mountains of PNG's interior, these islands are mostly flat, low-lying coral, with intensely cultivated interiors. We set off along an old airstrip used by Americans during World War II. An overgrown military plane wreck is visible in a ditch beside the road.

The few trees there are have large, spiky leaves and grenade-like fruit. 'That's pandanus.' Goom explains. 'We had to clear other trees to make gardens.' By 'gardens', he means plots of land that every family has and relies on for food, because they're all subsistence farmers. If they live by the sea, they fish also, but otherwise their gardens are pretty much their only source of food. He leads me to his family's garden. 'I work here when I'm not taking visitors around. I'm a *tokwaibagula*,' he tells me. To be recognised as a 'good gardener' here is highly prestigious.

Malinowski mentioned *lalogua* – wooden scaffoldings made up of tall vertical stakes and several rows of horizontal ones, from which the prize yams were hung. These *lalogua* would surround the *baku*, the dancing and ceremonial ground in the centre of every Trobes village. The more *lalogua* there were and the more bountiful the harvest, the more pleased the *baloma* (spirits of the dead) would be, since they'd feast on the spiritual essence of the yams. Conversely, if the harvest was poor and there was little food on display, the *baloma* would get (h)angry and show their displeasure through thunder, lightning and torrential rain, and would punish the islanders with storms and droughts, ensuring another bad harvest the following year. Which seems like a case of biting off the nose to spite the face, since it would mean less yam essence for the spirits, but what do I know?

'Do you still display yams in *lalogua* during the harvest?' I ask Goom.

'We keep our yams in yam houses. The big chief has the largest one, but the tallest one is in a village nearby. I can take you there if you want.'

I do.

'When we get to the village, I will introduce you to the chief. It's customary to give him a small gift.'

In the past, that would have been betel nut (the seed of the areca palm, a stimulant popular in PNG, judging by the puddles of crimson spit everywhere), but Goom tells me that these days 10 kina (US$2.50) would be more appreciated.

The yam house is a splendid, eye-catching structure in the centre of Togaku village. It resembles a tall and narrow log cabin, with a thatched roof, strands of large white cowrie shells, and the gables brightly painted in red, white and black patterns, with a bull's eye of black within circles of white and red at the end of each log.

We quickly acquire an audience consisting of the village's youngest residents, wearing torn, stained T-shirts and shorts which are falling apart. They, and a handful of women congregate on the large *buneiova* (covered platform) in front of the chief's house. The chief himself is an elderly man missing most of his teeth, dressed in a torn singlet and shorts. We exchange greetings. I'm then turned loose so that I can admire the yam house. Peering inside, I find a couple of shrivelled yams – all that's left of this year's harvest.

'There were no Milamala celebrations this year.' Goom is downcast.

'And no cricket either?'

He shakes his head.

Christian missionaries did their best to put an end to what they considered to be the islanders' carnal bacchanalia, and introduced them to the game of cricket in order to take their minds off sex and *kayasa* (ritual warfare). But Trobriander cricket is not a sedate pastime on the village green, or even the organised thrill of The Ashes. There is war paint involved, an unlimited number of players, singing and dancing mocking the other team after every out, shrill whistle blowing, plus non-standard batting and bowling practices. I'm sorry I don't get to see it.

There's a stone at the edge of Togaku village with a human face carved into it. Goom explains that it watches over the village and has benevolent powers. May I take a photo? Yes, but that'll be another 10 kina. The constant requests for money take some getting used to. Trobes islanders don't appear to be particularly materialistic – I see no modern conveniences among the palm-shaded thatched huts, no electricity lines, no running water, not even a single solar panel. But there's a strong sense that outsiders must pay their due if they wish to partake in the Trobes' culture, and this applies to everyone. Goom tells me that ritual gift giving has been part of Trobes' culture for centuries.

Trobriand Islanders have Polynesian roots and, before the advent of modern boats, Trobes traders crossed the open sea in their dugout canoes in order to exchange valuables such as volcanic glass from Fergusson Island and a rare jade-like stone from Muyua Island, as well as foodstuffs: fish, vegetables, pigs. The most famous of these trade routes is the *kula* ring, whereby a ceremonial exchange is conducted between eighteen islands of Milne Bay (Trobriand Islands are just one cluster among many). It involves trading *mwali* (white-shell armbands) for *soulava* (red-shell necklaces). The idea is to not hold on to any *kula* object for long and to pass it on, thereby building trusted trade partnerships.

'Does the *kula* ring still exist?' I ask Goom.

'Yes.'

'And do people still paddle their dugout canoes for hundreds of miles?'

'Some do. But others go in regular boats.'

The next day Goom walks me to Losuia, a scruffy little waterfront settlement that's the closest Kiriwina has to a capital. At the pier, several young men are loading crates on to a boat in preparation for a journey to Alotau.

'Are you sailing today?' I ask, eyeing the turbulent sea.

'We move with the spirits,' the boatman tells me, suggesting that they intend to wait for more favourable weather.

* * * * *

With Goom's help, I explore Kiriwina on foot over the course of several days, walking the dirt pathways connecting the villages, passing men with enormous bundles of firewood on their heads and women toting huge loads from their gardens. Goom takes me swimming in a sacred cave with a deep, crystal-clear pool, and introduces me to the artisans of Obweria village who carve elaborate walking sticks out of ebony – an extremely hard and brittle timber. We hang out with locals on the *haus win* (hangout platform) of various villages, and I chat to the missionary with betel-stained teeth, who is lounging around with the village elders, about the challenges of his work. In Yalaka village, I spot women trading what looks like patterned banana leaves, and Goom confirms that it's *doba*, banana leaf money that was once used all over PNG.

'The women take the leaves, put them on a wooden board with a carved pattern, and then run a scraper over the leaf and dry the leaves afterwards to make *doba*.'

'They use it as well as money or instead of it?'

'They use it if they run out of money.'

Apparently, a bundle of ten *doba* is worth 1 kina, making it a lot of effort for very little return.

It's a little overwhelming, being the only foreigner on the island. Wherever we go, I shake countless hands, am mobbed by hordes of children shouting '*Dimdim*! *Dimdim*!' and am accosted by curious adults who rub my arms to establish whether my skin colour comes off. The men pass my battered copy of the Lonely Planet guide to Papua New Guinea among themselves with great interest, trying to figure out the identity of the Trobes islanders in the photos. In one village, I am crowned with a wreath of flowers, like some sort of woodland sprite or faerie.

'So who exactly is a *dimdim*?' I ask Goom. 'Me?'

'Yes, white people.'

'What about Chinese, Japanese people?'

'They are also *dimdims*.'

'So basically all foreigners are *dimdims*? What about black tourists, do they sometimes come to Trobes?'

'Yes.'

'What do you call them?'

'N-----.'

This reminds me of an incident in Port Moresby on my very first day in Papua New Guinea. Horror stories about Moresby, the capital of PNG, abound, perpetuated by (mostly Australian) expats. You can't drive across town without getting carjacked. Don't even think about using public transport: it's suicide. Don't walk anywhere after dark. Better still, don't walk at all; take taxis. Better yet, get a private driver with a gun. 'But you should be okay to walk around downtown,' Nick tells me. He and his housemate Jared are two Aussie lads in their twenties who've offered to host me, sight unseen, after Nick met my Lonely Planet colleague Lindsay by chance in New Ireland.

Just like back in Kingston, I am pretty much the only pale face downtown, and feel uncomfortably conspicuous. People are openly staring at me – the barefoot higglers selling little bags of peanuts, the men with impassive faces lounging around next to a shopping centre. So I do what I did in Jamaica: I make eye contact, greet people, smile. Works like magic. People smile back, wave hello.

I make my way down to Ela Beach and watch families with kids splashing in the shallows. A teenage boy who introduces himself as Albert joins me, accompanied by a posse of half a dozen friends, ranging from ten-year-old kids to slightly older teenagers not much taller than me. They're all from the same neighbourhood, Koki. We sit around and talk.

'You guys not at school?'

'No.'

'Do you have to go to school?'

'No.'

It later transpires that Koki has recently been hit by a spate of tribal violence, with people from different Eastern Highlands tribes going at each other with machetes, bows and arrows. Schools are closed. Ah. There was story about this in a recent copy of *The National* lying on my hosts' kitchen table. It went something like this:

A toddler was leaning on a car. The driver started the car, the child fell over, and the mother started shouting: 'My baby! He killed my baby!' Two drunk guys chased the car, pulled the driver out and beat him to death. The child wasn't hurt. Then the relatives of the dead driver retaliated by torching fourteen houses, and his killers' families responded in kind.

Rival tribe members moving to the capital from remoter parts of the country often bring their deadly grievances with them.

Albert's teeth and those of his friends are stained red.

'You guys chew betel nut?'

Affirmative.

'Does it make you happy, chilled out?'

Enthusiastic nodding. One of the older kids casually cleans his fingernails with a switchblade. I'm slightly apprehensive. But apart from asking me for a couple of kina for cigarettes, they don't bother me. However, when they express the desire to follow me 'home', I shake them off. I can just imagine Nick and Jared's reaction if I turn up with a troupe of street urchins in tow. Before I leave, I ask their permission to take photos of them and they mug for the camera. Reviewing the photos on my viewfinder, they then make fun of each other's big noses and 'African' hair, and call each other 'n-----', seemingly as an insult. I'm not quite sure what to make of that. Prior to German and British colonial rule in PNG (1884–1975), Papuans had only fleeting contact with European missionaries, whalers, explorers and the like, though they were seen as racially inferior by these visitors. During colonial rule, Papuans were subject to discriminatory laws, and it seems that negative attitudes towards dark skin and certain physical features are deeply ingrained, though Papuans see themselves as higher up in the global racial hierarchy than other people of colour.

* * * * *

Since Goom seems to be easy-going, I broach the subject of Trobes' complex sexual relations. We're sitting around the table in the Butia Lodge lounge, and he's showing me how to use betel nut.

'You chew it. Here, take some of this' – he hands me some slaked lime wrapped in betel leaf, which goes in your mouth alongside the actual nut. I chew. It's really bitter, but after a little while I feel a not unpleasant warming feeling spread through me. Not enough to offset the ghastly taste or justify having a mouth like a vampire, though.

I turn to Goom.

'So when you were young, did you "make friends"?'

'Making friends' is a euphemism for having multiple sexual partners before marriage, which Trobes teenagers are encouraged to do.

'Yes,' He smiles. 'Many friends.'

Goom tells me that like other Trobes males, he moved out of the family home as a teenager and lived in the village *bukumatula* (bachelor house) along with the other young men.

'When I decided which girl I was going to live with, everyone knew, because we ate together in front of the whole village.'

Apparently, a couple is only considered to be properly married if they are seen to be sharing a meal. A good dining companion is not the worst criteria for a life partner, I think to myself.

'So after that, no more "making friends"?'

'Sometimes. During Milamala.' Apparently, a fling by mutual consent during the yam harvest is the done thing.

* * * * *

Since Kiriwina, its *kula* rituals, its oral traditions and magic are presided over by the paramount chief, and it's good manners to pay your respects, we walk to Omarakana village. We find the elderly man holding court on a chair outside his Western-style house, next to a beautiful yam house, and I present him with a small token (20 kina), careful to keep my head lower than his. And now that I've met one of the island's most important men, Goom suggests that I should meet the other.

'Would you like to visit the Rain Maker? He's a magician who makes rain when we need it.'

Of course. It's irrelevant whether I believe that certain individuals have the power to manipulate the weather. Here, on this island, it makes as much sense as anything else.

It may seem as if I'm taking everything in my stride, but what I'm feeling is a really profound sense of disconnect. Life on the Trobes is so vastly different from my regular life, or even from any other destination I've ever been to, that much of the time I feel as if I'm in some fantastical film or alternate reality, where I must suspend all judgement, not try to guess what'll happen next, and just absorb each experience as it comes.

'So how does he make rain?' I ask.

'When our land gets too dry, people come to him and bring gifts. He fasts for a day and then goes to the sea. He takes certain objects and places them under the reef, and says an incantation.'

'What sort of objects?'

'I don't know. Only the Rain Maker knows, and the one to whom he passes on his power.'

'Does this power, to make rain, come down from father to son?'

'Yes.'

The Rain Maker is not what I expected. I was on the lookout for a sorcerer in torn robes, with wild hair and a mystic's eyes. Instead, it's a middle-aged man in a discoloured old T-shirt who doesn't stand out from the rest of the village, with a betel-nut smile, an afro and a shy demeanour.

He accepts my gift and is happy to answer my questions, provided they don't involve the specifics of rain making – a professional secret.

'The rain we had this morning, did you do that?' He shyly allows that yes, that was his work.

'So how often do people ask you to make rain?'

'When the weather has been dry a long time, and the gardens need water.'

'And when you perform the rain-making ceremony, does the rain come that day?'

'Sometimes. Or sometimes it takes a few days.'

I don't ask him whether his incantations always work or whether there's a possibility that the rain that comes after a few days of doing his magic might be just a coincidence.

On my last night in Kiriwina, Agnes presents me with the first and best chilli crab of my life – a beast the size of my head, nestling in a bath of fiery-coloured sauce that's equal parts sweetness and heat – a treat all the more pleasurable because it's so completely unexpected in this land of tubers and Spam. It's accompanied by taro, sweet potato and the last of this year's yam – sweet and dense and tender and smoky from being baked on hot coals. It's a taste I will forever associate with this world of magical realism. Later, I will find bits of crab shell in my hair and sauce on my earlobe.

* * * * *

'I've eaten a fried tarantula once, in Cambodia,' my friend Brett told me over dinner at Saan, a Thai place in Auckland. 'It was crunchy on the outside, and bitter and creamy on the inside.'

I could have happily spent my entire existence not knowing what a fried tarantula tastes like. Or tarantula prepared in any culinary fashion, for that matter. I've been terrorised by arachnids my whole life. By the giant monstrosity above my bed in a thatched hut on Logea Island in Milne Bay, a few days ago, that had to be chased out with multiple cups of water, but continued to linger menacingly above the entrance to the hut. By the massive huntsman spider in the tree above my tent in Karijini National Park in the Australian Outback. By spider eyes, glinting balefully pale blue in the torchlight in the corner of my room at the tragically misnamed Friendly Guest House in the North Luzon highlands in the Philippines. By the tarantula that ambushed me as I picnicked on the banks of Lake Tinquilco in Chile's Lake District. As I saw the brown shape scuttling towards me, I hazily wondered how on earth a crab would find itself by a mountain lake before my brain caught up with me and I ran a four-minute mile. By the malevolent eight-legged entity on the Rupununi savannah in Guyana that blocked my way as I tried to step over an enormous puddle on a muddy road. Each time I tried to cross, the spider lunged towards my foot, and I jerked back, until I finally slipped in the mud and fell over on my behind in the puddle. Spider = 1, Kaminski = 0.

Most gastronavigators have a line that they will not cross. Spiders are mine. I have eaten some insects: dried grasshoppers drenched in chilli powder and lime juice in Oaxaca, and steak topped with giant, fat-bottomed ants in northern Colombia. Both put me in mind of dirty popcorn. But I sampled them more out of the conviction that a good travel writer ought to try most things at least once in order to give an accurate account of the experience, rather than in pursuit of gastronomic pleasure.

But I'll readily admit that it's somewhat illogical to be repelled by the idea of eating surface crawlers and yet munch on seafood with gusto. After all, prawns are but distant cousins of the woodlouse, while crabs and spiders look like close relations. There have been many crustacea in my life. *Centolla* (southern king crab) – the red-shelled monsters of the deep, plucked from the frigid waters of the Beagle Channel and brusquely loaded into crates by fishermen in Puerto Williams, Chile's (and the world's) southernmost settlement. The blue-shelled crab with a massively overdeveloped left claw, found lurking on palm trees on Batan Island in the Philippines. A bucket of small crabs, eaten with the shell still on, on Pirate Island off the south coast of Vietnam after night fishing in a squall with local fishermen. Black pepper crab with fellow foodies Shawn and Wyn in Singapore, where there are more restaurants than people and where everyone and their grandmother have an opinion as to where you should go for the best chilli crab (or white pepper crab, or black pepper crab, for that matter).

I ate my first ever crab at The Stinking Rose in San Francisco, aged twenty-four. Marlene, the then girlfriend of my death row pen pal James, took me on an impromptu driving tour of the Bay Area, and then introduced me to the restaurant where everything was infused with garlic, even the ice cream, and where giant Dungeness crab, roasted and drizzled with garlic butter sauce, reigned supreme. I loved the ceremony of it all – being given a crab bib to catch the shell fragments, the crab mallet and nutcracker-like implement to crack the shell and claws, the long seafood picks for retrieving the sweet white flesh hiding in the narrow legs. I occasionally wonder which early human first thought of eating such a forbidding-looking creature – in the same way that I wonder how many people died before they figured out that some species of cassava have to be squeezed dry of their juices in order to stop them from poisoning the diner. Here on Kiriwina, it takes me two hours to pull every last morsel of flesh from the wreckage of the shell, unashamedly licking my hands clean of sweet, piquant sauce. Just as in San Francisco, I come away with the firm conviction that crab, unlike cassava, is well worth the effort.

* * * * *

As I tuck into my chilli crab on Kiriwina, the first drops of evening rain begin to pummel the parched ground outside. The rain steadily increases in power and rhythm and shows no signs of abating. Later at night, as I listen to the sounds of the tropical deluge, I think of the Rain Maker and picture him muttering incantations into the storm.

* * * * *

The house of Ralf Stüttgen, German priest gone native and seller of indigenous artefacts, resembles a shipping container. It's unkempt and long in need of a paint job. A rusted car wreck sits next to it.

'Ralf came here before I was born,' my guide Chris tells me. Chris is a tall, shaven-headed Middle Sepik man in his early forties, impassive apart from occasional, startling roars of laughter. 'He spent decades on the Sepik, then married a local lady and settled down here.'

He bangs on the door, yelling 'Ralf! Ralf!' Eventually, the door is opened by a bespectacled, rail-thin old man with long white hair and one trouser leg rolled up to the knee, revealing a large sore on his calf. But though he looks frail, his handshake crushes my hand as he ushers me inside.

Every available surface of his home is covered with dusty masks and carvings from remote villages on the Middle Sepik – the part of PNG where Chris and I are currently heading. I stare. While some women salivate over handbags or shoes, indigenous carvings – particularly masks – have that effect on me.

When I was little, my grandmother's flat had a Tibetan demon mask hanging in the hallway, above her collection of Soviet badges. It was blue, with red-rimmed eyes, a third glaring eye on its forehead, its mouth open in a fanged snarl and its head topped with a crown of human skulls. An

Orientalist who consulted my lawyer grandmother regarding his divorce gave it to her as a gift. In later years, I learned that its brethren are used in the Cham, a millennia-old Buddhist ritual dance that brings blessings to the community, and that the mask's fearsome features are supposed to strike terror in evil spirits, while the five human skulls represent five negative human emotions – rage, ignorance, jealousy, attachment and pride. What masks represent – what they hide, what they symbolise, what they reveal – has been a source of lifelong fascination. As I grew older, I began to see parallels between these physical manifestations of the human condition, rendered in wood, clay, cloth or papier mâché, and the different visages that we, humans, present to the world, depending on the occasion. During my travels, I've amassed a collection of ritual masks from Nicaragua, Costa Rica, Borneo, Mexico, Japan, Mongolia, Tierra del Fuego – particularly devils, demons and skulls.

Guidebook research aside, my reasons for venturing to the Sepik river, in the north of PNG, are complex. When it comes to ceremonial masks and carvings, the villages along the middle section of the Sepik river are second to none. I'm looking to expand my collection. But I'm also heading into Papua's isolated interior to confront the petrified tangle of my roots as a traveller and my long-standing reliance on others for validation.

* * * * *

I move slowly around Ralf's living room-cum-museum, touching masks inlaid with cowrie shells, guardian figures, the carving of some strange creature with one leg in profile.

'That's the water spirit,' Ralf explains. 'It's rare to see him with just one leg.'

Leading me over to a detailed map of the Sepik river on the wall, yellow with age, he points at various exhibits and explains their origins.

'That one – with a cowrie shell outline – you can tell it's from the Middle Sepik because of the crocodile protruding from its mouth. The crocodile has a special significance to the people of the crocodile cult.'

There's one particularly striking vintage mask, topped with a thick thatch of cassowary feather 'hair'. I'm just not sure I'd be able to get it home, given that cassowaries are now an endangered species.

'You can carefully remove the feathers from the clay, hide them and reattach them once you get back home.' Ralf teaches me how to commit what may be a jailable offence in Australia and the EU.

Ralf also shows me woven yam masks used during the yam harvest in the Sepik region: 'By putting the masks on the yams, they give them a name, a spirit, an identity.' Looks like it's not just the Trobes that revere that russet-coloured tuber.

I'm on a mission to find a hook cult figure (a carving with an anchor-like hook at the end) for Jolyon. Since my early teens, he's taken on several unique roles in my life. My friend – though it's not a friendship of equals, given the disparity in our ages and the circumstances under which we originally met. My mentor – since I identified him as a source of wisdom and support very early on. My role model – the most adventurous traveller I knew while growing up, and whose exploits I sought to emulate. This was driven, I suspect, as much by my need to prove myself to him, at least during my early years as a traveller, as by my curiosity about the exotic and the unknown.

For years, he and I have been trading indigenous artefacts from our respective travels. He'd specifically asked me for this particular type of carving, and I take these shopping trips extremely seriously. At the time of the PNG trip, I'm nowhere near being able to examine my own reactions to him and his requests. Why my hands shook so badly when I brought him a carved figure of a female guardian from Sarawak, Borneo, that when I unwrapped the brown paper I knocked his phone off his desk. The mixture of pleasure and intense relief when he gave the guardian figure a prominent place in his study.

We'd fallen out several months earlier, over a misunderstanding. When I was in my late teens, Jolyon told me about another mentee of his who wanted to come travelling with him. He was against the idea because he felt he'd be spending most of his time bailing her out of trouble. I could understand that. Who'd want to be a babysitter? In my mid-twenties, as a rookie travel writer just starting out, I brought up the possibility of us travelling together, given our shared interests, and he told me in the nicest possible way to find travelling companions my own age. Back then, his accepting me as a travelling companion would've been the highest compliment, the utmost validation of my travelling prowess. I thought that not making the cut was simply because I didn't have sufficient travel experience. In my early thirties, as an experienced travel writer and traveller in my own right, I broached the subject again, approaching Jolyon as an equal with expertise of my own to offer.

'Are you categorically opposed to our travelling together sometime in the future?'

'No… but don't you think it would ruin things?'

At the time, I puzzled over what he meant by 'ruining things' and couldn't muster the nerve to ask for clarification for fear of appearing foolish. My shortcomings as a person, perhaps? That I wouldn't be sufficiently interesting as a travelling companion? Then, during our estrangement, in imagined exchanges with my mentor inside my own head – the place where we always have the cleverest responses, the best comebacks – I tried to figure out whether there was any way I could have interpreted that crucial sentence any differently at the time. And each time came away with my original interpretation: reluctance for reasons unclear to me rather than a categorical 'no'. Still, given the lack of enthusiasm, I wasn't going to ask again. And that would've been that, except that, years later, Jolyon was due to travel in South America and, aware of my expert knowledge of a specific region, approached me for some maps and recommendations. I obliged, and since I was due to be in the region for work, I offered to show him around if we were in the same place at the same time.

I saw my offering my expert knowledge as a way of repaying my mentor for his kindness towards me over the years, and felt hurt and wrong-footed when I received his negative response. I backpedalled wildly. Accustomed to deferring to Jolyon, I wasn't able to tell him that it was an honest mistake – that I genuinely hadn't realised, going on the information I had, that he was, in fact, opposed to our ever being travelling companions. Nor was I able to convey that, to me, there was a big distinction between travelling together and meeting up for a few hours while abroad. Jolyon and I never had conversations about our expectations of each other, what the rules of our interaction were, whether what we'd assumed to be true of one another was, in fact, accurate. I'd just taken for granted that he'd instinctively know what I was thinking. Whereas he'd assumed that I was applying the 'persistence overcomes resistance' approach to something that he'd already vetoed and understandably became upset. For much of my life, my knee-jerk response to male anger had been to placate. And my shying away from difficult feedback made it almost impossible to try and understand the other person's perspective. In the end, I sent him a long-winded apology and shan't leave the Sepik without the best possible hook cult figure I can find.

* * * * *

When I tell Ralf I write for Lonely Planet, he perks up. 'A Lonely Planet author came to stay with me here for a whole week in 1998. Then we both got the 'flu.' But try as he might, he cannot remember my colleague's name, and he waves us on our way along the 'Sepik Highway'.

The 'Sepik Highway' is a misnomer: it's a lonely, remote road with hardly any traffic. During the hours we spend on the road, which is spectacularly potholed, only a couple of PMVs (minibuses) pass us, heading to the market in Wewak. We pass roadside higglers selling betel nuts, fresh coconuts, sago parcels wrapped in banana leaf. From the little market town of Maprik, we drive up into the hills to an eerily deserted village, centred on a particularly beautiful *haus tambaran* (spirit house) – a pointed, thatched structure with an impressively decorated front and a tiny entrance. Chris looks around furtively to make sure there are no villagers about before he gives me permission to photograph it from the outside. This is not his tribe's territory and we could all get into serious trouble by being here without permission.

Chris himself is from one of the villages belonging to the crocodile cult in the Middle Sepik. That's where we're bound: the 'cultural treasure house' of PNG, where each village has its own artistic style.

On the final stretch of road to Pagwi, the gateway village to the Middle Sepik, our way is blocked by a procession. For a second I worry that we're facing a mob. Earlier that day, when we started out from Wewak, my stomach was knotted with apprehension when the men were loading up the pick-up truck with food and barrels of boat fuel, and I caught one of Chris's friends making sure his handgun was loaded and that he had extra clips of ammunition. But no, this crowd is singing, waving palm fronds, and carrying an image of the Virgin Mary. The man at the head of the procession is decked out in a grass skirt and cassowary feather headgear.

The sun is setting by the time all our supplies are loaded into the motorised dugout canoe in Pagwi, and fully dark by the time we moor the canoe by the steep mud steps of Kanganaman village – our base – where Chris's grandfather was once chief.

The guesthouse is the most rustic I've ever stayed in. A giant roach scuttles out of the living room. The kitchen's at the opposite end, with a couple of guest rooms in between. I commandeer the living room with the torn mosquito net, since there's some semblance of a breeze there. While Chris busies himself in the kitchen, I set up camp, unveiling my pop-up SansBug mosquito net tent that acts as a mesh cocoon against all creepy-crawlies. I blow up my camping mat, throw it inside along with my sleeping-bag liner, and am all set for the night. It takes me a while to get over my fear of falling through the floorboards, which are made of black palm and sag beneath my feet like a hammock. The guys are light-footed when they move across this floor, whereas my elephant-like footsteps make the entire place wobble.

Chris sets up a shower area for me behind a large sheet of plastic under the half-built house next door. A bucket of brown river water is provided for my convenience. Since nothing will induce me to wash alongside the locals in the river, with its man-eating crocodiles – not even Chris's mock-threats to throw me in – it's a step up.

Dinner is three kinds of tubers and tinned tuna ('tinpis'). I unveil my emergency bottle of hot sauce and a travel spice holder, so that I may have my 'tinpis' and carbs three different ways: curried, Cajun and jerk.

* * * * *

The following morning we're on the river, heading south to Chambri Lake. 'The normal waterway we use is too low,' Chris comments. 'We might not be able to get through to Wombun and Amboin.'

'Let's try.'

We pass a number of dugout canoes, filled to the brim with people and produce.

'They're heading to the market in Maprik,' Chris explains. It'll take them a long time, since none of these canoes are motorised. Unlike in the Trobriands and Milne Bay, when I smile and wave at people here few return my friendly overtures. I finally give up in embarrassment and stick to polite nods.

'Tell me about the market system,' I ask Chris.

Chris explains which village goes to which market and on which day, how people go to Maprik or do the overnight PMV journey to Wewak and often stay for a couple of days with *wantoks* (extended family or contacts) to make the most of their time. Since I'm looking to expand existing coverage of the Sepik region for the Lonely Planet guide, I have questions. Travellers coming to PNG can largely be divided into two groups: affluent birdwatchers and those with an interest in anthropology, who come on guided tours, and adventurous travellers, who get around PNG by shared minivan, plane and boat. I'm beginning to see that independent, cheap travel in the Sepik is doable, provided you're willing to risk riding a PMV along the 'Sepik Highway'. You can catch a PMV to the Pagwi boat landing and then negotiate passage to the village of your choice with the canoes picking up villagers returning from the market. Then, when you want to move on to a different village, you can either pay someone to paddle you down, or catch another market-bound canoe to Pagwi and then catch another canoe to a different village. Easy. But you need a lot of time to make this work.

'Do you often get hold-ups on the road to Wewak?'

'Not many. Sometimes, if people know that a PMV is carrying a local with a lot of money.'

'You mean these are inside jobs? Why don't the police catch the men responsible?' Chris has no coherent answer for me.

We take a Sepik tributary. On our right, on the steep river bank, there is a clutch of thatched houses. 'Amboin,' Chris announces. There's a shallow river section with water bubbling over exposed rocks. 'We can only get to Wombun if they help us push the canoe over. Shall I ask them?'

'Do it.'

Everyone piles out. Several local guys help Chris and the boat driver to portage our canoe, and we press on.

Near Wombun, we see numerous birds circling overhead: cormorants, herons, birds of prey. A fishy stench pervades the air as fishermen paddle their canoes by the river bank, pull in the nets, deftly gut the fish, throw the innards in the river and drape the fish over the edges of the canoe to dry. At closer inspection, all the fishermen turn out to be women.

'Where are all the men?' I ask Chris.

'Here on the Sepik, fishing is a woman's job.'

I wonder what qualifies as a man's job. Besides hunting, that is. Chris has already made it clear that Kanganaman's hunters will not take me with them on one of their jungle outings: 'Animals will hear you from the village.'

In Wombun, a small, appealing village, I cautiously ask permission to enter their *haus tambaran*, topped with twin heron carvings, wondering if I might be denied. *Haus tambaran* are traditionally the domain of men and taboo to women. But only local women, as it turns out. The men of the Middle Sepik have apparently discovered in recent years the commercial opportunities of allowing foreign women inside for a fee. Locals courteously invite me over the threshold and I take in the sandy floor, the brightly painted beams, the high berths that the men sit on to socialise, the hearths, the painted anthropomorphic wood carvings of deities – crocs, pigs, dogs, rats (all very obviously female, I note).

When we return to Kanganaman, Chris takes me to the large clearing, bookended by two *haus tambaran*. While we sit inside the smaller of the spirit houses, smoky from the fire in the hearth, he explains to me the significance of the female figures in general.

'Femininity is a sign of fertility.'

'What about her?' I point to the carving above the entrance of a woman with her legs spread.

'When we enter the spirit house, we leave everything behind. When we leave, it's as if we're reborn.'

There are more carvings here, too, and near the hearth I spot a fine example of a hook cult figure: a female, holding two crocodiles. It's exactly what I've been looking for. I ask them to put it aside for me.

Chris leads me back across the clearing. 'I've got a surprise for you.'

We approach the main *haus tambaran*, an open, two-storey building with a soaring roof, just as drumming commences and two remarkable figures slowly sashay out of the spirit house, bending this way and that, swaying, their grass skirts swinging. The dancers are wearing full-length *tumbuan* body masks, which encase them in a cone-shaped wicker framework, adorned with garlands of flowers and featuring two face masks with hooked noses. I've only ever seen these in the museum in Port Moresby. I watch their hypnotic movements, mesmerised.

Just as they stop, more drumming sounds come from the second, smaller *haus tambaran*. Children of varying ages, with painted faces, appear at the entrance. They are wearing grass skirts and rattling anklets; one boy has a particularly splendid headdress of cassowary feathers. Then a giant figure dressed as a cassowary emerges from behind the spirit house to the rhythmic drumming, mimicking the bird's distinctive walk, with the children dancing with great concentration around him, grass skirts flying.

* * * * *

'This is one of the villages where they practise the crocodile skin initiation, right?' I ask Chris.

'Right.'

'Why the crocodile?'

'Because we believe that the crocodile is one of our ancestors. That's why we swim in the river. We have nothing to fear from them.'

When the young men of the Middle Sepik reach puberty, they undergo a very painful initiation ceremony that marks their passage into manhood. It involves having a series of patterns cut into their torsos, shoulders and buttocks. The raised welts then heal to resemble crocodile skin.

'Do you think someone can show me their crocodile skin?'

'I've got crocodile skin!'

'Really? You never told me!'

Chris lifts up his shirt at the back so that I can see a pattern of bumps, arrows and a four-pointed star.

'How far does it stretch?'

He motions as if to pull down his shorts. I laugh.

'How long did that take?'

'One, maybe two hours. I'm not sure, because of all the pain. My uncle brought me here' – Chris points to the larger *haus tambaran* – 'and the elders of the village played sacred flute music to soothe us. Two of my friends passed out.'

'What did they use? A knife?'

'A razor blade. But my father's generation and older people, they'd have used bamboo knives.'

The young men of the village spend months recovering from the scarring ritual on the second floor of the main spirit house, their wounds moistened with sap from a specific tree and then covered with river clay to prevent infection. During their recovery, they learn survival skills from the elders – how to hunt, how to fish, how to make elaborate wood carvings, how to appease the spirits that protect the village.

Chris beckons a young man walking beside the clearing so that I can admire a particularly prominent pattern of ridges on his back and the four-pointed star pattern in the region of his waist. As I'm very tactile, I'd love to run my hands over these scars, to commit them to physical memory, but it would be entirely inappropriate to ask.

There's something intensely personal about touching someone's scars. When I was in Colombia, several years back, I was hanging on to the railings of a jeep as we were leaving Popayán for Puracé National Park. A striking Scandinavian woman with short-cropped blonde hair, sitting in the back, said to me: 'You've hurt yourself,' and then gently ran her finger along a freshly healed cut on my arm. That gesture was so electrifying, intimate and unexpected that I almost fell off the back of the jeep.

* * * * *

Over our standard dinner involving tubers, yet more tubers, and some Spam, Chris and I pore over my map of the Sepik. It occurs to me that since Kira Salak had managed to get down the Sepik way up from the Upper Sepik, there's no reason why the journey can't be repeated. In fact, there appears to be a rough road leading down from the town of Vanimo, on the north coast, to the Upper Sepik.

'Is it possible to go from Vanimo and then up the river?'

'Maybe. I've never been that far upriver. They speak different languages from me there.'

'But if you can get a canoe and fuel and supplies up there, then technically it's possible, yes?'

'Yes.'

'So maybe it's possible to go all the way up to the very source of the Sepik?'

Mentally planning my future expedition along the river, I get more and more excited. Surely it's just a matter of logistics: getting enough fuel, finding a guide that knows the Upper Sepik, a canoe, food supplies? Sure, it'd be really expensive, but I bet it can be done. The Middle Sepik is fascinating, but it's also relatively well trodden, by PNG standards. It would be truly something to go where no foreigner's footsteps have ever fallen. A thought for next time.

It's a breathless evening and there's no respite from the heat. I've already performed my evening ablutions. After a fairly unpleasant first night, begrimed and sweating on top of my sleeping bag liner, I perfected a shower system to get rid of a day's coating of sun cream, dried sweat and dirt. First, I dunk myself in the bucket of river water that the guys obligingly provide. Then, before turning in for the night, I 'shower' very efficiently, using hot, clean water from the flask that Chris boils every morning for my tea.

But tonight, in spite of that, I'm tossing and turning inside my mosquito net, sweating like a beast. Finally, I pick up the corners of my tent like a taco, take it outside and plonk it on the grass outside the guesthouse. Blissfully, a light breeze penetrates the mesh and I am just dozing off when am rudely awoken by torchlight. 'I was too hot so decided to sleep outside,' I explain sleepily. Chris is going on about showers. Half-asleep, I assume that he's concerned about my getting rained on.

'Don't worry, if it rains I'll go inside.'

'Do you want another bucket from the river?'

It finally dawns on me that he is actually suggesting that I shower yet again in a bucket of river water at midnight. Irritated, I snap that no, I don't want a bucket shower. All I want is to go to sleep.

At around 3am I'm awoken by loud cackling and chirping in the jungle and by the irrational feeling that I'm being intently watched. Everyone in the village is asleep. Woozy from sleep, I feel certain that I'm being observed by the spirits of the forest and am feeling rather exposed in the middle of the lawn. I should be sleeping better out here, where it's cooler, but I can't get used to the night noises. After a while I give up, drag my 'bed' indoors and sleep there.

* * * * *

The following morning, it's pouring down with rain. Terrific news for the parched land and the folks upriver who've been running out of food and drinking water. Chris is cooking breakfast. I am sitting on the steps of the guesthouse, cleaning my newly acquired wooden carving of a crocodile with a toothbrush. Since I have to pass through Australia on my way home, and they have extremely stringent rules about indigenous artefacts inadvertently contaminated with insect life, I'm meticulously dipping the toothbrush between each individual scale.

This peaceful domestic scene is interrupted by an apparition drifting into view. With a cloud of long, dark, wavy hair, the woman is dressed in a long-sleeved blouse, smart black trousers and black flats with pointed toes. Her make-up is impeccably applied, a handbag is slung over her shoulder and I can smell her perfume. She looks like she's just stepped off a city street. I, by comparison, am decked out in dirty cargo shorts, a formerly white shirt that's now hopelessly ingrained with PNG's red dust, and am barefoot, enjoying walking around with my toes sinking into the warm mulch.

The apparition introduces herself as Stamena, a Bosnian stewardess working for Swiss Air. My hungry brain immediately scrambles her name and changes it to 'Smetana' (Russian for 'sour cream'). She and her friend, the sporty-looking Rita, who is more appropriately dressed in jungle pants, shirt and trainers, are both keen birders and have come up the river a day after us.

'We were really looking forward to seeing birds of paradise, but now we've been told it's impossible to get to Wagu Lagoon because of the drought.'

'So what will you do?'

'After the Sepik, we're thinking of taking a PMV from Madang into the Highlands and trying our luck there.'

When I tell Chris about their plans, he scoffs: 'Taking a PMV is too dangerous. They should go as part of a tour.'

'But locals take PMVs all the time!' I retort. 'You know how you were complaining to me that PNG doesn't see enough tourism? Maybe the government should do something to ensure the basic safety of travellers trying to get around by public transport.'

EYEBALL TACOS AND KANGAROO STEW

* * * * *

The rest of my time on the Sepik is blur of village visits. One of my essential duties as a guidebook writer involves checking out accommodation, and I duly visit village guesthouses, where the guestrooms are invariably very basic affairs, with bare mattresses and woven walls. But their surroundings are the most remarkable I've ever encountered.

In Palambei, a large, splendid *haus tambaran* stands in the centre of a jungle clearing, crowned with twin spires. Inside, Chris points out the chair that the spirit of the village sits in and seven hearths – one for each of the village clans. There are several *garamut* drums here, beautifully adorned with pig, crocodile and hornbill carvings. Two drummers are standing by one of them. Without warning, they strike up a rapid, staccato rhythm, their hands a blur. They hold the sticks like pestles rather than drumsticks and strike different parts of the drum. Chris explains to me that the drumming is a way of communication between villages: announcing a death, inviting neighbours to festivities, announcing that visitors or enemies are on their way.

From Palambei, we walk further inland to Maringei, which isn't in the guidebook. The trail emerges in the prettiest village I've seen on the Sepik. There's a wide, grassy avenue running between the two rows of thatched houses. For the first time, I notice that locals don't just walk all over the grass where they please, but stick to the well-trodden dirt footpaths, and I endeavour to do the same. In the centre of the village stand the remains of an old *haus tambaran* – no roof, just several pillars. The carvings are still very much intact, including that of a male with optimistically proportioned genitalia.

Yentchen supposedly has the most attractive *haus tambaran* on the Sepik, its carvings faithfully copied from photographs taken by German explorers in the early twentieth century (*haus tambaran* occasionally have to be rebuilt). But we are several years too late. A fire had long left it in ruins, with only some of the pillars left intact and a soaring eagle, carrying a woman, visible at the top of what was once a roof.

* * * * *

Back in Kanganaman, the large *haus tambaran* looks eerie by night, lit only by the faint glow of fires from the hearths. Stamena and Rita are already there, sitting on one of the high berths. They pull me up.

'Where were you? We were worried!'

Four drummers step into position. One of them is Chris, shirtless. A staccato rhythm picks up, changing and shifting seamlessly to another rhythm, then another. It's hypnotic; I can't tear my eyes away from the blur of hands. The bodies of the drummers, lit by the dying embers, throw twisted shadows on the carved pillars. Then the drumming abruptly stops and two men step forward, holding giant flutes. They are closer to didgeridoos in size and played in pairs. The men stand, facing each other. Then one bends his knees a little, begins playing a plaintive dirge; the other picks it up. It sounds a bit off-rhythm to me, as if the second player is always playing catch-up, but there's something mesmerising about the repetition. The melodies – apart from one sombre one, that sounds markedly different from the rest – blend into one. The lead man always starts playing first, bends his knees as if about to curtsey, repeats.

With his legs bent, he reminds me of the carving that's waiting for me back at the guesthouse, wrapped up and ready for tomorrow's travel back to Wewak, and onwards to Cairns and the UK.

I wonder, when I present it to Jolyon, if he'll like it as much as the little guardian figure from Borneo. Whether it, too, will warrant a spot on his desk. I wonder if it'll be enough. But even if it isn't, I know that I've done my best to fulfil his request, and to try and make amends for our initial misunderstanding. I recognise now that during the course of our lives our identities and needs change, as do we as people. Jolyon's travels and his books have led me here, to this village on the Sepik, yet here I am, on my own. My apprehensions about PNG have proved to be unfounded and the country has proved to be even more extraordinary than I'd ever imagined. And perhaps I've been unfair to my mentor, too. After all, I never shared with him my evolving thoughts about travel, or my presumption that our roles would naturally shift during the course of our lives; I just expected him to read my mind. We'll talk about it when I get home. Perhaps we'll even laugh about it.

After seemingly an age of mesmeric dirges, there's silence and the spell is broken. Stamena and Rita come alive and we applaud, before walking back to the guesthouse in the dark, and sitting down for our final dinner of 'tinpis' and the holy trinity of tubers: taro, cassava and sweet potato.

CHAPTER 9
THE BLESSING OF BARON KRIMINEL

Darkness falls over Jacmel. It falls quite completely on this tight little grid of cobbled streets by the Caribbean Sea, the lit windows of our guesthouse the only points of light around. Must be another power cut. I am sitting in the garden with Anneline, a tall, athletic Londoner here for Haiti's Kanaval, discussing where we could possibly acquire white rum and candles for the evening's Vodou ceremony. We've got the black coffee and the plain toast for the feast of the spirits, but are missing some key offerings.

Earlier today, when Anneline was hand-painting a Kanaval mask in the little shop around the corner, shaven-headed, middle-aged shop owner Kiki sidled up to me. 'There's a Vodou ceremony on tonight. Do you want to come?' My answer is a foregone conclusion. I know how rare these authentic ceremonies are, even here in Haiti. For outsiders to be invited is rarer still.

'Would they mind us attending?'

'No, you just have to bring gifts for the loa.'

Kiki leads us two blocks from the guesthouse to someone's back yard. A humanoid figure made of earth, around my height, stands to one side. It's decapitated. It reminds me of that creature from the 'Arcadia' episode of *The X-Files*, summoned from the earth by the will of its master and unleashed against his enemies. I wonder what role it plays in Vodou rituals. At the back there's the space for ceremonies

– a packed earthen floor, a semi-circle of chairs, a plasticky-looking Tree of Life encircled by Damballah the serpent and topped with cattle skulls. It's propping up the roof, festooned with colourful plastic strips. The tree is symbolic: the loa – the Vodou pantheon – live in its upper branches. The symbolic effect is somewhat lessened by the fact that there are wires and power sockets dangling from it. It's a mobile phone charger station as well as the bridge between the human and the divine realms. Behind the row of chairs stand the papier mâché effigies of some of the Vodou pantheon, awaiting the Kanaval: Papa Legba, the guardian of the crossroads; Erzulie, the goddess of love; La Sirene, goddess of the sea; Baron Samedi, the leader of the dead. With their gaping mouths and incredulous expressions, they remind me of blow-up sex dolls. I quickly quell that blasphemous thought now that I'm on their turf, just in case they can read my mind.

Kiki introduces us to the *ougan* (Vodou priest), a compact, stocky man with a thin moustache. He shakes our hands, jokes around with Anneline (she's from St Lucia and can understand Haitian creole). The ougan has his own Facebook page, according to his business card. Sign of the times.

Brief introductions over, we leave. Kiki is to bring us back in the evening.

By nightfall, we still have no rum or candles. Peggy, the owner of our guesthouse, beckons a neighbour woman from across the street. There's an exchange in rapid-fire creole. The woman disappears into the darkness, only to come back with two candles and a bottle sloshing with dark liquid. Peggy admonishes her, pointing at the liquid. The woman disappears. Reappears with a bottle full of clear cane spirit. Kiki arrives, gets into an animated argument with Peggy about the alcohol. Apparently, the loa are very particular about their tipple, and prefer white rum to cheap cane spirit. 'Don't worry,' Kiki tells us in the end. 'There'll be rum and candles there.' We retrace our steps to the ougan's house, in almost complete darkness.

Lit by a dim lightbulb, the packed earth floor is crammed with about a dozen dancers, the women's heads clad in bright kerchiefs, colourful skirts swishing with the swaying of their hips. Their bare feet stamp in unison, their voices raised in a chant.

Several drummers sit to one side, their hands a blur as they pound out a complex rhythm.

Two doorways lead into the ougan's inner sanctum. The symbols of Baron Samedi are painted between the two – an eye, candles, a cross, a skull.

The dancing continues for a while before the ougan emerges from the left doorway, dressed wholly in white, with a scarf around his neck. Pairing up with one of the women, he walks slowly to the base of the tree. They look like a couple about to get married, both of them carrying white candles that they place at its base, the ougan's lips moving in what I imagine to be an incantation of some kind.

The dancers swirl and ebb around them.

The ougan disappears through the same doorway from which he entered. The drumming reaches a crescendo, the dancers in a frenzy. One of the drummers abandons his drum and staggers across the earthen floor as if drunk. Combined with the chanting, the whirl of limbs is hypnotic; I lose track of how long the dancing continues, until the drumming ends abruptly and there's a lull in the proceedings.

One woman breastfeeds, another smokes a hand-rolled cigarette. The young man who was staggering around the dance floor minutes ago comes up to one of the younger women, puts both hands on her breasts. Squeezes hard, possessively. She winces and shoves him away, stony-faced.

Kiki beckons me. I enter the left doorway into the ougan's inner sanctum – a tiny, whitewashed room dominated by an altar stacked with candles and sequinned bottles. Another door leads opens into the room next door. Permeating the stuffy air, a musky scent meets my nostrils. If the first room looks like it might be used by someone in the service of the Light, there's no doubting the purpose of this dark, sepulchral space. Dark magic, I think to myself. Fitting, given that Baron Samedi, in his various incarnations, leads the *ghede*, the spirits of the dead. There's a coffin upon the earthen floor, cobwebbed Vodou effigies made of wood, some other paraphernalia incorporating what looks like human femurs. In the fire pit lies a human skull. It brings home to me yet again that Haiti is darker and more macabre than I'll ever be. I'm out of my depth.

* * * * *

When I first felt the pull of Haiti, back in 2001, when I began studying the country's history, its reputation was an irresistible lure. This is a place shaped by the only successful slave rebellion and its aftermath; where black magic permeates the daily life of all strata of society, and where turning people into zombies is still listed as a crime in the official statutes; where animal sacrifices are common; where people are brought back from the dead by the ougan. Where the lines between the human and the divine, the land of the living and the shadowy world of the dead, are blurred. Coming here would be like setting foot in a magical realism novel. It would allow me to indulge my lifelong fascination with death, with mortality.

I think about death a lot. As a young child, I read the unabridged folk tales of different countries, my imagination permeated with Japanese *yurei* (unquiet spirits of the dead), Angolan cannibals who consume dead bodies, corpses coming back to life in Russian fairy tales. I went through a stage of obsessively asking my mother every night whether she was going to die, wanting reassurance that she would not. There have been several tragic early deaths in our family. My maternal grandfather, dead on the operating table at the age of forty-two during a routine operation after being given the wrong dose of anaesthetic. My other grandfather, drowned in the sea in Pärnu, Estonia, after having a heart attack. My uncle, crushed by a fallen tree while camping on a windy day.

I saw my first dead body when I was five years old. Growing up semi-wild in our little town on the outskirts of Moscow, we kids found what entertainment we could in the streets. Cut spruce branches trailing from the entrance of an apartment building meant that someone had died there. When the open coffin was carried through the streets, we followed. That dead man looked peaceful, but waxy and yellow, as if all colour had been leached from him. Later on, as an eighteen-year-old training to be a nursing assistant at Cambridge's Addenbrooke's Hospital, I learned that the discoloration is a result of the blood flowing downwards and pooling around the back in purplish-blue splodges. In time, I helped to lay out dead bodies and found that I wasn't squeamish or put off. One of my colleagues taught me to open the window when someone passed away, 'to let the soul out.' I liked that idea. I found myself working with the terminally ill, and felt privileged to be able to provide some comfort to those imminently bound for the other side, discovering that most people want some tenderness and reassurance, even if it's from a complete stranger, and often a hand to hold, even if they hadn't been the hand-holding type in life.

* * * * *

What was Haiti to me, back then? What did I know? What did I imagine? The torches of slaves snaking up the dark hillsides, the beating of drums carrying on the wind the promise of death and blood and fire and destruction to their French masters holed up in their mansions. Crackling heat from torched plantation houses, screams, blood glinting darkly on machete blades. The gaunt body of Toussaint L'Ouverture, slave revolt leader, the 'black Napoleon', twitching in its own waste in a cold stone cell in France, betrayed by the French, doomed to rot and die far from home. The palpable menace of the Tonton Macoutes, in the service of Papa Doc, who come for their victims under the cover of darkness, like the agents of Stalin's Terror, only more sinister. Papa Doc himself, who rasps like Baron Samedi and claims to straddle the gap between the people of Haiti and the loa. Bloodstains from animal sacrifices staining the dry, crumbling earth. Myself, twenty years old, in the back seat of a car on 72nd Street, Upper East Side, kissing Yves – my salsa dancing partner – with abandon, our ragged breathing sounding too loud in the quiet confines of the vehicle. Trying to wrap my lips, my tongue around the exotic, electric phrases that he teaches me. *Ki jan ou ye?* (How are you?) *Mwen grangou* (I'm hungry). *Mwen renmen ou* (I love you). The earthy, dark taste of rice with *djondjon* mushrooms at a Haitian hole-in-the-wall in Miami. Earthquake rubble on TV, the machine guns of UN peacekeepers, cholera, riots, rotting garbage, sunlight reflected mercilessly off corrugated iron roofs, desperate crowds surging, grasping for food handed out, the sharp smell of sweat.

But back in 2001 I would have found Haiti utterly overwhelming. Until getting banned from the United States pushed me to travel further afield, I was bound by my inexperience, my fear of the unknown and my need to control every detail of my trips, with everything planned months in advance. I was playing at adventure within the sanitised confines of American and Canadian cities, rarely stepping out of my comfort zone. Haiti thwarts all attempts at control, with its dark undercurrent, this underlying feeling that something explosive might happen at any given moment.

* * * * *

'Haiti is a country without a safety net,' my friend Paul – the author of the Bradt guide to Haiti – commented, when I told him about my initial impressions of it. How Haiti seems to be a heartbeat away from some dramatic and unexpected event.

* * * * *

When Kanaval arrives in Jacmel, I find myself making my way up the main street, packed with parade-goers, walking between monsters and devils and mythological creatures. A drone hovers above the crowd, filming the proceedings. Several kids in costume try to whack it out of the air with pieces of wood painted to look like guns, but they're too short. I duck away from the Lanset Kod lads, half-naked, covered in a black, sticky layer of charcoal and cane juice, playfully threatening to rub up against the spectators.

One of them offers to shake my hand. I refuse, but acquiesce when he rubs the tip of his blackened index finger against mine. Then I'm up above the parade on one of the rickety stands that local men have been feverishly building way into the previous night, dancing with a beer in my hand that one of the local DJs handed to me, looking at people hanging off windows and balconies across the street and wondering how much weight the flimsy stands can take before they collapse and crush us all.

Finally, all the monsters, exotic animals and dancers in swishy skirts have passed by, along with Haiti's new president, a banana exporter. He walks in the parade, flanked by bodyguards with machine guns who brutally shove drunk people out of the way. I decide to make my escape before all the marching bands arrive and find myself caught up in the dense crush of people moving down the street. I'm being pushed from all sides and cannot see above the crowd; it's a deeply uncomfortable feeling. Then a scuffle breaks out nearby; the crowd surges forward and I'm lifted off my feet. If I were to stumble and fall right now, I would be trampled to death. Adrenalin floods me and forces out the fuzzy beer buzz. It's terrifying. I do the only thing I can and stick my elbows out, to give myself a tiny bit of breathing room. After a few yards, my feet touch the ground again, but not before I get shoved right into a soldier with a machine gun. Luckily for me, he doesn't take offence.

But in the evening, I head out again, and hover near the entrance to the main street, the crowds as dense as ever. I lean on one of the massive portable stages playing merengue music and watch the action. Having somewhat recovered from my earlier scare, I decide to brave the crowd again, but a fight breaks out and people scatter like rabbits. I run as well, but not too far. My rubbernecking instinct is stronger than my fear. Hiding behind one of the massive wheels of the portable stage, I peek out at what's happening.

The constant adrenalin rushes are an addiction.

* * * * *

I wasn't ready for Haiti in 2001. Now, in 2017, I am. After Kanaval, back in Port-au-Prince, I amble down the steep street from Hotel Prince to the row of mototaxis parked in front of Hotel Oloffson. I straddle the back of one of the motorbikes without worrying about how I'll get back or whether I have the language skills to do what I want to do, and wave a skanky 100-gourde note in front of the driver. 'Vous connaissez L'Hôpital Français?' Affirmative nod. The motorbike roars to life. I scoot closer to the driver and grip the saddle with my thighs as we speed through the narrow, potholed, garbage-strewn streets. Given Port-au-Prince's perpetual gridlock, mototaxis are the only way to get anywhere. The ride is exhilarating: no helmets, the rush of air in my face, the reckless speed with which my driver takes corners, this constant balancing on a tightrope. We skid on some garbage and my knee misses an oncoming vehicle by an inch. A nervous energy thrums beneath my skin and everything comes into sharper focus as adrenalin floods my veins.

Some of my long-redundant French comes back, as well as a few words of Haitian creole learned from Yves, all those years ago in wintry New York. I get dropped near the hospital and make my way to the street of mechanics, where broken-down, brightly painted *taptaps* (miniature trucks with passenger seating in the back) and second-hand American school buses line the road. Across the street is a gateway hammered out of scrap wood, with an 'Atis Rezistans' sign on it.

I daintily pick my way through the shallow streams of fetid water in my flip-flops, trying to not to wet my feet. Fail, resign self to soaking feet in disinfectant later. Passing through the gateway, I step into a wonderland of twisted sculpture. Scrap metal, wood carvings, nails, bits of tyres, car parts and more have been assembled into an assortment of humanoid figures, some with heads and limbs fused together, some with eyes and lips nailed shut. I recognise their style: two of their brethren gave me nightmares in the garden of Hotel Oloffson on my first night in Haiti. There's a tall sculpture of a woman with a baby nailed to her; the baby boasts a pig's head.

They line the yard. They stare and leer from the corrugated iron roof of the artist's workshop in front of me. They squint and grimace from the staircase leading up to the concrete roof overlooking the shanty town beyond.

Their creator, the internationally renowned artist André Eugène, sits at the back of the yard, hands behind his head, watching me as I wander around, my mouth open in wonder.

I'm particularly smitten with one of his creations, the one with a missing foot, huge phallus and dapper headgear made out of a car part (or possibly a bucket).

'Why is he missing a foot?'

'Many Haitians lost limbs during the last earthquake. I meant to pay homage to them.'

'And the – ' I pantomime being in possession of an enormous penis. André spreads his hands, shrugs and grins, as if to say, 'Well, he IS Haitian.' We play the game, bantering, bargaining gently until we're both happy with the final price. André shows me around, pointing out a large, skull-topped sculpture, with a strategically positioned metal spring jutting out like a massive erection. It was recently displayed at an exhibition in Norway.

'You can see one of my works at the Liverpool Museum of Slavery,' he tells me, and this jogs my memory, because I have indeed seen it, last year.

In the semi-open space beneath the concrete roof there's a Vodou section. Bizarre arrangements involving twisted dolls' limbs on top of blackened dolls' heads, grotesque, squat figures with sewn-up torsos and painted human skulls.

'Where do you get the skulls?' I ask André.

'After the earthquake, many graves were cracked open, bones lying everywhere.'

It does seem to be fairly common practice to use human remains in Vodou paraphernalia. I've seen similar figures at the Marché de Fer, Port-au-Prince's nineteenth-century Iron Market, which has a labyrinthine Vodou section. The question which I don't dare ask, but which is foremost in my mind, is this: 'Do the dead mind?' Or, rather: 'Is it considered respectful and appropriate to use the mortal remains of strangers in one's art, or is this the shady territory of grave robbers?'

André leads me through the beaded curtains into the depths of his workshop, where a human skull, painted black, sits upon a sequined platform with a cross behind it.

It's clearly a symbol of Baron Samedi, my favourite of the loa pantheon – the one in charge of the dead, the dapper gentleman with a cane, who likes strong rum and a good joke. A part of me covets André's skull sculpture, and I even idly ponder the practicalities of importing human remains into the UK. However, I also feel a certain amount of superstitious disquiet at the thought of parting someone's remains from their homeland and possibly being pursued by some vengeful spirit for the rest of my days.

I have given my passing some thought. While I, personally, don't mind the idea of my skull or my ashes roaming the world way after I'm dead and gone, that may not be true of most people. And here there's no one and no way to ask.

* * * * *

Twenty-first-century Port-au-Prince lacks the glossy sheen of my younger self's daydreams of Haiti. It's a snarl of squat brick houses, smog, never-ending traffic, mounds of garbage. Yet when I take a mototaxi up into the hills, to Pétion-Ville, I begin to appreciate the raw beauty of the city's setting – the steep hills plummeting down to the sea, the lush vegetation covering the surrounding mountains, the brightly painted jalousie shanty town that clings to the steep mountainside and reminds me of Bolivia.

And when a mototaxi takes me even higher, towards the L'Observatoire de Boutilliers restaurant and viewpoint, Port-au-Prince spreads out below me. Lit up by the setting sun and set against the deep blue of the Caribbean Sea, it seems almost ethereal and more than makes up for my first impressions of Haiti.

* * * * *

My first day in Haiti didn't end well. That evening found me having dinner on the terrace of Hotel Oloffson in Port-au-Prince, the grand colonial edifice that served as inspiration for Hotel Trianon in Graham Greene's *The Comedians*. Time seemed to stand still in the wrought-iron detail, the chandeliers above the grand, open-air terrace. I sat in the corner of the shaded patio, looking out over the lush grounds, and imagined Mr Brown dallying with his lover, Martha Pineda, right here, all those decades ago. The clandestine whispers.

The setting was wonderful, the meal – some elderly prawns, prepared creole-style – mediocre, and the rum punch unpleasantly strong. I was strung out already – from the long day's travel, from the incessant gridlock and noise that has the city in its grip, from being skewered by people's stares as the only pale-skinned person around. Not hostile, exactly, but not friendly either.

A tightness constricted my throat and chest and left me winded. The rum punch was a mistake. Whereas an occasional strategic glass of wine can numb and insulate me against the worst of my periodic downward spirals, the rum took me over to the other side, flaying me, stripping me of my defences, turning me into a raw bundle of nerve endings. The alcohol served only to amplify the feelings of inadequacy, loneliness and loss.

I've been travelling alone for much of my adult life and largely prefer it that way. Few share my love of the macabre, my tolerance for physical discomfort and for endless hours on public transport, my willingness to pack as much into my trips as possible. I trust myself implicitly to make decisions to keep myself safe. I trust my instincts about the people I meet. I'm uniquely suited for the work that I do. There's an old photograph of me, sprawled casually across the rooftop of a bus, somewhere in the Cordillera in the Philippines. The caption below reads: 'Born to do it.' It's partly braggadocio, it's partly the court jester playing to the audience, but it's also the truth. I'm comfortable with the long hours, the solitude, the incessant movement, the having to make a myriad decisions every day. Drop me anywhere in the world, and I'll land on my feet. Regardless of the continent I'm on, I'm very rarely out of my depth. Landing in yet another new city in Indonesia/Uzbekistan/India I bounce out of the airport or train station, negotiate with drivers without breaking stride or turning my head, and am on my way in two minutes flat. Trinket sellers and street personalities generally give me a wide berth as I walk briskly, with a slight swagger in my 'don't mess with me' walk, my lips pressed tightly together, my nostrils flared, reflective glasses deflecting stares. They recognise purpose in my movement that sets me apart from other foreigners and try their luck elsewhere. I'm generally content with my own company and enjoy solitude. But sometimes, without warning, I'm floored by how alone and isolated I feel.

At times like that I begin to question everything. My life's choices that have landed me on this solitary road. My purpose in life. Whether I will die alone and far from home. During the worst of times, every bad decision I have ever made comes back to haunt me: too much time wasted on dead-end entanglements, not enough time and effort invested in relationships that meant the most to me, every misstep, every failure that I'd hoped in vain to turn into a triumph.

As always in such circumstances, my thoughts turned to my losses.

* * * * *

I toss and turn on the sofa in our beige, impersonal holiday flat, unable to sleep. We've had an explosive row, you and I – the worst of our lifetime. It was over a seeming triviality – a triviality to me, at least, a mundane practical matter. But to you it seemed to symbolise everything that has been wrong with our friendship for a very long time now. The room – a space that you have just violently left – feels devoid of oxygen. I want to pack up and leave and not look back. The acknowledgement of that feeling is accompanied by a rush of intense shame, because you're one of the people dearest to me. You're 'my other wing', like Gabriel was to his twin sister, Native American lawyer Annawake, in Barbara Kingsolver's novel *Pigs in Heaven*. Inseparable since we became friends as teenagers, we've confided most things in one other, soothed each other's hurts and disappointments, rejoiced in the other's successes. You taught me one of life's most valuable skills: the basics of self-awareness, how to question my own reactions. I'd give so much not to feel this way. And yet, I want to be anywhere but here.

You are my conscience, my moral compass. You know almost everything about me, from my most depraved fantasies to my deepest, most heartfelt desires. I know your vulnerabilities. You know mine, too. And maybe that's part of the problem.

When and how did it begin, this unravelling? Were two damaged people always destined to hurt one another? Surely we are not prisoners of our upbringing? Or was it precisely because we came from troubled backgrounds and subconsciously expected each other to provide all the love and stability that we lacked elsewhere, that we were always destined to fall short, to let one another down?

I judged you harshly when we were growing up, for your excesses, seeing them as weakness, and failing to understand that you were in pain and self-medicating because of all the rejections and losses you'd suffered during the course of your young life. Perhaps you'd felt rejected by me as well. You judged me, too, for my tumultuous relationships with entirely unsuitable men, and didn't see that they were knee-jerk reactions to my own upbringing. I'd wounded you with careless remarks and actions without meaning to. One time, you likened my admiration of my mentor to a lewd act, reducing a lifetime's respect to something cheap and tawdry. Your comment was intended to wound. You saw that it did, and the brief, triumphant gleam in your eye gave away that you knew that I knew. 'I just wanted to hurt you,' you told me later, and I knew that to be absolutely true. One question I never asked you was 'why?'.

I never told you this, but a part of me understood, empathised. There's a perverse, dark pleasure to be had from knowing someone intimately, and knowing which words would do the maximum damage. I've done it to my mother, lashing out over childhood hurts, then watching her blanch and recoil as if slapped. Afterwards I'd be revolted with myself, remorseful, apologetic. Was it the same for you?

How do you move beyond the knowledge that someone can know you better than anyone, and not always mean you well? That they would deliberately use your vulnerabilities against you? Blood relations are supposed to forgive you, to take you back, no matter what. But what of the family we choose for ourselves? Is friendship supposed to be unconditional?

Over the years, miscommunication between us hardened, calcified. Both of us felt dismissed and hurt by the other at one point or another, but neither of us said anything, or if one did, the other would react with hurt and anger and shut down the conversation. Because all of us, without exception, are sensitive to criticism from those whose opinion we care about, and these emotions interfere with our ability to truly listen, to hear the other person out. As more time passed and both of us felt unheard by the other, this sense of disconnect became compounded, and we finally reached a place where we just didn't feel safe talking to one another about subjects that would make us vulnerable. And when things were good between us, neither of us wanted to do anything to rock the boat.

I'm still there in the morning, of course. I wouldn't have left you alone in an unfamiliar country. I've been awake much of the night, thinking of the things I need to tell you. How horrified I am that we seem to be mirroring the shouting, the tears, the beseeching supplication, the self-recriminations that I'd observed at home for so many years of my life. But I'm also furious. I don't deserve this. This can never happen again. And it doesn't. By the morning, I've steeled myself to talk to you, with apprehension twisting my gut. But you pre-empt me, and everything is once again left unsaid. You apologise for yelling at me, tell me you'll never do it again, and hug me tight. 'You're my best friend,' you tell me with some desperation. You are mine, too, and yet I can't reach you. Something important feels irreparably broken and I don't know how to fix it. Or whether it can be fixed at all.

We limp on together for another three days in agonised inarticulacy, strangers to each other, digging our bare feet into the fine white sand, eating lobster, rice and beans on picnic tables by the sea, talking about inconsequential things. We're unable – or unwilling – to address the gaping chasm between us. Perhaps we lack the vocabulary to do so, or perhaps we're too mired in our respective past hurts. On your last day you have your eyes closed during our journey to the airport, shuttering yourself against any attempts at conversation. I accompany you, but I don't stay. It's galling that two people who know each other so well – who love each other so damn much – have nothing to say to one another. It'll be another two and a half years before we see each other again, and by the time we do, the intimacy we'd shared for over twenty years would be gone.

I leave Cancún, and bum around the rest of the Yucatán Peninsula, spending several weeks aimlessly walking the streets of Mérida, Campeche, and other towns whose names and streets I've now forgotten, refusing all communication barring sporadic calls with my sister, and breaking down in the privacy of my room. It feels like a bereavement, which I suppose it is.

Our society places much greater emphasis and importance on romantic relationships than on friendships, suggesting that the latter are somehow less intense, less important. That we are not complete unless we experience intimacy in a romantic context. 'We're just friends,' people say. Yet for me, there is no 'just' about it. My close friendships have been the most intimate and enduring of my life's relationships. There's the common belief that friendships should be easy, that we always know what the other person is thinking and what their expectations of us are. That if there's conflict, it means the friendship is not working anymore. But surely, a friendship is defined not by a lack of conflict, but by how two people seek to resolve it. Whether they are prepared to fight for the friendship, to have the difficult conversations, to trust each other enough to talk through what transpired and try to understand the other person's perspective. Even if their own perception of the situation differs considerably. We were not prepared to do that. At least, not then. And there are no shortcuts to rebuilding.

I've never experienced the dissolution of a marriage, yet from what divorced friends have recounted, this unravelling of ties that bound and supported me for so many years is as painful and devastating as any divorce could be.

* * * * *

The diners at the other end of the terrace are a family. Possibly. Six adults, two children. How old are the children? Six? Seven? The boy chases the girl around the table. He catches her, pulls the ends of her cornrows. She squeals, turns, thumps him in the chest with a small fist. He starts bawling. One of the men gets up, walks over to where they are, talks to them with endless patience in a low voice until they've calmed down. Perhaps it's the trick of the dimming evening light, but from the back, the loping, long-legged stride and the silvering hair are so familiar to me that my heart does a painful lurch. I take another large swig of the rum cocktail, turn my head slowly from side to side, watch my surroundings wobble and swim around me.

Upon my return from Papua New Guinea, the hook cult figure on which I had pinned so much hope gathered dust in the garden shed. I emailed my mentor to tell him that I'd fulfilled his shopping request, and received no response. In the end, I posted it to him, convincing myself that that was the right thing to do, when what I really wanted was the carving – a painful reminder of our estrangement – out of my sight. The silence stretched on for months. I couldn't bear it, so I filled it with letters of explanation, entreaties and apologies that tried to address what I imagined he was thinking and feeling. Thinking that, if only I could find the right words, then surely everything could be fixed. A supplicant, seeking to shoulder all the responsibility, because that was easier than admitting to myself that someone I'd admired so much, for so long – someone who watched me grow up, who bore witness to everything of importance that happened to me, whom I trusted to understand me and know me as I really was – turned out to be only human, and unwilling or unable to hear me and understand me when I needed it the most. I hadn't realised until then how dependent I'd become over the years on two men – my best friend and my mentor – for advice, for comfort. How stripped down I was without it. In the rawness of my grief over the demise of my closest friendship, over my life exploding, I was unable to keep things in perspective, or to extend to Jolyon the same empathy that I needed from him at the time. My need to be heard and understood directly fed Jolyon's need not to have to do either of those things. It felt like yet another trusted figure in my life was abandoning me. In a reflexive panic, I tried to cling on, when what he most likely needed from me was breathing space. And holding on was like trying to grasp water.

Finally, a terse typed note arrived in the post.

'I'm afraid I really don't want to see you.'

Not for years? Not ever?

* * * * *

I think that most of us – maybe all of us – live with a deep-seated fear of judgement. From strangers, or from people we think highly of. Most of all, I live in trepidation of the voice of judgement inside my own head. It finds me when I'm at my lowest ebb and tells me what deep down I have always feared: that I'm a mediocrity, a disappointment, that I don't measure up. That I never have and never will. And there's nothing I can do but ride it out.

The harpy in my head closes in.

Wallowing again, I see. How unattractive. Don't you ever get tired of this – this mawkish self-indulgence?

But I hate feeling like this... I don't mean to push people away...

And yet you've been looking to others your whole life for approval, for validation. That's a hell of burden to place on your friends: making them responsible for your own personal happiness.

I really care about the people in my life. I would do anything for them...

Except what you don't really want to do. The people in your life don't need empty, grand gestures from you. They don't need you to take a bullet for them, they don't need your fucking kidney. What they need is your understanding, your empathy, a sign that you hear them and that you respect their wishes and their points of view, even if they make no sense to you.

But I find it difficult to read people, to understand what they are trying to communicate…

What, you're the only person in the world with poor social skills? Learn new ones. If you're not clear about something, ask. Don't expect people to make allowances for you for the rest of your life.

And so it goes. The arsenal of tricks that I employ in my day-to-day life to cloak my insecurities, my self-consciousness, my social awkwardness – the self-deprecating humour, the deliberate exaggeration of my clumsiness, the carapace of buffoonery that I sometimes wear like armour, the playing to an audience for laughs – none of it works here. Against this voice, and this voice alone, I have no defence.

What I keep seeking, I realise, is a reprieve. By trying to overcome my character flaws, by landing the next travel gig, by showing that I still have what it takes by climbing that mountain, I silence the voice in my head. But it's a silence I have to keep earning.

The harpy is relentless.

How's that book coming along – the one you were going to write all those years ago? Do you really think that you're capable of original thought, original turn of phrase? That in your life you will have achieved something of importance, or substance?

Do you remember how hungry you used to be for inspiration? it continues. *How as a university student you scribbled down that James Baldwin quote about earning one's death by confronting with passion the conundrum of life? How you wanted to do something tremendous, meaningful with yours? What the hell happened to you? Look at you,* it snarls. *You're drunk. You're defeated. What would ... say if he were to see you now? Would he still feel glad to have known you, or would he recoil with revulsion?*

I'm finding it hard to breathe. I can feel my bloodshot eyes burning. I roll my eyes skywards to try and put an end to the waterworks – it's a trick I learned from you, many years ago. The medication you were on made you emotional and prone to tears. You found it irritating and embarrassing, so whenever you'd look up to stop feeling tearful, I'd tease you gently: 'What? What? Is it a bird? Is it a plane?' and be rewarded with a watery smile.

* * * * *

We're having one of our early morning conversations that I've come to cherish. You're telling me about how when you were handed your death sentence – when you were told that the messages from your brain to your muscles will become interrupted until you can no longer move or breathe – you had two choices. To travel the world, see the sights, and then come home and wait to die. Or to keep working, until you could work no more. You chose the latter.

'So is that life's ideal purpose?' I ask you. 'To be useful to others for as long as possible?'

'To be useful without vanity,' you clarify. 'What you do has to be its own reward. If you expect acknowledgement and praise, if you do it for any reason other than the conviction that it is the only right and proper thing to do, you will always be disappointed.'

You tell me about your work in some of the remotest parts of Africa, the satisfaction of completing your task and knowing that improved means of irrigation mean that there will be no famine this year, or the next. Of initiating younger colleagues into the mysteries of irrigation engineering. Of raising your sons, and sometimes getting an illuminating, rewarding glimpse of the men they would grow up to be.

I see parallels between you and my mentor. I'm inspired by both your examples. And I try to walk the same path, but my ego and my fears get in the way.

* * * * *

My tasks include helping you wash and dress. More often than not, when I get to know people at the end of their lives, they are usually old, and often befuddled. You are neither. We talk, and find common ground over music, politics, travel. You show me your stamp collection. On impulse, I track down a couple of stamps that you've been missing and surprise you with them. You put me to work lining the stamps up along the square paper, licking the hinges and sticking them down, my clumsy fingers trembling in case I mess up your page.

We discuss travel writing as a viable career, and you tell me that it doesn't quite fit your formula for true happiness: a good, stable family life, a home and a job you love. I allow that yes, being on the road much of the time would make the first two difficult, but point out that the formula for true happiness may be different for different people. You don't disagree. But you urge me not to rule out parenthood, 'because it's a crime for intelligent people not to reproduce.' You bring up your own example, and how having children was the most remarkable thing you'd ever done, the most worthwhile.

Do you have any regrets? Some.

'If I'd have known... I'd have travelled more, like you. For leisure. I'd have spent more time with my sons. In our household the division of labour was very traditional. But then I'd watch my younger colleagues and see that there's a different way of doing things.'

I'm drawn by your confidence, your lack of self-consciousness, your ability to find humour and light in the darkest situations, by how comfortable you are in your own skin. You conduct yourself with the grace and ease of someone who's spent his entire life cherished by others – the brilliant husband, the treasured friend. You're the kind of person that others naturally gravitate towards, drawn by your genuine warmth, your kindness towards others, your willingness to help out. You're well travelled, well read, resourceful, principled. Funny, too. Sometimes your deadpan remarks have me literally crying with laughter.

But what draws you to me? Unlike you, I'm an acquired taste.

You're interested in the inner workings of my mind, you tell me. You ask difficult, probing questions, and have this way of giving me your complete attention, your chin resting on your steepled fingers. 'Parisian gargoyle,' your elder son calls that pose. I always answer you honestly, even if the truth is uncomfortable. You never dodge any of my questions, either.

I go away on a travel writing gig to Chile. When I come back, you can no longer hold your cup of tea by yourself. The backs of your hands are covered in prominent veins, the muscle beneath wasted. When I rub moisturising cream into your arms, I can feel each bone beneath your skin.

'I'm on death row too, you know,' you tell me, half in jest, half in warning, after I regale you with stories about my death row pen pals. Having had more experience than me when it came to losing people you know, you want to spare me the devastation of your death. But more than anything, it's your family that you wish to protect – from the distress and helplessness at seeing you occasionally undone, sad, frightened. You don't want to die. I'm honoured to lend you my ear, to be useful to you, when you need to speak of your fears of what's yet to come.

I've started doing something I've never done: I pray. I beseech any deity who may listen, promising them anything – *anything!* – if they keep you around for a bit longer. *Carve years off my life, and give them to him.* But only in private. If you can face the end with such stoicism, the least I can do is pull myself together and be as supportive as possible.

'It's brutal to think that I'll be dead soon,' you tell me matter-of-factly over lunch one day. And it is. I am present, along with your family, when it happens. Your breathing mask is removed from your face and your eyes snap open and for several endless, terrible heartbeats it seems as if you are still trying to breathe, to fight, to live. Then your eyes close, and your mouth goes slack. The man – the vital, breathing, wonderful human being – becomes a shell. I will carry that image with me for the rest of my days.

'He really loved you, you know,' your younger son tells me. I've kept it together until then, but then the tears come and they don't stop as I cycle frantically through the stillness of that warm June night, sobbing silently until I'm winded, gasping, retching with grief. What do I do? *What do I do now?*

* * * * *

A choked sob brought me back to the terrace of Hotel Oloffson and it took me a few seconds to realise – the horror! The embarrassment!

– that the sound came from my own throat and that my eyes were spilling over. I was glad that the diners at the end of the terrace were having a raucous time, oblivious to me, and that the waitress had disappeared. Any gesture of concern on their part, and I'd be reduced to an unholy mess of blotchy skin, ropy saliva, snot and tears. I wonder why a show of distress is so much worse in front of others. After all, vulnerability is human, and I accept that it sometimes overwhelms me. A performance poet friend of mine told me once that being an introvert is not a fear of people per se. After all, when you stand on stage with the microphone in front of you, you have complete control over what happens next. 'What we fear,' he said, 'is the loss of control and having others bear witness to our humiliation.'

I gulped air like a fish and concentrated on breathing deeply. Slowly, the constricting feeling in my throat and chest subsided. I decided that I'd rather conduct any further meltdowns in the privacy of my own quarters. Making my way through the dark gardens, I ran smack into some Vodou sculpture. As my eyes adjusted to the darkness, I could see that there were two fetishes – one with nails hammered into his face, another looking as if it's trussed up in chains.

The image of the mutilated little wooden horse from *The Chestnut Soldier* by Jenny Nimmo – a book from my childhood – popped into my head. The horse's lips cut off, its teeth frozen in a snarl, a tormented demon trapped inside. The fetishes seemed to radiate pain and malevolence. One of them, the empty turtle shell topped with a blackened baby doll's head pierced with nails, made me recoil and stagger backwards.

I tasted bile in the back of my throat. My vision swimming, I rushed out of the gate, tripped on the uneven pavement on the street and almost fell into an uncovered manhole. I twisted my body to one side at the last moment, landed on my knee and elbow in some unspeakable gunk – coagulated vomit? animal waste? – grazing my arm, wincing. Hurrying up the steep, narrow street to Hotel Prince, as a crowning touch for the evening I was menaced by a skinny, barking dog – all sinew and prominent ribs and ill intent. I snarled back at it with fury born of fear, daring it to attack me so that I could take my pain and anger out on something. But it was more frightened of me than I was of it. It skulked around me, looking for my weak spot, finding none and slinking off.

I huddled in my hotel room and had no wish to leave it, ever.

* * * * *

Back at the ougan's fire pit in Jacmel, I'm tempted to raise the question: does Baron Samedi know all of the dead, or just the Haitian dead? 'Have you seen him?' I want to ask. 'Have you seen my friend?' A part of me wonders if you are still out there, somewhere, in some tangible form, recognisable as yourself. But that is not what I believe.

I'm ushered out of the inner sanctum back into the tiny room with the altar, the dribbling occult candles, the sequined bottles. Kiki produces a round plate made of tightly woven straw – akin to the utensil used in rural southeast Asia for sieving rice. There's a dark stain on it. I stare at it in confusion. Is it for the sacrifice? Yes, of sorts. I'm expected to make a financial contribution towards the proceedings, towards the rum and the candles. Quite a hefty one, too – 3,000 gourdes (the equivalent of around £30). 'This is a shakedown,' I think. How well they planned it! When you're put on the spot like that, it's difficult to bargain or argue. I pay up, somewhat grudgingly, and am released back to the drumming and the dancing.

A new drummer joins the musicians. The drumming reaches fever pitch. The women continue chanting, their dresses swishing rhythmically as they whirl around the packed dirt floor.

One of the men steps forward towards the Tree, bends from the waist, and proceeds to draw a complex symbol of Erzulie on the floor with cornflour. A heart appears, then surrounding whorls, then a grid across the heart.

Blue candles are lit and passed around to each of us. One by one, we make our way to the base of the Tree, melting the bottom of our candles on the flames of the preceding ones to help them stick down. I cup the flickering flame with my hand, stick it down, then stare into the flame and repeat my wish, over and over, until a gust of wind blows it out.

After a lengthy absence from the proceedings, the ougan re-enters the fray, dressed entirely in crimson. He issues instructions in a deep, rasping voice, each sentence preceded by three sharp, throaty inhalations. He appears to have been possessed by Baron Kriminel, one of the incarnations of Baron Samedi. It's a surprisingly thoughtful manifestation: he motions towards the Tree, and a couple of the dancers move their charging mobile phones higher, out of reach. A bottle of rum makes the rounds. All the dancers take a sip and then it's our turn. I put my lips to the bottle after Anneline; the sip burns my throat. It's strong, overproof stuff, about as pleasant as drinking paint stripper. Baron Kriminel then takes the mostly full bottle, tilts his head to one side and appears to pour the rum in his ear.

He then repeats with his other ear. Staring all the while at the Tree, he strikes a match and breathes out. A cloud of flame bursts forth towards the Tree. He walks around to the other side of the Tree, strikes a match, breathes fire.

The bottle is empty. The ougan looks displeased. In a swift movement, he brings the bottle down on his own head. The bottle shatters, shards of glass flying everywhere. The ougan doesn't seem to be any worse for wear. He staggers past me, the jagged bottle in his hand missing my face narrowly; looks at it thoughtfully, takes a bite out of the glass and begins to chew. There's no blood. What is dead cannot bleed. If this is some kind of trick, it's a really good one. I've heard that if Baron Kriminel doesn't like the food or drink that he's given, he sometimes begins to take savage bites out of the very body he's possessing, tearing chunks out of the flesh, so maybe the ougan got off lightly.

The ougan staggers through the red door marked 'Kriminel'. The drummers launch into a new, frenzied routine. The women keep swaying; one older woman in particular is dancing with complete abandon, her head swinging from side to side.

Kiki beckons me. I'm ushered though the same doorway that the ougan just passed through. Fire burns in the fire pit. I think of Dante and the gates of Hell. The skull is gone. I stand cautiously on the edge of the fire pit, wary of being in such a confined space with the ougan, a man almost certainly drunk, and apparently possessed by an incarnation of Baron Samedi. The air seems to crackle with expectation. Baron Kriminel clasps my hand, then hooks his elbow around mine. Unhooking it, he firmly takes my face in his hands, slowly inclines his head towards me. His face is inches from mine. I can see a tiny muscle twitching madly beneath his left eye as two black, bloodshot orbs peer into my eyes. A momentary flutter of panic. What is he… ? Will he bite a chunk out of my face? Will he kiss me? Will he pull me into the fire between us?

But no. He rubs his forehead against mine, anointing me with his sweat. He gives three sharp gasps, then proceeds to say something in his deep rasping voice. Kiki translates that Baron Kriminel offers me his blessing and his protection. I bow my head to the loa in acknowledgement of his gift and both Kiki and I are dismissed from his presence.

'What about the animal sacrifice?' I ask Kiki. Earlier he was saying that the ritual was due to culminate with a shedding of blood, typical of Vodou ceremonies. I know from attending a bullfight that I don't enjoy witnessing pain and death inflicted on animals, but feel that I should stick around for the whole proceedings, so as not to fail some fundamental test.

'That will be tomorrow. No knives, just teeth.' I get an unpleasant mental image of the glazed-eyed dancers, sinking their teeth into the throat of a squealing pig or goat. My friend Paul witnessed an animal sacrifice at a Vodou ritual during his year spent researching the country.

'I wish they'd sharpened the machete first. There was an unnecessary amount of sawing.'

What if they ask me to participate? What if I have to drink blood? I picture myself holding a warm, twitching, feathery body of a chicken in my hands, bright arterial dribbles on my lips and neck, a sour coppery tang in my mouth.

* * * * *

Fast-forward to the Pint Shop in Cambridge. 'Why would you even think that?' asks Paul. 'When you visit a Catholic church, do you normally take a swig of the communion wine? Why would you take part in a ritual that means nothing to you?'

Touché, I think. Though I did drink the rum.

* * * * *

The dancing looks set to continue late into the night. Anneline and I feel that we have witnessed as much as we want to, so we take our leave. Kiki walks us back via the waterfront promenade.

Power is still out. Gentle murmurings drift from the groups of people huddled on the benches and the promenade wall. Lit candles lend the scene a somewhat surreal, intimate air. Monstrous shadows dance on the walls of the dark houses from the guttering candles within. Somewhere out in the darkness, waves lap against the beach. The air smells of sea salt and rotting garbage. We walk along the silent street, passing a doorway lit with neon that leads into a darkened bar. Inside, dancers gyrate to the pulsing beat. Kiki wants us to go in; he's drunk and buzzing, and wants to party, most likely with Anneline and me funding the drinks. We refuse, and Kiki is silent all the way back to the guesthouse.

Anneline excuses herself, jetlagged and catatonic with exhaustion. And I sit in the dark garden by myself, wanting to probe, pick apart, and digest the night's experiences before they fade from memory.

I see you in the fragrant darkness, as clearly as if you were sitting across the table from me, your features luminous and the dark blue of your eyes almost black in the absence of light. I'm not surprised to see you here. You appear in the strangest of places.

I'd like to tell you all the things I've been meaning to tell you before we ran out of time, and everything that I've learned since. That I still love to travel as much as I did when I first started out. That I'm still hungry to see more, that I love the challenges of my job. That I occasionally have my doubts about the value of my work to humanity at large. That I travel to places like Haiti, like India, like Papua New

Guinea, because it's a surrender – a relinquishing of control that I don't permit myself elsewhere. It's a palpable relief to let go, to be passive and just do whatever these destinations expect of me. They are volatile, challenging; they have the power to overwhelm me, to rob me of control, to push my boundaries. They wrongfoot me, take me out of my comfort zone and transform me. They are what I instinctively feel I need to break free from the confines of my flaws and the suffocating hair shirt of my own skin.

There is no one sitting across the table from me on this balmy night in Haiti. I wish I believed what Haitians believe: that the dead walk side by side with the living, that they have a tangible presence, that they can be summoned. But you're not here. There's nothing tethering you to this earth, not even the solidity of bones in the ground. You're nothing but atoms now.

A line from a poem* at your funeral stayed with me: *The dead live on forever in the living*. But it's not forever. The only place where you exist now, as I knew you, is in my increasingly unreliable recollections. Once I go, so will you.

---

*'If I Be the First of Us to Die' by Nicholas Evans.

CHAPTER 10
HONORARY WONGUTHA

Meekatharra is infamous in the white Australian imagination. The husband of one of my closest friends likes to make fun of this unprepossessing little desert town that serves long-distance truckers and the mining community. He is from near Sydney, and he's never been to Meeka, but it tends to make the news for all the wrong reasons. Mainly, Aboriginal-on-Aboriginal violence. So when I pull up in Meeka one blistering January afternoon, after hours of driving south from Karijini National Park, my expectations are not exactly sky-high.

There's a meditative quality to this solitary road trip that started in Perth and has taken me through a blur of coastal towns, all the way up north to the mining hub of Port Hedland, where I took a sharp right inland and pressed on south, deep through the Outback – the vast, largely unpopulated, arid heart of Australia. Most days, I get up at dawn to beat the heat, and drive for five or six hours, sometimes vying for highway space with road trains – the wheeled leviathans of the desert – but most often alone, enjoying the silence and the monotony of the landscape: red earth, green scrubland, endless blue sky, arrow-straight road cutting through desert for hundreds of miles.

It's late 2018, and I'm still recovering from a severe bout of pneumonia contracted the previous year while on a work trip. Unlike many of my colleagues, I'd managed to avoid serious injury and illness on the road for much of my life. So when a persistent dry cough kicked off one evening in Lamu, Kenya, I ignored it. But it didn't go away.

Within days, there was some difficulty breathing and intermittent fever. Did I go to the doctor? No. I went on a safari instead.

When I returned to the UK, my wonderful GP, Dr Townsend, informed me that if I hadn't come to see her when I did, there was a good chance that I could have died. She told me that my lungs sounded 'like crunchy snow' and that I had severe pneumonia, put me on bed rest for weeks, and then called me every night to make sure I hadn't shuffled off this mortal coil.

Months later, I was finally diagnosed with a chronic respiratory condition, of which there had been hints over previous years. I'm still clawing my way back to relative health. During the long months of recovery, amidst numerous setbacks, I was choked both by my faulty lungs and by anger over my body – my formerly robust, dependable body – betraying me. I'd breathe in sometimes, and it was as if the air would hit a barrier, refusing to go all the way in. I'd try again, with the same results, my body flooding with adrenalin, feeling as if I were drowning inside. When antibiotics didn't seem to be working, and terms such as 'pulmonary fibrosis' and 'possible lung transplant' were tossed about, I wallowed in despair, thinking that I'd rather not be here than live a vastly diminished life.

What frightened me wasn't the prospect of no longer existing. It was the visceral fear and helplessness that I found objectionable. I was angry that I couldn't overcome my illness by sheer force of will. For the first time since I was a child, I found myself utterly dependent on others.

Six months after my initial illness, the lung biopsy results were cautiously encouraging. Still, I lost my nerve for a while, and couldn't see myself travelling properly again. No more 'machete' gigs for me, I thought. No more Haiti, or India or PNG. Then, I cautiously agreed to a gig in the Channel Islands, and after an excellent respiratory specialist taught me how to manage my condition, I'm doing my best to get back to my normal working life. With the mellow pace of my Australian journey, the fresh sea and desert air, I feel my strength returning, bit by bit, while the remoteness of any human habitation gives me respite from the claustrophobia of bed rest, hospitals and the alarming background jangle of Brexit.

My mission, for Lonely Planet, is to explore Western Australia with fresh eyes, with a particular emphasis on Aboriginal culture. I've visited every single Aboriginal art gallery en route, every sacred site in the national parks, and have spoken to every Aboriginal tour operator in my bid to learn as much as I can and to do Australia's original inhabitants justice. The Goldfields are entirely missing from my guidebook. Mount Magnet, Cue, Meekatharra – small mining towns off the Great Northern Highway that time appears to have forgotten, soporific in the 40+° heat – are a blank spot on my map. I would be remiss if I failed to investigate them.

* * * * *

First impressions of Meeka: super-wide main street, Wild West saloon-style motels. Very quiet. The girl at the tourist office/library directs me to Made in Meeka, a local gift shop on the corner. 'You'll want to speak to Anna,' she tells me.

The sign on the door says: 'Shop hours may vary due to Fires, Car Crashes, Menopause, Dog Situations, Mood, Lounge Room Dancing and Nana Naps.' There's also a billboard outside advertising haircuts for dogs and humans for $20. 'It'll grow back' appears to be the hairdresser's motto.

Inside, my mouth drops open at the sight of the bright, vibrant Aboriginal canvasses on the wall depicting watering holes, goannas (big lizards), emus. I then get distracted by railway 'dogs' (iron fastenings), prospecting magnets (with a sign that says 'Seriously: don't touch the sodding magnets') and local postcards themed '10 Things to Do in Meekatharra'. Sample: 'Visit Our Medical Facilities. Once you've ticked "pub fight" off your to-do list, it's handy to know that the regional hospital is within easy staggering reach of all three pubs.' It's the sort of shop you walk into intending to buy some postcards, only to emerge hours later wearing an 'I Kissed a Bungarra and I Liked It' T-shirt and laden with rusty horseshoes for luck.

I recognise the cheerful proprietress as Anna Johnson, author of *Don't Try This At Home: Our Life in the Outback*, displayed at the local library/tourist office. She's also owns a B&B – 'Basic, perfect for your readers: shared bathroom facilities and likely ghost sightings.'

'How many ghosts do you have?' I'm thinking that she's kidding.

'Let's see: angry prostitute, distressed prostitute – related to a guy who hanged himself out back... we had to have the place cleansed, it had a really dark aura... mischievous little girl – we've had some unexpected poltergeist activity around – objects going missing, then turning up where you already looked, being poked in the back of the leg... oh yes, and a mangled guy out front – three completely unrelated people saw him. Sounded like Jim Campbell who got run over by his own truck in 1863.'

'Why the prostitutes?'

'This building we're in is over a hundred years old; it used to be a pioneer bakery, plus a boarding house, and boarding houses tended to double as brothels.'

I tell her I'm trying to get a feel for the Outback and for Aboriginal culture.

'You should head south. Big Aboriginal artist community in Mount Magnet, plus a good museum. Also, have you heard of Walga Rock? No? It's the largest gallery of Aboriginal rock paintings in Western Australia. Less than an hour out of Cue.'

'Is Meekatharra really as bad as its reputation suggests?' I feel that Anna wouldn't mind a direct question.

'Personally, I love it here. The place really grows on you. Here you get people from all over. I stopped for a drink seven years ago and never left.'

Anna tells me that she's originally from Vancouver Island, that she's lived in Australia for thirty-five years and that one day she'd had enough, sold all her worldly possessions, bought an old bus, loaded up her dogs and cat, and exchanged a corporate life in Melbourne for the uncertainty of life on the road. I read in her book later that she was a film maker and director, responsible for many episodes of the soap operas *Home and Away*, *Shortland Street* and *Neighbours*, including the episode where Madge dies. 'Yes, I killed Madge!' she crows when I ask her about it.

Not an insignificant chunk of Meeka's population comes from elsewhere. They've all found their way here from other parts of Australia or further afield, and ended up staying, for one reason or another.

'A German girl came here, a backpacker. She fell in love with our resident flying doctor. We also have some of the best-looking policewomen in Australia, including a surprising number of lesbians. Some of the local guys try to make a move on them, and we're, like: "You have more fingers than teeth, John. Even if she didn't bat for the other team, why would she be interested in you?"'

Anna is also a volunteer firefighter: 'All emergency services, apart from the flying doctor, are staffed by vollies here.'

In a small, isolated community of just over six hundred people, everyone plays their part. Government cuts play a part, too: 'Half the people here can't afford their own teeth and have to crowdfund medical treatment for their kids.'

I continue to admire the Aboriginal art on her walls, while three large dogs of indeterminable pedigree – Anna's canine adoptees – come out from behind the counter, nuzzle and lick me, beg for belly rubs.

Having talked to numerous Aboriginal artists in Geraldton, Roebourne, Port Hedland and Newman, I recognise some of the symbolism in these traditional Aboriginal paintings. They are essentially maps of the country, with massive appeal to a map nerd like me. In fact, before Aboriginals had access to canvas, these maps were drawn on the ground – to show the locations of important landmarks, to point kin to good hunting grounds or a source of water. The paintings are typically executed in a style similar to pointillism. Concentric circles mean 'waterhole', but can also mean 'community' or 'settlement'. The U-shapes are people. The U-shapes with spears next to them are men; with digging sticks, women. Animal tracks mean one thing, while the whole animal depicted means another.

Anna points at the wall: 'Most of these paintings are by Beryl Walsh. Her mother was Avy Curley, famous activist for Aboriginal rights.'

Even I've heard of Avy, who'd raised eighteen children and was awarded a state honour for her activist work. Anna shows me a beautiful and fragile bark painting done by Avy that's strikingly different from the bright, bold works of her daughter.

Anna points the artwork of a young woman who recently walked the length of the rabbit-proof fence – some 1,240 miles.

'Oh, I've just listened to *Follow the Rabbit-Proof Fence*!'

Australia-themed audiobooks have kept me company during my long drives. I've gone from the gory account of the bloodbath and mutiny aboard the *Batavia* in 1629, to tales of family, belonging and being mixed race in *Growing Up Aboriginal In Australia*, to *Follow the Rabbit-Proof Fence*, the story of three mixed-race Aboriginal girls who were forcibly taken to a mission school in the 1940s and who then escaped and walked home along the fence, living largely off the land. The fence, erected in the early 1900s, was meant to keep rabbits, emus and other agricultural pests out of Western Australia. I find a dramatic account of it at the Mining and Pastoral Museum in Mount Magnet the following day, along with tales of the Emu War of 1932, which was lost… by humans.

'Daisy, the youngest of the three girls, recently passed away,' Anna continues. 'We wanted a state funeral for her but didn't get it.'

Conversation turns to Aboriginal communities in general.

'Which peoples live here? Do you say "peoples" or "tribe"? Is it okay to just talk to random people and ask them about their culture?'

The reason I'm asking Anna all these questions is because she has numerous friends among the local Aboriginal communities and also, within Aboriginal culture, asking questions is not the done thing. You're supposed to absorb knowledge by listening to your elders.

'Don't worry, the Aboriginals have a great sense of humour and they don't mind if you fuck up as long as you're genuinely interested and respectful. "Mob" is safest. "Which 'mob', or 'skin', or language are you?" People are happy to talk to you. They'll banter with you and might try to hit you up for some spare change or a cigarette, so just joke with them. That's the thing with living in a small town. You might see someone – Aboriginal, or one of us transplants – getting drunk and yelling, and then you see them the next day, and you tell them, "You were a mess last night," and they'll be like "Yeah, I was, sorry about that." In Meekatharra you're accepted for who you are. In a bigger place, you might see someone who looks like a down-and-out, and give them a wide berth, but here you learn that people are rough diamonds. There are lots of different facets to people, and that same down-and-out will help you put out a fire, or help you fix your car. There's a guy here with mental health problems who got away from the family home the other night, took his clothes off and ran up and down the main street, shouting. In a big city, he would've been Tasered and put in jail, but here the police just called his family and helped get him home.'

Like many visitors new to Aboriginal culture, and mindful of the trauma they have suffered over many generations, I worry about causing distress by asking the wrong thing, or using unintentionally offensive terminology. In Geraldton, while talking to Margaret Whitehurst, a Wajarri artist whose painting I was admiring, I asked her if she spoke Wajarri, and she looked very uncomfortable. 'Not really. I was sent to missionary school.'

'I felt like such a heel,' I recount to Anna. 'I really should've known, going by her age, that Margaret was likely to have been one of the "Stolen Generations".'

Between 1910 and the 1970s, the Australian government pursued the misguided policy of assimilation, believing that the Aboriginal lot could be improved if only they were part of white society. Aboriginal children were forcibly taken from their families, put in church-run mission schools and taught to reject their heritage. They were forbidden from speaking traditional languages, and what little they were taught about Aboriginal culture often instilled in them a sense of deep shame. Neglect, psychological, physical and sexual abuse were common. Some kids were adopted by white Australian couples, in spite of having living family of their own, and forced to work as unpaid domestic servants, while others were returned to their biological families with a complete sense of disconnect, unable to communicate due to lost language skills, with no skills that would allow them to live off the land, but not accepted by white society either.

'They typically received very little in the way of education,' Anna continues for me. 'And even those fortunate enough to be genuinely loved by their adoptive parents still went through the trauma of abuse at mission schools, as well as losing their birth family. My Yamatji friends have told me as much. And you can't learn to "be white". It would only take one "I'm not gonna be friends with you coz you're an A*o" at school to bring across to these kids that they didn't fit in, and never would.'

Meeka's Aboriginal community comprises a number of 'Stolen Generations' individuals, and the repercussions of generations of trauma are still very much being felt.

'Quite apart from the cultural knowledge never passed on by the elders, with generations of children snatched away, many parents never got over having their children taken from them. They'd turn to alcohol as a crutch, or worse. And many of these stolen children never grew up in a supportive family environment and had nowhere to learn proper parenting skills themselves. So there are a lot of problems here with drugs, and alcoholism, and domestic violence – women versus women, men versus men, adults versus kids and dogs, et cetera. Sexual violence. A lot of crime, too. Mostly break-ins. They send the kids to steal, because underage kids can't do time. There are some businesses that are broken into several times a week. Meeka's a small place, so everyone knows who did what. Lots of fighting, too; there are two Aboriginal mobs that live around here – one on the north side of Main Street, one on the south side. They fight.'

This echoes what Scharlette told me years ago about the majority of her clients. Cycles of trauma.

'Hey, head on down Consuls Street by 6pm to the pop-up kitchen run by Mission Australia. They feed anyone that needs feeding. Ooh, it's trifle tonight!'

I take Anna up on that. On my way I pass several boarded-up houses, a burnt-out car, some dwellings with sagging porches and household detritus cluttering the front yards. But the line for the chicken and salad and trifle is orderly and the mood jovial, with those waiting to be fed joking around with the Mission Australia team. They feed me also, having more than enough food for everyone.

'We're here every Thursday,' one of the charity workers tells me, a cheerful Aboriginal lady in her forties. 'It's not enough to compensate for the regular diet of takeaway fried chicken, Coca-Cola and two-minute noodles. Still, it's something. It's common for folks around here to have heart surgery by the time they are forty, plus diabetes is rampant, kidney failure. But we do what we can.'

Walking back in the fading light, I pass by the bar at the Royal Mail Motel, full of miners, Mission Australia workers and Aboriginal folk playing pool. An easy camaraderie reigns. No shouting or fighting – at least not tonight.

* * * * *

I drive south to Cue, a historic gold rush town. Taking a left on the Beringarra–Cue road, I pass the derelict buildings of the ghost town of Big Bell that flourished and died between 1937 and 1955, and head further into the bush. My destination is Walga Rock, a granite monolith second only to Uluru in size. More importantly, it's a sacred site for the local Aboriginal communities, and I need to see it.

The road turns to gravel and sand and meanders through scrubland-dotted desert. My mobile phone signal disappears. Some thirty miles west of Cue, I'm completely on my own. It's an unsettling feeling. Were something to happen to my car, it would likely be days before I'd be found, so I'm travelling with gallons of water and a stash of camping food.

'If you break down, whatever you do, don't wander away from the car,' Anna instructed me. 'Every year we have people die that way. They walk off to try and find help and very quickly get heatstroke.' Including trans-Australia truckers, who really ought to know better. I take what precautions I can: in the national parks, I take to the hiking trails at dawn. I carry way more water than I think I need. I leave notes under my windscreen wipers to announce where I'm headed when I go bushwalking, in the unlikely case that someone might find them. But there is little I can do about the possibility of automobile malfunction.

'You can set your spare tyre on fire.' Anna's not kidding. 'If people see smoke, they'll come and investigate.'

I reach Walga Rock without incident. The low, sloping granite monolith towers above me. Beneath the cliff overhang there are dozens of images, engraved or painted in freehand on stone: spirals, goannas, spears, boomerangs. There are handprints, too, outlined in red. Some emu footprints. From visiting the ancient Bidjara and Karingbal rock art sites in Carnarvon Gorge in Queensland, I know that these would've been made by the artist blowing a finely ground mixture of powdered pigment and water against their hand or the object, held static against the rocky canvas. What's remarkable about this is that the two art sites are some six millennia apart, yet they tell similar stories. Many of the images at Walga Rock are over ten thousand years old, compared to the mere 3,500 years of art in the Carnarvon Gorge.

These are tales of hunting and ancient trade routes, of the Dreamtime serpent, of evil spirits, of first contact with the outsiders. Just like the stencil art of a rifle in Carnarvon Gorge that warned of the arrival of Europeans and their fearsome firepower, here I locate an object of enduring mystery. It's a painting of a what seems to be a two-masted nineteenth-century steamship. It's believed to be the SS *Xantho*, a pearling ship that sank near Port Gregory in 1872. But before it did, it was home to Sammy Hassan or Sammy 'Malay', a sailor from Indonesia or thereabouts, who either chose to stay on the Australian mainland after he ceased to be employed by the pearling industry, or else was abandoned among the Aboriginal people instead of being repatriated. He left his mark here with this drawing, further confirmed by what may be Jawi, an Arabic-Malay script, directly beneath the image of the ship.

I contemplate the hand and emu footprint stencils. Several years earlier, I encountered a riot of 'jazz hands', ñandú (Patagonian cousin of the emu) and puma prints on the walls of Argentina's Cueva de Las Manos, dating back some seven thousand years. Patagonia's ancient inhabitants and Aboriginal Australians inhabited different continents and different time periods, had never met each other, and yet they chose to express themselves in almost identical ways. What does this tell us about humanity in general?

Still pensive when I find myself back in Cue, I decide to hide from the noon heat inside the Queen of the Murchison, Cue's retro guesthouse and café that looks like a cowboy saloon. There are saddles and tack on the wall, and other assorted gold rush paraphernalia. But the canvas above the bar stands out starkly against them all. It's an Aboriginal painting with some circular motifs (waterholes? togetherness?), strung together with what looks like diffused lightning. Unlike most canvasses from the Goldfields – all reds and russets and yellows of the desert – this painting is almost entirely black. An intense black that's more than the mere absence of other colours. A hypnotic darkness that sucks you in.

Correctly guessing that I'd like to buy it, the proprietress apologises that it's not for sale. 'But I've got another painting by the same artist, if you're interested,' she tells me, and produces another canvas – also black, also with circular motifs. But whatever magic the artist had captured in the original painting, the ephemeral muse – it's missing here. It's just a flat, black canvas.

* * * * *

'So what does it mean to "go walkabout"?' I ask, as the van sets off along the main street of the mining town of Kalgoorlie-Boulder. The others fall silent for long enough to make me think that I've put my foot in it, again, but then Linden – a stocky, mustachioed Wongutha man my age – speaks up, choosing his words carefully.

'It's a derogatory term used by white Australians in relation to Aboriginal people, meaning that they cannot be trusted to turn up to work. That they are lazy layabouts who sometimes go missing for days without explanation.'

'How did this term come about?'

'Aboriginal society is governed by many internal rules and obligations that outsiders don't necessarily know anything about. "Walkabout" was originally a reference to disappearing into the bush in order to go on a ritual journey, and that still happens. But more often than not, an Aboriginal individual may have pressing obligations, such as attending a family funeral, and may not feel like explaining the minutiae of their lives to non-Aboriginals.'

Since there is so much that I don't know, I'm glad that the Brownley family does not take offence over my endless questions. They run a series of cultural tours, aimed at introducing outsiders to Aboriginal culture, and they're taking me out into the bush for the day.

Before we leave Kalgoorlie-Boulder, we stop near Kingsbury Park. Linden shows me a mural by a prolific local Aboriginal artist, Jason Dimer. Green creeper vines stretch along the length of the building against an earth-brown background, bearing teardrop-shaped green fruit that gives half the town its name. Kalgoorlie is a Wangai word meaning 'the place of the silky pear'.

I recognise the motif, because I spotted it the previous day when I stopped by the Bush Blossom Gallery that showcases art by Aboriginal peoples that live in or near Kalgoorlie, such as Ngaatjatjarra, Wongutha and Ngadju. Monica, the friendly curator, was happy to point out pieces by local artists, such as Jason Dimer and Vera Dimer, Jason's daughter.

'Artistic talent frequently runs in the family,' Monica explained, when I pointed out the similarity between their paintings, all telling their family's stories and reflecting their cultural ties to the land. 'But oftentimes you'll have the grandmother's or grandfather's work featuring traditional images and themes – bush tucker, hunting/gathering, Dreamtime – and then the grandchild produces something utterly contemporary.'

I could see that she was right. While many of works had been executed in traditional dot style, some of the most vibrant canvasses were postmodern and abstract, bringing to mind Kandinsky or Jackson Pollock. Some paintings are by internationally renowned names, such as Dr Pantjiti Mary McLean, whose massive canvas has pride of place on the back wall. But I prefer the traditional dots, concentric circles and Vera Dimer's creeper vines to McLean's distinctive naïve style.

* * * * *

Trevor, Linden's father, points out a clinic on the corner, and tells me: 'This one caters to Aboriginal patients.'

'Are there separate medical facilities for Aboriginal and non-Aboriginal patients?' Seeing my look of query, he explains: 'The medical staff are sensitive to their patients' needs.'

'What do you mean?' I'm still puzzled. 'Are there major cultural differences when it comes to medical treatment, or… ?'

Linden jumps in: 'There are cultural aspects to medical treatment that can include language. In remoter parts of the Outback, there are places where Aboriginals don't speak great English because they interact almost exclusively with members of their own community. They may feel intimidated if they find themselves in a large, English-speaking hospital, like the one in Kalgoorlie, or might not know the medical terminology and may not be clear about the particulars of their medical treatment. This clinic has Aboriginal staff who act as cultural interpreters.'

I tell the Brownleys how in the town of Wiluna, further north along the Goldfields Highway, I came across the statues of Warri and Yatungka, whose lives have been immortalised in a book, *Last of the Nomads*. Warri was depicted holding a spear and shading his eyes with his other arm, looking out into the distance, while Yatungka sat at his feet with a basket full of bush tucker. Their story is remarkable. They both belonged to the Mandildjara tribe and fell in love, but since Aboriginal law forbids, under pain of death, union between people from the same 'skin group' (each Aboriginal 'mob' consists of five or six different 'skin groups'), they eloped. They disappeared into the desert and survived for decades by hunting and gathering. In 1977, they were found, close to starvation, by a Mandildjara elder, with explorer Stan Gratte, after a severe drought hit the region, and were subsequently forgiven and allowed back.

'This is a very rare case,' Linden tells me. 'The penalties for breaking the strict rules that govern Aboriginal society may seem very severe to outsiders.'

'So does Aboriginal law come into conflict with Australian law sometimes?'

'Yes, and that's when problems arise. For example, my second cousin was caught stealing from another Wongutha. The elders then negotiated an appropriate form of payback, which is vital for restoring balance. Basically, when there's a grievance, payback is both appropriate and expected.'

'So what happened?'

'He had to return what he stole and then the family of the victim broke both his arms.'

'Harsh.'

'Perhaps so. But there's often a lack of trust on the part of Aboriginal people towards Australian law enforcement. In remote areas in particular, Aboriginal law is sometimes the only way for victims to get justice.'

* * * * *

It turns out that our picnic destination is the vast salt flat that is Lake Ballard, a half-hour's drive from the one-street former gold prospecting town of Menzies, north of Kalgoorlie-Boulder. Several nights earlier, before arriving in Kalgoorlie, I'd camped here overnight, just yards away from the salt flat. Trudging across it – my sandalled feet quickly abraded by the salt crust and caked in mud – and then climbing the hillock in the middle of the 'lake', I observed the eerie panorama of ghostly-white swirls of salt merging with the red outback dirt, and the fading sunlight glinting redly off the eerie, human-shaped metal sentinels. The fifty-one metal humanoids are part of Antony Gormley's 'Inside Australia' work, the sculptures based on laser scans of Menzies' inhabitants.

Later, watching the celestial river of the Milky Way through the mesh of my pop-up tent, I considered that this was as off the grid as it gets in the developed world. No one knew where I was, there was no phone signal, and there wasn't another human for miles around. There is something about sleeping out in the open: your primeval instincts kick in, even though there is nothing hunting you. You're hyper-sensitive to every gust of wind, every clandestine rustle in the undergrowth. Not for the first time, I felt watched.

It's happened to me several times during this trip. Once when I got lost in the rocky hills of Murujuga National Park while admiring carvings and paintings of turtles, kangaroos, ospreys and fish dating back some thirty thousand years. Another time, I was at the Python Pool – a waterhole of spiritual significance to the Yindjibarndi people, fringed by red rock cliffs in Millstream Chichester National Park. Finally, in Karijini National Park, during a dawn excursion into a beautiful, narrow gorge, when I had to overcome my dread of dark water and swim along a trench that was too deep for wading. Each time, I got the impression I was being observed – not in a hostile manner, but with considerable curiosity.

I remember reading Bruce Chatwin's *The Songlines* as a teenager, and falling in love with the poetry of the Aboriginal stories of creation. When writing about Aboriginal beliefs, Chatwin relied largely on information gleaned from non-Aboriginals, so it's entirely possible that some of his information was presumptuous and that he'd employed plenty of poetic licence. But still, I was enchanted by the idea of ancestral beings, walking the empty land, and singing all life into existence.

While camping at Lake Ballard, my dreams were extra vivid. I dreamed of these 'songlines', except that instead of their being invisible threads, connecting all living beings to this ancient land, I visualised them as crackling, slow-flowing white lines of electricity – the way I once pictured the shivers running down my spine during an out-of-body experience, after sampling the hallucinogenic ayahuasca jungle vine in Peru. 'Like electric molasses,' I carefully wrote down in my notebook, once I'd returned from my travels out of my mind.

At dawn, groggy and half-asleep, I fully expected to see vast grooves left in the parched earth by Goorialla the Dreamtime serpent, crawling across the land as he did through my night-time world. It wouldn't surprise me in the least if this land were indeed alive and sentient.

* * * * *

While Trevor and Marcia – Linden's mother – are setting up the campfire, Linden shows me how to throw a boomerang. It's not what I expected. For starters, it's barely curved and doesn't come back when you throw it.

'We have different boomerangs for different types of game,' Linden explains. 'There are fishing boomerangs, boomerangs to bring down kangaroo… and if you're trying to bring down a heavy animal, you really don't want a returning boomerang.'

I take his point about not wishing to get clobbered by a heavy chunk of wood and recall seeing the heavy hunting weapons, shaped like a Nike 'Just do it!' tick, at the Kalgoorlie-Boulder museum.

'This one's good for hunting goanna. Dad can bring down a running goanna at thirty paces.'

When I have a go at throwing, I manage to hit a nearby tree. Not the tree I was aiming for, but still. I tell Linden about my fruitless search for an authentic returning boomerang in Kalgoorlie and beyond.

'There are very few Aboriginal craftsmen left who know how to make one. Mostly old blokes, living out in the bush. It's a dying art.'

It is in Western Australia, anyway. When I'm over on Australia's east coast, and swing by the Dreamtime Cultural Centre in Rockhampton, on my way to the Carnarvon Gorge, the guide demonstrates how to use a returning boomerang, and when I try it out, it truly comes back. Like magic. Apparently, returning boomerangs are still quite commonly made by the Darumbal people.

Linden produces something that resembles a wooden paddle, pointed at one end and with what looks like a claw bound to it with animal sinew at the other.

'This is a woomera,' he tells me. 'A spear thrower,' he explains, when the term is met with a blank look from me. 'It helps you throw a spear with more power than if you were just using your arm.' He demonstrates. 'Also, back in the day, you'd use it as a mini shield. To deflect enemy spears in battle.'

'Oh! Actually, I have seen these – at a gallery in Kalgoorlie-Boulder.'

But when I tell him about the contents of the gallery – a wealth of canvas paintings, displays of woomera, even a few vintage boomerangs – and about my encounter with the Stetson-wearing proprietor who claims to know the Aboriginals, Linden frowns.

'He is not a great advocate for Aboriginal people despite his history with our mob. He places a low value on Aboriginal art and artefacts and buys it from us for far less than it's worth. He knows that many artists live hand to mouth and often need the money up front.'

'So he exploits them.'

'Yes. He knows that it's worth far more to collectors than what he pays for it, so he sells the art and artefacts for a higher price and makes a quid for himself.'

* * * * *

Trevor calls us over. The campfire has been reduced to embers and a couple of gently glowing logs, and he is stirring the kangaroo stew in a red Le Creuset casserole dish while damper (traditional soda bread cooked on hot coals) cools on a fire-blackened iron rack.

Marcia ladles everyone a generous bowlful and we all settle down to eat. Mouth full, I express my enthusiasm for this rich, meaty concoction, fortified with potatoes and bits of bacon. Kangaroo is stronger-flavoured and gamier than beef or lamb, but is a surprisingly tender meat, given how springy and well muscled the animal is. When I mop up the gravy with the spongy, smoky bread, and ask for seconds, Marcia looks at me with approval.

Trevor then makes a short speech in Wongutha, which Linden then translates. '… You are now my daughter, and this is your mother, and this is your brother.'

This is entirely unexpected. In Aboriginal society, how you relate to everyone else depends on your kinship group, whether you're male or female, whether you're young or old. Your duties and obligations, as well as taboos, stem from your place in the community. And while I'm sure that they say this to all the visitors to introduce them to the complexities of Aboriginal culture, I'm still momentarily pierced by wistfulness as I get a brief glimpse of what it must be like to live in a world defined by very precise rules, within which your own place is guaranteed and secure.

'Your "skin group" is Garimada, same as your grandfather and your brothers,' Trevor continues. 'That means that you may not marry a Garimada.'

'It's to prevent inbreeding,' Linden clarifies. 'You're not supposed to marry your first cousins. That's why Warri and Yakungka had to run away; they were first cousins.'

'If you were staying with us for longer,' Marcia interjects, 'we'd take you camping overnight in the bush, dig for witchetty grubs, cook goanna.'

'Do they taste like chicken?' Because for some reason, that's everyone's reference point when it comes to unfamiliar sources of protein.

'The goanna does, yeah,' Linden says. 'Like oily chicken. It has this delicious layer of yellow fat – good as a moisturiser, too. But the grubs are kind of nutty, especially if you roast them.'

When I saw a bucket of writhing, aesthetically repellent white sago grubs at a market in Sarawak, Borneo, their appearance did little to convince me of their edibility. But I'll try most things once.

'So do many Wongutha eat bush tucker, then?'

'Not just Wongutha, but most Aboriginals who live in the Outback. We hunt at least part of the time. "Go bush" when time allows. And it's not just for the nutrition – though it's better than the processed food we buy at the supermarket. It's a direct link to our culture, and to country.'

When I first came to Australia, years ago, friends in Sydney told me that no one really eats kangaroo, crocodile, etc – that it's just novelty fodder for tourists, just like breaded 'gator bites in Cajun restaurants in the States. But they couldn't have been more wrong. For Aboriginals, the consumption of bush tucker is one of the most profound ways of reaffirming their identity. Which further underlines the profound disconnect between largely white, coastal, urban Australia with its European roots, and the ancient cultures that have called this continent home for over sixty thousand years.

Earlier in the trip, I'd talked to 'Capes', aka Darren Capewell, an Aboriginal guide who conducts cultural and nature tours on traditional Nhanda and Malgana lands in Shark Bay, on the west coast, and he told me that he takes groups of youths – both Aboriginal and non-Aboriginal – out on the land. They camp wild, and he teaches them Aboriginal history, how to identify bush tucker, how to find water in a desert environment, how to play the didgeridoo. Some Aboriginal kids who've grown up in large towns have never seen a witchetty grub, or lit a campfire, or listened to Dreamtime stories. Without Capes's help, they'd still be missing those essential ties that bind them to their ancestral homeland, and reaffirm their place on it – just like the Stolen Generations, who carry their losses around with them like amputated limbs.

'We killed this kangaroo a couple of days ago,' Trevor tells me. 'That's enough stew to feed the whole family for a few days.' Apart from Linden, Trevor and Marcia have four other sons, plus daughters-in-law, assorted grandchildren.

'Kangaroo is not just a good meal,' Linden explains. 'For different mobs, different types of kangaroo are their totem animal. They have great cultural, social and spiritual significance for us. For the Wongutha, it's –' and he lowers his voice to tell me which kangaroo type is special. 'But you mustn't tell anyone,' he admonishes.

And so, dear reader, I'm not at liberty to divulge what type of kangaroo I've consumed.

'Come back next time, and I'll make you kangaroo haggis,' Marcia promises when the Brownleys drop me off in town in the evening. Haggis! Scotland meets Outback Australia in one delectable, offal-heavy dish. Surely, that's reason enough to return.

* * * * *

Later, in Esperance, on Australia's south coast, I pop into the Karnpi Designs Art Gallery and pause to admire the works of Sophia Ovens Junnburramudja, a talented Aboriginal artist originally from the Kimberley. Unlike Outback art that reflects the parched desert from which it springs, many of her paintings depict the ebb and flow of coastal waters and the movement of marine life in the shallows. When I get talking to Pauline, the gallery owner and Sophia's mother-in-law, it turns out that she knows the Brownleys and is the same 'skin group' as me: Garimada.

She greets me as kin.

CHAPTER 11
DINNER WITH TOM JONES

Every morning, I get up at 7am and pad down Sukhumvit Soi 12 in my flip-flops to the street food stalls at the end of the lane, breathing in what passes for air in Bangkok, with its distinctive scents of exhaust fumes, temple incense, salty fish sauce, sour tang of pickled marinades and lime, fragrant smoke from streetside grills. My destination is a diminutive stall where a middle-aged lady sells grilled chicken-heart skewers. We *wai* each other while singing out: 'Sawadeeka'. After five days of the same routine, I'm a regular. I hold up two fingers, exchange some coins for two skewers and then trot down Sukhumvit Road, past the Asok skytrain station, munching on the hearts. I dash across the busy intersection, ahead of the morning stream of motorbikes. Minutes later, I step into Artis Coffee, a quiet, air-conditioned oasis, for my morning cup of Thai highland coffee.

Bangkok is my kind of city. It's been my gateway to southeast Asia since I was nineteen years old. I remember walking barefoot on the warm hardwood floors of my hosts' home and along smooth marble in the Temple of the Reclining Buddha. Thai women cooing admiringly over my friend Heather's alabaster skin, and wanting to have their photo taken with her six-foot frame. Discovering for the first time in my life that there are countries where I am medium height. Being tricked into chewing on a couple of raw bird's eye chillies, then having the flames in my mouth soothed with iced coffee and condensed milk. Being anointed with flour, pelted with water balloons and squirted with water pistols by festive locals during Songkran festival. Speeding along the Chao Phraya river in a spray of murky water, past an architectural mishmash of slums and skyscrapers, waterside hotels and temples, and admiring the slender, elegant spires on the tips of the multi-layered roofs of the Royal Palace. Watching traders selling fresh produce from their boats at a floating market, while food sellers cooked noodles over small braziers directly in their water craft and then washed the dirty bowls in the river. But most of all, I remember the feasts.

I originally came here to stay with my friend Sonia, and the Leong family forever changed my views on hospitality and food. Sonia – who'd go on to become a well-known comic-book artist – and I met at university. We lived in the same hall of residence during our first year and bonded over our mutual love of edged weaponry. Cooking together in the shared kitchen, we cut the fat off smoked bacon in order to munch on it in front of fellow student Rachelle, who disapproved of our 'chewing the fat' (as we called it, being nineteen years old and hilarious in our own eyes) in particular and of us in general – including our habit of throwing knives at the communal noticeboard. 'You amuse me. Come live with me,' Sonia said, and so we became housemates in our second year as well. She taught me to sashimi my salmon and tuna and eat the slices raw, with soy sauce and considerable relish.

The Leongs were the first serious foodies that I met, their passion for eating matched only by their propensity for feeding their guests until they creaked at the seams. And what I liked the most is that in their home, as their guest, I was absolved of all responsibility. I wasn't asked about my dietary preferences and I didn't have to make any decisions about what to eat. All that was expected of me was to turn up and partake.

EYEBALL TACOS AND KANGAROO STEW

'Here' – Anna Leong (Sonia's mum) showed me how to approach hotpot during a family meal in their high-beamed dining room, expertly picking up raw prawns, or fish balls, or see-through slices of Wagyu beef, or noodles, with her chopsticks, and then cooking them in the vat of broth that was bubbling away merrily in the middle of the table. 'Then you dip it' – she indicated the small bowls filled with soy sauce and chilli oil. I followed her lead. At a table piled high with dishes – fried giant mantis prawns; entire steamed barramundi, Thai-style, criss-crossed with spring onions and dotted with bird's eye chillies; fiery fish head curry with okra; Kerala fish molee; Hainanese chicken rice, and other delicacies, all new to me – when Anna saw me flagging after third helpings, she encouraged me to eat more, even volunteering to peel the remaining prawns for me.

The Leongs made no allowances for my delicate palate, and I learned to eat *som tum* (spicy papaya salad) the way the Thais do, at first sweating and blinking away tears of capsicum-induced pain, but resolved to build up my spice tolerance. When we drove south of Bangkok, and stopped at some nondescript shack on the beach, I admired the way Anna pointed at the fish and seafood tanks, instructing the chefs how she wanted them prepared, followed by a swift parade of dishes, fragrant with holy basil, galangal, chillies and lemongrass, placed in front of us on the picnic tables.

Under normal circumstances I'd have been content to dally awhile in Bangkok, writing up my research in the hangout spaces at The Commons 'lifestyle mall', where you can plug in your laptop and demonstrate how busy and important you are for the benefit of onlookers. There's also an international food court featuring everything from lobster mac and cheese and poke bowls to some of Bangkok's best ice cream at Guss Damn Good, kickass coffee at Roots, and even an artisanal kombucha tap – the height of yuppiedom.

But then, the unthinkable happens. I run out of work.

The bane of my travel writing existence has been effective time management. Unlike many of my colleagues, who'd do their guidebook research well in advance of their deadlines, with ample time on the road, and a leisurely few weeks writing up at home, I've often done much of my writing up while travelling. It's a habit I got into very early on, while writing for Rough Guides, since deadlines were very tight, and carried it over to Lonely Planet. But I was always unfailingly over-optimistic about my own productivity. Which sometimes led to rationed sleep in order to meet deadlines, with writing up from one gig bleeding into the research of the next. On one memorable occasion, exhausted by a week of three- and four-hour nights, I passed out with my face in my dinner at a Middle Eastern restaurant in Medellín, Colombia, causing a commotion among the serving staff.

I'd planned to spend a leisurely fortnight in Bangkok, finishing my write-up of my Western Australia research, but I manage to finish with a week to spare. For over a decade, my 'holidays' have been spent at home, trying to make up for months of lost time with friends and relatives. But since my non-changeable flight back to Europe is not for another ten days, I make a spur-of-the-moment decision to go on an impromptu holiday. Having eavesdropped on some backpackers, I've learned that there's a motorcycling instructor named Tom living in the middle of nowhere in Laos. So I decide to scooter across Laos in search of him, and learn to ride once and for all.

* * * * *

On the wall of the COPE (Cooperative Orthotic & Prosthetic Enterprise) visitor centre, a map of Laos bleeds with a myriad red dots, each representing a location bombed by the United States Air Force between 1964 and 1973. Two million tons of bombs were dropped on Laos, making it the most heavily bombed country in the world. It was an unacknowledged war, waged on Laos because of the alliance between the country's Communist government and that of North Vietnam, and designed to disrupt the supply chains on the Ho Chi Minh Trail. A third of the bombs – around 75 million or so – failed to explode on impact and continue to cripple Laotians, decades after the war, with ninety-eight percent of the victims being civilians. Around me, there are installations made of cluster bombs, old-fashioned prosthetic limbs dangling from the ceiling, household utensils and sculpture fashioned out of unexploded ordnance. In 2016, Barack Obama stood where I'm standing now, and pledged $90 million for the clearing of the bombs. In the meantime, COPE – a non-profit – provides prosthetic limbs and rehabilitation to the maimed.

It's a sobering introduction to Vientiane, a spread-out jumble of golden stupas, concrete housing, French colonial villas, Buddhist temples and grandiose stone gates that sits on a bend in the Mekong river. It's the sleepiest Asian capital I've ever been to, and I'm getting used to scootering here before embarking on my grand odyssey between Vientiane and Luang Prabang, the country's ancient capital in the north. The subdued, reserved greetings and occasional outright indifference of Laotians are jarring after the smiling exuberance of Thais. Perhaps decades of living under communism is to blame. To me, even after years of seeing the familiar hammer-and-sickle flags fluttering on the breeze in Vietnam, this juxtaposition of Communist imagery and tropical scenery is still rather surreal.

Upon arrival, I engage in two activities: procuring a scooter for my journey and chicken-heart economics, having spotted several stalls selling chicken-heart skewers. In Bangkok, there were two chicken-heart sellers at the end of my lane. It took me a couple of days to figure out that I should be buying them from the older lady, with eight hearts per skewer, rather than from the stingy guy (five hearts per skewer), with the skewers costing exactly the same – ten baht (25p) – and the best price being just over 3p per chicken heart. Here in Vientiane, a skewer of three hearts costs 1,000 kip (around 9p, so around 3p per heart). Laos is generally around twenty-five percent cheaper than Thailand when it comes to accommodation and food but not, it seems, when it comes to chicken hearts. Go figure.

Of the handful of scooter rental places, only TL Motor Bikes will let me take their rental scooter on a long journey and do the trip one way. On my final morning in Vientiane, they take my passport hostage, promising to return it to me at my guesthouse in Luang Prabang, and strap my rucksack and my pop-up mosquito net tent to the back of the scooter with some fraying cables. It's only 210 miles, so I figure that a week should be plenty, but there's potential for things to go wrong. If my passport (with Laotian visa) fails to reach me, I may be spending a great deal more time in Laos than expected.

* * * * *

Getting out of the capital is a chore and traffic is hellish, with roadworks, convoys of fume-belching lorries and epic amounts of dust. Outside Vientiane, ugly concrete gives way to lush countryside. Though much of the time I'm sailing merrily along the smooth, paved sections, occasional cratered stretches of road make me wish I'd worn a sports bra. Small villages composed of dun-coloured houses, sleepy dogs and dragon-embellished stupas come and go, hugging both sides of the main Highway 13, a sleepy single carriageway. Roadside stalls selling fruit beneath the shade of vine-wrapped trees seem timeless and familiar. I could be anywhere – Central America, Mexico, Jamaica – until the greenery-clad karst, those distinctive, lumpy southeast Asian mountains, appears in the distance.

On the approach to Vang Vieng, the road becomes crowded with schoolchildren cycling home, the girls carrying parasols with one hand while expertly navigating their way between the potholes. And maybe because I've been in the saddle all day, and my concentration is beginning to wander due to the heat and the exhaustion, while the road deteriorates at the same time, my front wheel hits a pothole at the wrong angle and I vault over the handlebars, landing in a heap in the middle of the road. I thank my lucky stars that because the road is so rough, everyone is driving slowly, and that the lorry behind me has time to veer around me. I'm bleeding from multiple shallow forearm and leg wounds, but am otherwise unharmed. My scooter is dented, but functioning. A friendly young man stops to help me reposition my luggage, and I gingerly make my way to my hotel.

Years back, I first learned to ride a scooter on the Malaysian island of Langkawi. And by 'learned to ride', I mean I watched a couple of YouTube videos, figured that a fully automatic scooter shouldn't be hard to master, and took advantage of the fact that the only qualification required to rent a scooter there was answering 'Yes' when asked 'Can you ride a scooter?' I then made my wobbly way around the streets of Kampung Lubok Buaya and beyond, got cocky on a jungle road after it rained, took a corner too steeply, skidded on some wet leaves and toppled over, trapping my leg beneath the scooter, pulling a muscle in my leg and shredding my forearm. I then spent a couple of days resting my leg in between bouts of research on makeshift crutches (my hiking poles). At my guesthouse, a fifty-something Swedish backpacker nicknamed Jimi (apparently, his curly blonde hair = Jimi Hendrix), offered to rub Deep Heat into my affected leg. I let him. He seemed nice, and rather lonely. It wasn't until he started telling me the same inconsequential anecdote about sushi that he'd told me the day before that I had a horrifying vision of my own potential future in which it was I who was aged fifty-something, still adrift, living out of a bag somewhere, and telling the same lame story to young backpackers to pass the time. Spooked, I hightailed it to Penang the following day, makeshift crutches and all.

* * * * *

Dramatically positioned on the banks of the Nam Song river and surrounded by leafy, humpbacked karst mountains, Vang Vieng reminds me a lot of Phong Nha, the Vietnamese village I'd visited years earlier. Phong Nha is the gateway to Hang Son Doong, the world's largest cave, and I was there to interview Brian, member of the British Cave Research Association. Brian had conducted a full survey of Hang Son Doong after its discovery by a local man, and thought that there might be even bigger caves in the little-explored hinterland.

'We have plans to look for other caves, but we are waiting for the bombs to be cleared,' he told me. In Phong Nha, as in Laos, you'd see people on the streets with missing limbs, hobbling around on wooden crutches like the Soviet veterans of the Afghan war during my childhood.

EYEBALL TACOS AND KANGAROO STEW

'This was the most heavily mined part of Vietnam during the Vietnam War,' Brian informed me. 'Every year a couple of kids die from digging in the jungle and coming across unexploded ordnance.'

When the first bomb went off that evening, I landed flat on my stomach between the two beds in my room, and cowered there for a bit. Then, when my ears stopped ringing from the explosion, I peered out of the window cautiously, and found that the world hadn't gone to hell. It was Tet, Vietnamese New Year. There were revellers out in the street, and once I got somewhat used to the deafening bangs around me, I joined them, and was promptly accosted by some local ladies clutching a jug of fermented rice wine, complete with long drinking straws for sharing the booze with strangers. The explosions around us were caused by throwing unexploded bombs into bonfires.

'Do people sometimes get hurt?' I later asked my guesthouse owner, and she allowed that yes, sometimes the bombs misfire. This made the 'little Johnny burned his finger with an improperly handled sparkler' type accidents from Bonfire Night back home sound positively tame.

* * * * *

There are no bombs going off in Vang Vieng but, like Phong Nha, it's a backpacker magnet, offering river tubing, rock climbing, caving and swimming holes that are all imaginatively named Blue Lagoon. As a younger traveller, I always packed as many new experiences into my trips as I could, living as if each trip were my last. But now, having cleaned, disinfected and bandaged my scootering wounds, I decide that I don't want to get in the river and infect my scrapes with goodness knows what waterborne horror. Instead, I arrange to get a bird's eye view of Vang Vieng from a hot-air balloon.

Just before sunset, we backpackers stand around in a large group in a field on the outskirts of town watching the balloon handlers fill them up with hot air. The balloons jerk upright, and we are herded into the tightly packed baskets. It's a far cry from my experience of ballooning at sunrise over the Maasai Mara in Kenya. Then, there were just a few people in each basket, and as we glided above the savannah, the silence was broken only by the occasional 'whoosh' as the flames were turned up, while herds of wildebeest and zebra flowed across the green expanse beneath us.

By contrast, hot-air ballooning in Vang Vieng is terrifying. Our balloon flies really low to start with, with the pilot glued to his mobile phone and the basket missing the tops of buildings by a cat's whisker. At one point we brush against a tree canopy and there's a collective intake of breath. I suspect that our pilot doesn't have enough fuel to have us soaring high for much of our trip. When we finally descend, we barely miss some electricity wires and crash-land in some bushes, having overshot the field that our pilot was aiming for. But all things considered, seeing the roofs of houses, the pointed pinnacles of stupas, the pearlescent ribbon of river separating the town from a patchwork of green fields, and the dark karst looming in the background, was worth the stomach-clenching fear.

* * * * *

'Could you do me a favour?' Tom messages me. 'Pick me up some Anchor butter, salted?' I've touched base with the one-man motorbiking show that is Uncle Tom's Trails, and before setting off from Vang Vieng for Kasi, his base, I do some last-minute food shopping for him.

'I hope it won't melt en route,' I comment.

'You should be okay. Crappy road at the moment, so allow yourself a couple of hours.'

An experienced motorcycling instructor thinks that the next leg is crappy. My wounds still aching, I'm wary of further wipeouts. Some of the route is duly purgatorial. Since the Chinese are constructing a new railway that connects Laos to China, road sections are being improved for better lorry access, and tarmac abruptly gives way to mounds of gravel and stretches of mud – obstacles around or over which I wobble with difficulty. But the rest of the time, I'm enjoying the near absence of traffic – remarkable, given how this is the main road between Laos's two biggest cities – with palm trees, jungly karst and rice paddies on either side of the me.

Driving into Kasi, a nondescript huddle of houses straddling the Nam Lik river, I cross the bridge and look for the sign on the right-hand side. I knock, and the door is opened by Tom Jones, the legendary Welsh singer.

How do I know it's Tom Jones? Why, because I've seen him in concert many years earlier. Until my friend Heather brought up the impropriety of my playing Cher's 'The Shoop Shoop Song' to her seven-year-old daughter (because it teaches the wrong lessons about what constitutes a healthy romantic relationship), I hadn't really stopped to dissect the lyrics to songs, including Tom Jones's most popular hit, 'Delilah' – a justification of stalking and murdering an unfaithful woman. Back when I saw him play Wembley Arena, I was more concerned about a portly man in his sixties uttering 'I think I better dance now' during a cover of Prince's 'Kiss', and then slowly unbuttoning his shirt. The strip-tease sent members of the audience, which consisted mostly of middle-aged women, into paroxysms of rapture, with flurries of underwear bombarding the stage.

But instead of bursting into 'It's Not Unusual', Tom calmly greets me with 'D'you want to come in and choose your motorbike?'

* * * * *

'Why did you let go of the clutch?'

'I don't knooowww!' I wail into the mic attached to my helmet.

It's the third time it's happened, just like when I was learning to drive a car and repeatedly making stupid, nervous mistakes I'd never make again as a qualified driver. In fact, it's worse, because I'd taken several motorbike lessons in the UK, and had never, ever taken my hand off the clutch before.

For hours, Tom's had me doing loops on a wide dirt road behind his house, driving around cones, changing gears. Getting used to Ruby, a red-and-black 125cc Lifan Vanguard GT, built for diminutive riders like myself, before we take the show on the main road. It's been going fine. I've been reaching biting point without revving the engine too much, changing gears smoothly, turning without knocking over the traffic cones, accelerating when instructed to.

Tom is an excellent, patient instructor. The first thing he does when I straddle the motorbike is correct my riding posture.

'Look what your arms are doing' – Tom points to my elbows, sticking out at right angles. 'No wonder you were wobbly.' He's referring to my wipeout near Vang Vieng. 'Relax your shoulders, keep your grip gentle.' I see the difference almost immediately. A loosened-up posture makes it much easier to execute riding manoeuvres.

But now that I'm trying to descend a small hillock, then rev the engine at the right time before ascending it again, everything is going wrong. Tom continues talking to me in his calm and measured way and eventually, something finally clicks and I sail back up the incline with my hand on the clutch.

We ride along quiet, picturesque country roads, which is precisely the motorbiking I've been wanting to do. Learning to drive in the UK and going from figures-of-eight in a car park to doing 60mph on an A-road in two lessons, ahead of lorries and other assorted traffic, was terrifying. I won't have formal qualifications at the end of my time with Tom, but at least I'll be able to ride at my own pace in countries that don't ask for riding credentials.

* * * * *

'Want to join me and my friends for dinner?' Tom invites me as I peel off my borrowed leathers, boots and helmet. Exhausted after hours of riding, I'm happy to let him take charge of the evening meal, and not have to go looking for sustenance, or even wonder what to order in a country whose cuisine is unfamiliar to me and whose language I don't speak beyond 'hello', 'thank you' and 'sorry'.

'Just come to the café across the street from my garage,' Tom instructs, first installing me in a spotless guesthouse run by his neighbour. She speaks no English, so she and I communicate in the universal language of smiles.

Tom's two friends appear, laden with home-cooked food, while Tom supplies sausages that I saw my landlady grilling outside her house earlier, and chilled bottles of Beerlao.

We're a peculiar quartet – me, a Tom Jones lookalike (who's also Welsh, incidentally, and has actually won prizes for his physical resemblance to Wales's famous baritone), and Sai and Tik, a young mechanic and his wife. They open container after container of amazing dishes that Tom identifies for my benefit. Two types of sticky rice, spicy duck stew with dill, sun-dried liver – firm, chewy and slightly sweet – morning glory with garlic, some sort of edible flower stuffed with pork, bamboo with mushrooms… So this is Laotian food – spicy and fragrant, with subtle French influences.

The dill – a European herb – is somewhat of a surprise, until Tom reminds me that Laos was a protectorate of France till 1954. While the three of them chat animatedly in Lao, I eat slowly, savouring unfamiliar flavour combinations. Lulled by the warmth and generosity of my companions, knowing that for tonight I can shelve my prickly self-reliance and not fret about my safety, and mellow from the beer buzz, I think about food trails left by ingredients that crossed continents over the centuries and irrevocably altered the cuisines they touched. Who can imagine Italian cuisine without tomatoes? The Irish culinary repertoire without potatoes? Indian curries without chillies? Hanoi's street food stalls without filled bánh mì baguettes?

My companions' laughter brings me back to the present. I accept the proffered container of spicy duck stew with both hands – as taught by Tom – and Tik motions for me to clean up the remains with clumps of sticky rice. My palpable enthusiasm prompts more mirth, and Sai says something to Tom while glancing at me. Tom explains that in Lao, 'greedy piggy' translates as 'dog'. But they are glad I like their food, he hastens to add.

When Sai and Tik leave, Tom and I sip the warm dregs in the bottoms of our bottles, and I ask him what brought him to this little working town with no hint of tourism, in the middle of the Laotian countryside. What keeps him here? I'm always keen to learn what motivates individuals to cross the world and move to remote places.

'I fell in love with the terrain here while motorbiking across southeast Asia. Off-road riding here is absolutely terrific. And I really like the people – some have very little, but if someone wants to build a house or just needs help, everyone pitches in.'

'Was it hard? When you first moved here, I mean? Not knowing the language…'

'Yep. A steep learning curve. Ten years on, I'm still learning the language. But there's genuine interaction with locals here, which you don't get in bigger, more touristy towns. They accept me here. I'm part of the community.'

* * * * *

The mountain range north of Kasi looms ominously in the back of my mind. To reach Luang Prabang, I have to cross this range, ascending a particularly hairy, unpaved section where lorries struggle with the incline. When one of my friends did this journey a couple of years back, that's where he wiped out, badly.

During the morning ride, Tom notices that I'm distracted. I confess to him my fear of the mountain road.

'Tell you what: we'll cut our morning lesson short, and I'll ride up with you to the top of the pass instead.'

My grateful expulsion of breath is audible.

Tom secures my gear to my scooter with brand new cables, and we ride up and down hairpin bends, past cultivated fields and jungle-clad mountains, until the road narrows, the incline steepens and thick fog shrouds the road's uppermost bends, the eroded, ochre-coloured mountainside towering above us.

'Just take it easy,' Tom cautions. 'Go slow and steady.'

He demonstrates. I follow his example. Paved road disappears and the two of us bounce on dirt and gravel in the cloud of dust raised by the lorry that passed us.

We stop and watch it ascend with difficulty along a stretch that looks almost vertical from our vantage point, its engine roaring. The lorry strains and falters, strains and falters. For a few heartbeats, it looks as if it could go either way. I frantically look for a place to dive to safety. The burnt-out lorry wrecks on the hillside below testify to the fate of drivers who didn't make it. But then, a final rev of the engine moves it beyond the precipitous section, and it's our turn.

'I'll go first,' Tom tells me. 'Just aim for that gap' – he points to the slightly less vertiginous, narrow stretch between twin mountains of gravel.

He kicks his motorbike into gear and surges uphill, skidding a little as he negotiates the steepest section.

Tom's voice in my ears: 'I'm through. Go ahead, I'm watching you.' I grip the handlebars and rev the clutch. My scooter jerks forward, while blood pounds in my temples and I hold on for dear life.

The scooter wobbles, bucks under me, and slides sideways on the loose scree. But just when I'm expecting to topple over, it bounces over the top of the incline, and holds its course.

I come to a stop and wait for the shaking in my limbs to die down. Shortly after, we reach the viewpoint at the top of the pass, obscured by fog.

Tom shakes hands with me, and wishes me well. As if heralding that my biggest challenges are now behind me, the clouds clear, giving me an all-encompassing glimpse of the valley below. The rest of my journey to Luang Prabang takes place on a beautifully paved road, past rice paddies, small villages and banana tree plantations.

Luang Prabang is a delight. It reminds me a bit of Hoi An – my favourite place in Vietnam, with its sedate pace of life and colourful lanterns lighting up the streets in the evenings. Except that Luang Prabang – the former royal city – is even more laid-back, less peopled. I message TL Motor Bikes in Vientiane to let them know where I am, and send a triumphant message to Tom:

'Made it to Luang Prabang! 4½ hours! Lovely ride! And I didn't even do Mick Jagger's funky chicken!'

Relieved to be on two feet again, I wander along the bank of the mighty Mekong, the quiet, frangipani-fringed streets, and pad barefoot along the smooth stone of riverside temples. Periodically check my phone for any messages from TL Motor Bikes. Nothing.

I dine out on minced pork with herbs cooked inside lemongrass, papaya spring rolls with a spicy fermented fish dip, dried buffalo meat, and betel leaves stuffed with aubergine paste and steamed local greens, and do my best to ignore the gnawing, growing fear.

My phone remains stubbornly silent.

In the evening, I end up at Icon Klub, decked out with black-and-white photos of Hollywood greats – the thimble-sized former haunt of my friend Iain, a fellow travel writer. Elizabeth from Transylvania mixes dirty martinis and margaritas with salty banter behind the dark-wood bar. It's my favourite sort of watering hole: quiet, mellow, the kind of place you end up lingering for hours. In an alcoholic haze, while trading travel stories with a middle-aged Hungarian lady and a young French woman, I dimly register the beeping of my phone.

It's Tom.

'Very proud of you… well done. And so fast, awesome.'

* * * * *

DINNER WITH TOM JONES

The following morning, there's a knock on my door. It's the guesthouse receptionist, brandishing my passport.

CHAPTER 12
THE ARCTIC CALLS

Arriving in Iqaluit, the capital of Nunavut, on Baffin Island – Canada's largest island, which sits between the Canadian landmass and Greenland – felt like entering a new country. The three-and-a-half hour flight north of Ottawa took us over a snow-mantled expanse of bare rock, dotted with dark meltwater lakes, and threaded through with a spider's web of icy fjords. The windswept, huddled look of the town by the water, with its unpaved streets, road signs in Inuktitut (an Inuit language, inscribed in phonetic symbols that Moravian missionaries helped to develop in order to convert the Inuit to Christianity) and snow-flecked tundra beyond the settlement all added to this sense of otherness.

In 2016, when chosen to update part of the Lonely Planet guide to Canada, I opted for the country's northernmost extremes without hesitation. Having absorbed a steady literary diet of folk tales of different cultures, including Inuit (or Eskimo) as a kid, I later moved on to accounts of Arctic exploration. I was drawn to descriptions of extremes, particularly the extreme north and the extreme south, and was captivated by the exploits of those who attempted to chart the unknown. It was about as far from the drab reality of our little Soviet town as you could get. I bussed it from Toronto to Vancouver as a backpacking teenager, but Nunavut – Canada's newest, largest and northernmost province, a sparsely populated, labyrinthine mass of fjords, islands and tundra nearly the same size as Mexico – was out of my reach back then, so I seized my chance to see places I'd never get to visit otherwise.

Again, there's the small matter of my eyes, shaped like my mother's. When she was little, kids in her class would tease her and call her 'Chinese'. After joking about that particular genetic imprint for years, telling my friends that I have a low tolerance for alcohol probably because I've got some Native American ancestry down the line, I finally decided to put my money where my mouth is and forked out for a DNA test with 23andMe. The results were taking forever to arrive.

In Iqaluit I was met by Jovan, employed by National Parks Canada, who gave me a tour of the town in his pick-up truck.

Iqaluit was abuzz with news.

'We've found HMS *Erebus* two years ago, and we think we are really close to finding HMS *Terror*,' Jovan told me. Of all the Arctic mysteries, the 1848 disappearance of Sir John Franklin's two ships has been most enduring. They became trapped in ice off the coast of King William Island, during their search for the Northwest Passage, and then both the ships and their crews disappeared without a trace. No expense was spared over the decades that followed to find out what happened to the expedition, but all efforts were in vain until 2014, when a combination of Inuit oral history and modern archaeology and science finally led to the discovery of HMS *Erebus*, almost perfectly preserved in shallow waters, some fifty miles south of King William Island.

Brimming with excitement, and originally thinking that I could perhaps interview underwater archaeologists in Gjoa Haven on King William Island, and travel to remote Inuit settlements such as Naujaat, Cambridge Bay and Grise Fiord, way north of Iqaluit, I was very much deflated to find out that my travel budget would just about cover return flights to nearby Pangnirtung and Kinngait (formerly Cape Dorset). 'Nearby' is a relative term. Distances between Nunavut's settlements are considerable. Beyond the few miles of gravel and tarmac in Iqaluit and the other Arctic towns, flying is the only way to travel and it's a terrific way to drift into insolvency.

'It's probably just as well that you decided not to camp,' Jovan continued, referring to the waterside patch of tundra in the Sylvia Grinnell Park that we'd just left. 'A polar bear rampaged through the campsite three days ago.'

I was profoundly relieved to be installed in one of the shared houses normally used by the National Parks Canada staff, since they were away on field trips in Quttinirpaaq and Ukkusiksalik National Parks up north, monitoring polar bears and musk ox – hairy prehistoric cattle that once shared the Earth with the woolly mammoth.

In the end, even my humble plans to fly to Pangnirtung and Kinngait were scuppered by the weather, as the fog caused by the July melt of the ocean ice grounded all flights. I ended up spending eight days in Iqaluit, wandering the dusty streets and the waterfront path, communing with croaking ravens that perched on a pair of enormous whalebone ribs that framed the tundra. I haunted Iqaluit's art shops, admiring the intricate scrimshaw, the bizarre, fanged shaman figures crafted from porous whalebone, the figurines of polar bears, walruses, igloos, Inuit hunters. The *inuksuit* (tundra markers), carved from midnight black-green soapstone, captivated me the most. They were shot through with lines of lighter green, like northern lights turned to stone.

Iqaluit grew on me. There's something about Canada's Arctic that draws a diverse crowd from various corners of the world, in contrast to my rather homogenous experiences in the extreme north elsewhere. The taxi driver who picked me up was a Lebanese refugee. He'd lived in Montreal prior to coming here, and liked it better, 'but there's much more work here.' Another taxi driver I got talking to was Somalian. Did he mind the cold and the months of darkness? No. After endless civil war back home, and a year and a half of hardship trying to reach Canada, the climate was a small price to pay for a peaceful life and a chance to provide for family left behind, he told me. From my National Park housing I moved on to Couchsurf with Theresa, a GP-anaesthesiologist who doubled as a gourmet chef, hanging out with her and her medic friends at the Black Heart Café, a speciality-coffee-and-pastrami-sandwich pocket of hipsterdom. And where in the world but Iqaluit could you attend a music performance by a Zimbabwean gospel singer fronting an Inuit band?

* * * * *

Inspired by a photo of a two-year-old Inuit girl tucking into some raw whale blubber in the *Nunatsiaq News*, Iqaluit's local newspaper, captioned 'Little Sawyer loves muktuk', I set off to find Iqaluit's 'country food' store, hoping to sample traditional Inuit fare. 'Country food' is a broad term that covers Inuit staples of seal, ptarmigan, arctic char, beluga whale and basically anything else that can be fished, trapped, hunted or harvested on the tundra and off the ice floes. But either the instructions I'd been given were off, or my sense of direction was, and I found myself at the Nunatta Sunakkutaangit Museum by the waterfront instead. Giving myself a break from the incessant dust and the cold, I wandered inside to peruse displays of traditional Inuit clothing, sleds, tools and weaponry. A porous, rather creepy likeness of an Inuit woman in a hooded parka, holding a decapitated seal's head

– both carved out of old whalebone – was holding my attention when another visitor spoke to me.

'Remarkable, aren't they?' The speaker was a tiny woman of Indian origin, and by 'tiny' I mean shorter than my own 5ft 0. 'Look at these' – she pointed to some familiar-looking objects with narrow slits for eyes. The Thule (ancestors of the Inuit) figured out centuries ago how to avoid snow blindness while hunting or just travelling on snow and ice by making snow goggles out of caribou antler or wood. I got into a spirited conversation with her about this remarkable testimony to human ingenuity and capacity for survival in one of the world's most inhospitable regions. We moved on to talk about hunting and the traditional Inuit diet. It's hard to imagine another culture whose diet has been as profoundly shaped by their natural environment as the Inuit.

'I'm really disappointed that I haven't been able to find traditional Inuit food in restaurants around here,' I confessed. 'Well, unless you count arctic char and grilled caribou at the Granite Room,' naming Iqaluit's fanciest dining establishment, way out of my price range.

'And you won't,' Shefali told me. 'The restaurants around here cater to government workers, folks working in mining and mineral exploration industries, and the occasional tourist. Inuit themselves don't eat at the restaurants, and you'd probably be disappointed in what you'd find in an average Inuit kitchen. "Country food" is eaten only on special occasions. For the most part, they eat a lot of junk food, which results in corresponding health issues.'

It turned out that Shefali was a doctor – an anaesthesiologist – from Saskatchewan, doing a stint at Iqaluit's Qikiqtani General Hospital – a large building painted with colourful animal murals that I passed the previous day. She invited me to dinner at the Frobisher

Inn, the chunky, austere monolith on the hill above where I was staying, and I gladly accepted. Sometimes, a chance meeting with a complete stranger offers a profound mental and emotional connection for a short, intense period of time. You talk for hours, more candidly than you would with most people in your life, and then likely never see that person again. Perhaps precisely because of that.

Shefali and I got a window booth in the Frob Kitchen, overlooking Iqaluit's mishmash of residential buildings, the white, igloo-like dome of St Jude's Cathedral, and the dark, bare rock spurs jutting out into the bay. She told me about some emergency cases she'd handled, such as a man she had to resuscitate on a plane, and an unfortunate injury here in Iqaluit. 'Sometimes things get rowdy after hours at the Legion and there are fist fights,' she informed me, referring to the Royal Canadian Legion that's locally renowned as the most hopping spot in town, attracting a motley crew of local Inuit, Somalian refugees and professionals from various corners of Canada. 'I once had to patch up a guy who got punched in the face and whose eyeball literally burst.' I winced, imagining the sickening squish of jelly.

Workwise, she split her time between Saskatchewan and Nunavut – where medical facilities are often limited and chronic health problems are endemic, and one has to find creative solutions while being sensitive to patients' cultural needs.

'This is the only hospital of any size in the whole of Nunavut, with massive distances between remote communities. So oftentimes, things like diabetes, heart disease and alcohol abuse-related liver malfunctions go untreated until it's too late,' Shefali said. 'For any serious surgery, they have to come here or even be flown south as far as Ottawa, which can be incredibly intimidating for someone who's only ever lived in a remote settlement of four hundred people. Here, the government provides free accommodation for family members travelling with the patient, because sometimes it's a mother of several children who can't be left alone, or an elderly person who's never been away from their close-knit community.'

This sounded very much like the Aboriginal experience in remote Outback communities.

We discussed how the human body is a remarkable machine that's geared towards survival – how it manages to adapt to any environment, and how for centuries, the Inuit managed to cater to all their nutritional needs by eating game, vitamin C-rich whale blubber, and berries in summer.

'Though Inuit have the legal right to hunt and pursue a traditional way of life to a certain extent,' Shefali continued, 'for many it's just not practical in their day-to-day lives. Plus, there's high unemployment and high rates of alcoholism, along with domestic violence and pretty shocking suicide rates. And a small income or unemployment cheque means that it's prohibitively expensive to buy healthy food.'

I shared with her my impressions of a book I'd just finished that had a profound impact on me: *The Long Exile* by Melanie McGrath. In the 1950s, the Canadian government decided, based on their own very limited knowledge of the Arctic and the paternalistic belief that they knew best what was good for the Inuit, to relocate eighty-seven Inuit from the east coast of Hudson Bay (Quebec) to Resolute Bay on Cornwallis Island and to Grise Fiord on Ellesmere Island – Canada's most northerly landmass. They promised them a land rich in game, ignorant of the barren landscape in which the Thule had only managed to subsist millennia ago, when the climate was warmer. The Inuit have traditionally relied for survival on their small, close-knit communities and on ancestral knowledge of hunting grounds, passed on to younger generations, whereas these settlers were dumped in places they had no knowledge of. They were told: 'if you don't like it up north, we'll send ships for you, and bring you back home.' Of course, that didn't happen. Among the deportees was one Josephie Flaherty, the unacknowledged half-Inuit son of Robert Flaherty. Flaherty Sr made a film in the 1920s, *Nanook of the North*, that captured the global imagination, but unlike that of the mythical Eskimo protagonist, Josephie's desperate struggle for survival was anything but Edenesque.

'Some of the earliest memories of his eldest daughter, Martha, who was five at the time, were about becoming her father's hunting partner. Inuit have to hunt in pairs. They'd go out into complete darkness and cold like you wouldn't believe, because if she didn't, her mother and her little brother and sister would have nothing to eat,' I continued.

Shefali listened attentively.

When Josephie had a nervous breakdown, his daughters became a frequent target of his rages. He died in exile, but his children came back south, and Martha became an outspoken advocate for Inuit rights.

'I can't even begin to imagine what they went through,' Shefali spoke up. 'Or how I'd maintain my sanity during months of complete darkness.'

Nor could I. Endless darkness does something to the human brain. In Norwegian, there's even an expression for it, which loosely translates as 'the Arctic calls'. It's when someone seemingly sane begins to do odd things. Obsessively counting the tinned food in their cupboards, over and over, or deliberately walking off a cliff. Maja-Stina – one of the two Norwegians I met on a Trans-Sib train – and her husband moved to Spitsbergen, Svalbard, where they, too, get to experience months of complete darkness (only two and a half months a year, mind). They assured me that it's more than bearable. 'We have movie nights at each other's houses, and Spitsbergen's a great place to raise the kids. Very close-knit community. We have to watch out for polar bears, though.'

Shefali confided in me her passion for her work in First Nations communities, during the course of which she'd go above and beyond the call of duty. 'Sometimes you get to know a patient over a long period of time, and you become friends. And then they pass away. One of my patients was terminally ill, and she'd asked me to fulfil her lifelong dream. So I took her boys to Disneyland. They're teenagers and they'd never been out of their small Métis community before, so they ran wild.' She smiled.

In turn, I told her of my past life as a nursing assistant, before I became a travel writer, of my own friendship with a terminally ill patient, and subsequent bereavement.

'I greatly respect people who do this for life,' I confessed. 'But I couldn't. You don't get used to loss.'

Shefali's eyes glittered with mirrored emotion.

By the time she and I parted company, it was almost midnight. Recognising a fellow independent traveller in me, she invited me to join her in Rwanda one year, where she does an annual residency while doubling as a squash coach for local children. We embraced like old friends, and I slowly made my way down the hill through the Arctic twilight.

* * * * *

At night, the shipping container warehouses that squat on the edge of the bay are briefly plunged into twilight as the sun dips below the horizon before rising again above the broken ice and the unpaved streets of Kinngait (meaning 'mountains' in Inuktitut) just a couple of hours later. It's not quite Grise Fiord – Canada's northernmost civilian settlement, numbering 148 souls – where the sun just circles endlessly overhead for weeks on end before disappearing for several months, but impressive nonetheless. A combination of jet lag and 'white nights' means that I'm wide awake in the wee hours of the morning, contemplating the settlement from my balcony at Dorset Suites, pretty much the only hotel in town. The hotel sits on a craggy little outcrop, the hilly topography of Kinngait dotted with colourful single-storey houses. Many buildings are on metal stilts because of the permafrost. I savour the moment. It has taken me three years to get here.

As it's my second trip to Canada's northern reaches, I'm better prepared for the Arctic's travel challenges, and hit Kinngait at the very beginning of my trip, allowing room for error, and the weather cooperates. I have three tasks on my agenda: to meet some of the town's Inuit artists, to find some authentic Inuit food, and to hike to the historic Thule remains on Mallik Island across the bay. The previous day I wandered by the gleaming new Kenojuak Cultural Centre and Print Shop, hoping to catch some artists at work, only to find the place inexplicably closed, with a cryptic sign on the door: 'Walrus and polar bear penis bones. Size doesn't matter. $60.'

When I ask Silaqqi, the cheerful young hotel manager, about it, she cackles madly.

'Polar bear penises are a lot smaller. Who'd want to be a bear? Walrus is bigger!' She calms down. 'Walrus penis bones have traditionally been used as clubs here in the north, and our artists use them for carvings.'

She shows me the Dorset Suites collection of Inuit art, the hotel's crimson walls decked out with framed original prints by some of the town's most famous names: bold, cheerful owls and loons by Kenojuak Ashevak, coloured pencil drawings by Pudlo Pudlat. Kinngait has been renowned for its Inuit art since the late 1950s, when its resident artists pioneered modern printmaking. In recent years, Inuit stencil prints, lithographs and soapstone and whalebone sculpture have enjoyed a rocketing surge in popularity worldwide, mirroring a similar rise in demand for other indigenous art, such as Aboriginal paintings.

Second time lucky: when I walk by the Kenojuak Cultural Centre in the morning, I run into a compact, mustachioed Inuit man in his fifties, getting into a pick-up truck. It's Joemie, the manager. When I tell him that I'm very interested in seeing local artists at work, he invites me to accompany him. 'I'm going to look for some carvers, to take pictures, and then I can show you around.'

I hop in.

Apparently, on a fine summer day like today, you'd often find men sitting outside their houses, working chunks of white marble, black marble, soapstone and serpentine stone with power tools on makeshift tables made of giant cable spools. Disappointingly, the streets turn out to be carver-free, apart from a single teenager hunched over his power tool and chunk of stone. 'It's because there's no wind today,' Joemie explains. 'They like to work when it's windy, because it blows away the stone dust.'

When I remark that the artists seem to start young here, judging by the boy we'd passed, he nods.

'Many get started when they are kids, and the skills are passed down from father to son. One of our best artists is David Pudlat – he's only fourteen years old but he's been drawing and carving for years, and his work sells at the co-op.'

'Do they work inside in winter?'

'No, outside – they're used to the cold. There's no room to work inside the houses.'

'Your summers seem rather brisk.'

Joemie laughs.

'This is nothing. Now, last year we had a really cold summer. But this year the ice is melting early and my wife has already found a mosquito in our house.'

Arctic mosquitoes are the most voracious I've ever met. I've already had an encounter with them while looking for bison in the Wood Buffalo National Park near Fort Smith in the Northwest Territories. The second I stepped out of the car, a dense cloud of bloodsuckers enveloped me like a living shroud, biting me right through my hiking trousers and shirt, getting in my eyes, nose and mouth, and generally not giving a damn about the all-natural citronella bug spray that I'd generously doused myself with. I lasted about thirty seconds before darting back inside my vehicle and slapping madly at my face.

It's the same during Nunavut's brief summer, according to Silaqqi.

'When I have to go outside, I put on two pairs of pants and a sweater, no matter how warm it is. I just hold my breath and run,' she told me.

The photographic mission becomes an impromptu tour of the town. Joemie drives me up a dusty road into the hills for a grand view of the bay. I ask him about hunting and 'country food'.

'There is a quota on polar bears and narwhals (Joemie pronounces it 'nar-whales'), but not on walruses or seals. We also fish for char. Have you tried *pipsi* – dried char? It's like fish jerky.'

'No, just cooked char.'

'It's good raw too, like sushi. Slightly salty if you catch it in the sea.'

At a picnic ground a short drive from the settlement, there are some bleached bones on the beach.

'That's the spine of a bowhead whale. We caught it in 2007.'

'Do people here hunt whale every year?'

'No, the licence is too expensive. It's a shame, because nothing beats *muktuk* (raw whale blubber). You cut the nar-whale open, and it looks like watermelon inside. Marble-white skin and fat, pink flesh. My wife, she chops it up into small pieces and we eat it raw, or sometimes with soy sauce.'

They hunt belugas, too, with harpoons on motorised boats, exactly as their ancestors would have done (minus the motors).

I express my repeated disappointment over my inability to find 'country food' anywhere.

'The best place would be at an Inuit celebration. Eating whale's a real delicacy for us as well. Back in the day, my grandfather would go hunting for whale with the rest of the men, and one whale would feed the whole community for months.'

I ask Joemie about *igunaq*, seal or walrus meat, buried in the ground in summer, where it ferments through the autumn and freezes in winter, ready to be consumed during the lean spring months.

'I love it. It has a really strong flavour to it. But my grandkids' – Joemie assumes a child's expression of disgust – 'want burgers and fries instead. And don't even talk to them about *kiviaq*!' *Kiviaq* is essentially a giant sausage made by stuffing a seal skin full of auks (seabirds), beaks and feathers and all, squeezing the air out, sewing the whole thing up and fermenting it for seven months or so under a heavy stone in the permafrost. Even with my firm belief that you have to break bread with people and eat what they eat in order to truly immerse yourself in their culture, the idea of chomping down on a partially decomposed bird gives me pause.

'We hunt caribou sometimes also,' Joemie continues, 'but in recent years we haven't seen many around. They say it's climate change or whatever. When I was a kid, my mum would make *akutaq* – she'd whip together caribou fat, seal fat and berries – it was creamy and sweet. Better than ice cream! And we'd dry the rest of the caribou, turn it into *mikku*.'

During our drive back, we run into Joemie's elderly parents, piling into a van with some women and children. Greetings in Inuktitut are exchanged. 'They're going camping,' Joemie explains. The ice has broken up, and there's a flurry of activity by the bay. Motorised canoes are being loaded up as families prepare to navigate between ice floes en route to camping grounds.

'My folks like living above the bay. That way they can see what's coming in. They call me at 5am sometimes: "Come quick, son, there's belugas in the bay!"'

Back at the Kenojuak Cultural Centre, Joemie walks me around the very modern, multi-room art centre, where several artists are busy drawing or else inking plates for lithograph printing.

'The Canadian government set up the West Baffin Eskimo Co-operative here in 1958, when I was very little,' Joemie explains. 'It was a way of providing work for the local community, and the first generation of artists drew and carved what they saw in their everyday life – animals, hunting scenes. Now we have dozens of artists working full-time. Recently, I suggested to the artists that maybe they should try doing something more contemporary' – he ushers me into a spare room – 'and here's the result.' He grins. Among the carvings, there's a small soapstone TV and an Inuit man in a hooded parka, carved out of serpentine, happily plugged into a tiny iPod and a pair of minuscule white marble earphones.

Some travellers object to this intrusion of modern life. They deem these carvings less 'authentic' than traditional hunting scenes, as if the Inuit exist in some time warp. But these carvings are an accurate reflection of what it means to be a twenty-first-century Inuit.

I mention to Joemie the massive mural of Kenojuak Ashevak's wonderful 'Enchanted Owl' that greeted me upon arrival at Iqaluit's new airport. He nods.

'She was one of our best artists, and it's great that she's recognised for her talent now, but she died in poverty, without reaping the rewards.'

He glances around the workshop.

'I hope that our young people are recognised for their talent while they're still alive to enjoy it.'

I hope so too. There are depressing parallels between the challenges faced by Inuit artists and Aboriginal Australian ones: undercutting of their craft by the proliferation of imitation art, inadequate protection of cultural property, unscrupulous art dealers.

* * * * *

I ask Silaqqi if it's okay for me to go for a wander in the hills surrounding the town, having been emboldened by my stay in Pangnirtung – a dusty little town built around a former whale blubber processing station, dramatically located on a fjord – prior to my arrival in Kinngait. I turned up in Pang with no accommodation booked, and Markus, the tiny German owner of Fjordview B&B, who reminded me of Engywook from the film *The NeverEnding Story*, generously laid out a mattress for me on the floor of his office. In the evenings, I hung out with his guests, a film crew from Toronto that was shooting an alien invasion film, and with Markus himself. He'd previously been employed as a nurse in Iqaluit, then became convinced that 'working for the man' in any capacity was wrong. In Pang, he was trying to educate visitors genuinely interested in Inuit culture about the challenges the community faces, and wasn't impressed by the apathy displayed by most outsiders.

'Every year, cruise ships plying the Northwest Passage dock here, the passengers roll out, stare at locals, and make very little effort to interact with them.'

He packed me off to the Uqqurmiut Centre for Arts & Crafts to chat to the local weavers, producing Inuit tapestries on their looms, and then sent me on a lofty hike up Mount Duval above the town for a bird's eye view of the fjord, assuring me that I was unlikely to get stalked by polar bears.

'Peter Kilabuk – a local guide – is dropping off some hikers in Auyuittuq National Park tomorrow,' Marcus told me when I returned, uneaten. 'Why don't you go with him?'

The following day, as the motorboat neared the soaring cliffs looming on either side of the fjord, and the water changed from aquamarine to slate-grey as the sea met the summer meltwater, Peter commented that normally, at this time of year, the fjord is still ice-bound. The climate has been noticeably changing over the years, and here in the Arctic, that's felt particularly keenly. Hikers bound for Nunavut's most accessible national park have traditionally only had a window of several weeks to complete a snow-free trek, but that's no longer the case. Up close, the cliffs looming on either side of the fjord were off-the-scale enormous. The two hikers – two teachers in their twenties from Toronto – were already tiny specks in the distance, having begun their sixty-mile trek through the deep valley of 'the land that never melts'. Peter pointed to a twin-peaked monolith: 'That's Mount Asgard; it appeared in the parachute scene from *The Spy Who Loved Me*. I brought the film crew here.'

'Are they likely to run into any polar bears on the way?' I was anxious for the teachers' welfare.

'Polar bears only tend to hang out at the north end of the valley, by the coast. There's an emergency shelter by the fjord; the guys will wait there to be picked up. We hardly ever get polar bears around here, near Pang; there's nothing for them to eat.'

But Kinngait is not Pangnirtung and Silaqqi looks at me as if I've suddenly sprouted horns.

'Are you nuts? There are bears around. You need a guide with a shotgun.'

'We don't go tenting anymore,' she continues. 'Or if we do, we stay next to a cabin. We used to camp wherever we pleased, but these days it's just too dangerous. When I was little, my friends and I used to play on the hills across the bay and on the ice. Nowadays, I don't let my son even near the water.'

Polar bears have been getting closer and closer to human settlements over the years.

'What do you do if they get close to town?'

'People scare them off. If you shoot one above the quota, you're not allowed to keep it. If it's a female, that's minus two from the next year's quota.'

Encouraging the Inuit to pursue their traditional way of life, the Canadian government exempts them from national restrictions on hunting and allows a yearly quota of animals.

'One time we caught a seal and left it under cover near the tent,' Silaqqi tells me. 'We woke up to find a young bear eating it. It didn't even move. It wasn't afraid of us at all. Then our little dog – a dachshund – went and sat by it. And it ran away, but only when the dog started barking at it… One of our neighbours found their summer cabin with the window gone. Not broken – missing; the bear peeled it right off.'

I tell Silaqqi about my first impressions of Churchill, Manitoba – the 'polar bear capital of the world' that tourists converge on every October to trundle through the tundra in special bear-proof safari vehicles. But hungry bears hang around in the summer, and there's even a polar bear 'gaol' where they put repeat offenders.

She shudders.

'Churchill is the scariest place. Everyone leaves their doors unlocked because if there's a bear, you want to get into the nearest house, quick.'

I know what she means. The *nanuk* ('great white being') was very much on my mind as I walked around Churchill, hypervigilant, on the lookout for hiding places. An internal monologue took place constantly, along the lines of: 'There's no point in crawling under this car because the bear will just flip it over, but I can scoot under the foundations of that house.' You can't outrun, outswim or outclimb it, and it actively hunts humans.

The following day, Silaqqi drops me off next to a nondescript house along the coastal road. A slight, mustachioed Inuit man in his sixties emerges, carrying a rifle. Pootoogook beckons me to follow him past the twisted metal and burnt-out car carcasses of the town dump, and on to the ice.

'If you see any yellowish ice moving, tell me,' he instructs me. 'Because that'll be a bear.'

Kinngait is not actually part of Baffin Island, where the majority of Nunavut's settlements are located. It sits on a small rocky island of its own, south of Baffin Island's Foxe Peninsula, and the uninhabited Mallik Island is its closest neighbour. On the ice, as I waddle after Pootoogook in my loaned rubber boots, I feel very exposed. Pumped full of adrenalin, I imagine that this is how Inuit hunters must have felt much of the time. Stalking prey while trying not to become prey. But there are no polar bears to be seen as we make our way along the pebbled strip of shore hemmed in between the ice of the bay and reddish-brown cliffs.

Pebbles give way to spongy tundra. A wooden boardwalk skirts a small, seasonal lake, leading to the remains of several *tuniqtait* – winter houses of the Thule – with their attendant detritus from ancient feasts: mounds of bones and shellfish rubble. Only the stone foundations remain, but Pootoogook explains that they would've had roofs made of whale rib bones and animal hides, topped with sod for insulation, plus earthen walls.

'See this long, narrow entryway? They'd block the passage from the inside to stop the cold air from coming in.'

'But what would they use for heating?'

'They'd have used soapstone lamps with walrus fat for light and heat. It was warmer a thousand years ago.'

When we cross the island, Pootoogook points out something that looks like a large stone cairn.

'Old fox trap. When my wife was a girl, it was her job to check her family's traps.'

He must be older than I thought. I'd read that these hollow stone pyramids with a hole in the roof have been out of use since the 1940s. The Inuit women would place meat inside as bait, and once the fox climbed in, it was stuck.

A short walk away is an *inukshuk*, a vaguely human-shaped tundra sentinel made of stones.

'It means "shellfish found here",' Pootoogook explains. 'Different *inuksuit* mean different things. My ancestors built them to tell each other if there's danger here, or good hunting. To show each other the way.'

I stare at the *inukshuk*. So did mine. Perhaps.

Weeks after spitting in a test-tube and mailing it off, I got my DNA results from 23andMe. Most of the findings – my being an Ashkenazi Jew – were expected. There was one big surprise, though. Some 0.01 percent of my DNA on my mother's side was attributed not to Mongolians, as I'd suspected, but to Alaskan Inuit! 23andMe update their results as they get more data, and they eventually clarified this to mean 'indigenous Siberian from the extreme Far East', namely, Yupik Eskimos, or Russian Inuit, though this cannot be confirmed with any degree of accuracy. When the ancestors of present-day Alaskan and Canadian Inuit crossed the Bering Strait, the ancestors of the Russian Inuit stayed put. I've been wracking my brains ever since, trying to figure out how I could have a full-blooded indigenous Siberian ancestor dating back to the eighteenth century. The only plausible explanation is that my mother's family was exiled from Western Russia to Siberia, and that one of the women had a baby with an Inuit man. It had to have been a Jewish *woman*, because Jewish men who fathered children outside the Jewish community were typically ostracised, along with their offspring, whereas children of Jewish women were accepted, regardless of paternity. Then somehow, this hardy Jewish woman made it back to Western Russia along with her child, and this child turned out to be my great-great-great-great-great-great-great-great-grandparent. So this tundra survival lore is potentially part of my story too.

Pootoogook and I get back to town without seeing any polar bears, to my relief and disappointment. I also failed in my quest; Inuit specialities are nowhere to be found.

But all is not lost: it's musk ox meatloaf night at the Dorset Suites. That'll have to do.

CHAPTER 13
EYEBALL TACOS
AND RENEGADE SAINTS

The taxi drops me by Café Praga. There, hunched over her notebook and busy scribbling away, is Celeste. She sees me approaching and smiles. We hug. I order *chilaquiles verdes* – tortilla chips smothered in tomatillo salsa, topped with white, crumbly cheese and accompanied by the ubiquitous, comforting brown smear of *frijoles refritos* (refried pinto beans). It finally feels like I'm in Mexico proper.

Celeste is the cool older sister I've always wanted. Her life reads like a novel, and she's one of the very few women writers I know who's fearless, resourceful and happy to take on 'machete' gigs in remote places. In other words: my ideal role model. I originally met her in Paramaribo, Suriname, in 2012, while covering the Guianas for a rival guidebook. Together, we did test-tube shots of rum at Paramaribo's rum distillery, and compared notes on our ventures into the Surinamese jungle. I ended up road tripping across French Guiana with Celeste and her aunt Kem, which involved cuddling sloths in a sloth sanctuary and watching a Russian rocket take off at the space centre. I watched with admiration as Celeste nailed a large tropical cockroach with her sandal at twenty paces at Restaurant La Petite Maison in Cayenne – a skill she'd perfected during twelve years spent on a remote Tahitian atoll – and she taught me how to get red wine out of a white shirt (rub salt into your bosom). Since then, we've met in a variety of places, ranging from Melaka and Singapore to Brighton, and now here we are in Tijuana, one of Mexico's dodgiest cities.

I survey Avenida Revolución – TJ's main drag. It's lined with pharmacies, cafés, tacky gift shops selling Guatemalan ponchos. Three blocks north of us is the gleaming metal Arco Monumental that's one of the first things day trippers from San Diego see when crossing the border into Mexico. I've been walking this same street for almost two decades. For an eighteen-year-old backpacker, Tijuana was a foray into a more chaotic, more colourful world. Pungent markets with mountains of chillies and hanging piñatas, donkeys painted to look like zebras, posters advertising woman-on-woman action in seedy bars, the smell of exhaust fumes, spicy food and piss – the last particularly noticeable when you traverse the bridge across the Tijuana river.

Tijuana provided me with my first introduction to Mexican food. I tried prawn ceviche here – from a cart on a street corner, gastric repercussions be damned. As a nineteen-year-old, I also had my first ever blowout meal in TJ, in a decades-old restaurant inside some elegant colonial building where the dark, earthy flavours of ink-black *cuitlacoche* (corn fungus) mingled with a silky web of melted cheese and tangy tomatillo salsa. But it's the tacos that made the biggest impression during my first and subsequent travels in Mexico.

They are deceptively simple, these yellow or purple tortilla circles made of cornflour, water and salt. 'Maize has kept Mexico fed since before the Aztecs,' the proprietress of the family-run Tortilleria Zaragoza, a small tortilla factory in Mazatlán, told me during an earlier research trip to Mexico's Pacific coast. She demonstrated how the corn was first soaked in limewater (undergoing nixtamalisation) before being hulled, in order to maximise the amount of nutrients humans could get out of it. It was then ground into flour, and turned into tortillas. 'The Aztecs knew this but the Spanish conquistadores didn't,' she continued. 'So they ate corn plain, and died of malnutrition.'

Hot from the griddle, with a myriad toppings and drizzled with a rainbow of fresh salsas – nothing captures the culinary diversity of Mexico's different regions quite like these wonderfully inexpensive edible morsels. I've eaten them topped with *flor de calabaza* (squash blossom) and goat's cheese in Mexico City, *cabeza* (possibly beef cheek, or some other part of a cow's head) in Sayulita, *cochinita pibil* (slow cooked pork, Maya-style) in Tulum, fried tripe in Puerto Vallarta, cabrito (roast goat) in Monterrey, crunchy breakfast tacos topped with stewed *machaca* (Sinaloan dried beef) from El Veneno (the Poisoner) in Mazatlán… Celeste interrupts my waxing nostalgic about my taco map of Mexico by saying: 'I'm glad you're so enthusiastic about tacos, because that's what we're having for lunch.'

I'm shadowing Celeste for a few days while she researches TJ for a guidebook chapter on Baja California. My job is to provide insightful food and drink commentary as she reports on TJ's renaissance as a serious foodie destination, complete with edgy new fusion restaurants, craft beer breweries and, of course, old-school taco joints. Tucked away down a small street behind Mercado Cuauhtémoc, the taco joint in question is a simple scattering of white Formica tables and plastic chairs, with bowls of fresh tomatillo salsa, and one speciality on the menu: cow eyeball tacos. Celeste feigns a lack of hunger, assigning the role of food taster to me.

The tacos, when they arrive, are surprisingly inoffensive. I'm not sure what I expected. Perhaps an entire eyeball, looking at me accusingly from its warm tortilla pillow. Instead, it's chopped-up, miscellaneous meat with a pleasant, soft texture and delicate flavour, studded with bits of crunchy white onion and fragrant with fresh cilantro. Later on in the trip, when I leave Celeste to do my own research along Mexico's Pacific coast, I reprise my eyeball consumption at what has become one of my favourite eateries of all time. It's La Flechita Roja, a nondescript 24-hour taco stand on the busy main road in Zihuatanejo – the little seaside town where Andy and Red allegedly meet up at the end of the *The Shawshank Redemption*. Insomniacking, I'd perch on a counterside stool in the wee hours of the morning to observe Mexico's classic nose-to-tail dining. The two cooks would methodically grill and chop snouts, brains, gelatinous parts of hooves, eyeballs and tongue, gruffly serving tacos topped with the stuff to truckers and other assorted night-time clientele.

'Not bad,' I comment to Celeste, picking at the remnants of the eyeball. 'But it's only the second most memorable meal I've had in TJ. The last time I was here, ten years ago, I found myself whizzing around on the back of some random guy's motorbike, with a roast chicken strapped to my back.'

Celeste laughs.

So I tell her about my Couchsurfing stay with Chay, a secretive American guy in his late twenties, in a dodgy part of TJ a few blocks west of the main drag. I briefly wondered if I'd ever be seen alive again when the gate of his marble home swung shut behind me, since Chay was decidedly cagey about what he did for a living. And I did see Mexican guys briefly dropping by his mansion all hours of the day before disappearing again. But he proved to be an interesting host, putting me up in one of his many empty rooms, teaching me to shoot his BB gun and keeping me fed. Dodging TJ's chaotic traffic on his motorbike added a frisson of excitement to our forays for takeout.

'The last time I had a girl ride pillion, she fell off,' Chay would tell me conversationally, turning his head towards me while riding, while I mentally screamed at him to keep his eyes on the road.

There were other Couchsurfing adventures as well.

When it rained, the steep cobbled streets of San Miguel de Allende, lined with seventeenth- and eighteenth-century stucco houses in shades of vermilion and ochre, became a water slide. I'd fallen over quite spectacularly during my walk into the colonial heart of town from the bus station on the cactus-studded urban fringes. I wasn't entirely sure why I'd ended up in San Miguel, beyond liking the sound of the name. Before arriving there, I emailed a fellow Couchsurfer, L'Africa, an African American woman in her early twenties, asking if I could crash at her place.

She wrote back. 'I'm away at the moment, but you can stay with my boyfriend.'

When he opened the door of his art studio to let me in, her boyfriend, E C Bell, turned out to be a compact man in his sixties, with a quizzical look on his face and a halo of wild steel-grey hair, reminding me of Doc from *Back to the Future*.

His studio, where he'd made up the sofa for me, was a shrine to L'Africa. There were wall-to-wall paintings of her, her image captured in all her naked glory. Against the backdrop of a seafoam-green wooden door, stretching to greet the morning sun that illuminated her concave stomach and her pendulous breasts. In a doorway, leaning casually on the door frame, her bare feet pressed tightly against one another. On all fours, back arched, seemingly tossing her mane of black hair over her shoulder. E C caught me looking at that one. 'That's my favourite position… ahem… pose,' he hastily corrected himself and cackled.

Turned out that L'Africa was his muse as well as his lover.

'We moved down here from Charleston, South Carolina,' E C told me. 'Charleston's my home town, but they're not very tolerant of interracial relationships up there.'

'What about her family?'

'Oh, I get on great with her folks. They're the same age as me. But there wasn't much of a market for my art up north.'

Whereas here, EC fits right in. San Miguel has been a refuge for artists and other bohemians for decades, largely thanks to the efforts of Stirling Dickinson – a Chicago native and local oddball who moved here in 1937 and ended up founding an art institute in a local convent.

EC took me for a wander around San Miguel, through the thickets of nopal cacti on the hillside above town, along the narrow cobbled streets. We ended up dawdling in the Jardín Allende, the park next to the main square in the heart of town, its topiary overlooked by the pointed neo-Gothic spires of the Parroquia de San Miguel Arcángel. As dusk fell, taco stand activity around the square reached a crescendo, with competing plumes of fragrant smoke rising from the grills.

We joined a line of locals leading to a stand where a middle-aged woman was spooning nopal, *chicharrón* (fried pork rinds) and chicken stew on to corn tortillas, warmed on the griddle by her daughter. I munched mine, standing up, in silent contentment.

'I love this place,' EC confessed, and I nodded in agreement, thinking he meant the taco stand. But no – he was talking about San Miguel.

'I first came here in the '70s,' he continued. 'I needed to away out in a hurry.'

'Oh?'

'I just came back from Nam,' he explained. 'One day you're shooting at the Viet Cong in the jungle, and the next day, it's "Hi Mom". I was all kinds of fucked up. Then I came home, and nothing. No government support. No therapy for what we went through.

No acknowledgement, even. Some of my buddies ended up killing themselves. Drinking themselves to death, or worse. I knew I had to get away when a guy cut me up in his car and ended up with my machete pressed against his throat. So I came here.'

Back at EC's place, we end up sitting on his bed in the sparsely furnished, surprisingly austere – given the exuberance of canvases downstairs – bedroom. Later, when I'd recount this encounter to friends back home, and tell them how within ten minutes of meeting my host, I found myself being shown naked photos of him and his lover, taken by an internationally renowned photographer, they were convinced that EC was trying to seduce me, and that I was naïve for thinking otherwise. But while the people closest to me have better social skills and are generally better at reading people, I feel I have the edge over them when it comes to interaction with those who operate outside the confines of society's norms. The oddballs. I see them as life's fellow travellers and have boundless empathy for them. So I understood exactly where EC was coming from when he wanted to tell me about his life. Two divorces, four beautiful daughters, his worries about L'Africa. He was just lonely and missing his young lover.

'Maybe she'll meet some hot young guy in Charleston…' he said mournfully, staring off into the distance, his voice trailing off. So I listened to him, while cradling a handful of black kitten – EC's other companion, Pancho. Later, as I lay on the sofa in the main studio space, with the kitten purring loudly and kneading my chest, I sleepily contemplated how there's nothing in the world that's softer or sharper than a cat (ow, ow, my boob).

I was sorry to leave.

* * * * *

The evening finds me and Celeste in a reflective mood at a rooftop beer bar, nursing our respective flights of craft beer while looking out over TJ's rooftops and the metal Arco Monumental. Beyond it is the United States border, which I may not cross. The setting sun illuminates the underside of gathering storm clouds.

My Tijuana visits of years past took on darker hues, as well. Across the street from the café where Celeste and I had breakfast is Hotel Caesar's, a nondescript-looking but locally legendary place, where the Caesar salad was invented by chef César Cardini in 1927. Hollywood celebrities would flock to the wood-panelled restaurant/bar during the Prohibition era in search of both the salad and booze. I've tried the salad once. But, more memorably, I stayed at Caesar's on three occasions between 2005 and 2007, in order to meet up with Forrest, the troubled man from across the border whom I was trying to save from drug addiction. There was the agony of uncertainty, the endless pacing of my generic, beige room. (Will he turn up? Will he 'get lost' on the way to TJ again?) One time, Forrest failed to turn up and, propelled by anger, I decided to head south rather than wait around.

'It pushed me to travel further afield,' I continue, wondering what Celeste must think of my former timidity. She'd gone to university in Chiang Mai, backpacked for months in Indonesia and sailed off to live on a remote Tahitian atoll, all in her early twenties, whereas it wasn't until I was twenty-five that I made my major solo forays into the non-English-speaking world. 'I'd take Greyhound buses from TJ all over Mexico,' I tell her.

There was the 24-hour jaunt to the very bottom of Baja California, and watching the sun set over a natural stone arch in the sea near Cabo San Lucas. The sunrise over Mazatlán on the Pacific coast from a hilltop viewpoint. My face painted – for the first time in my life! –

as a *calavera* – a skull – during the Day of the Dead celebrations in Puerto Vallarta, giddy from the revelry of the crowds on the *malecón* (waterfront promenade) and the cup of firewater that someone handed me at the local cemetery. What a wonderful idea, I thought at the time: going picnicking amidst the gravestones and exchanging gossip with one's departed loved ones, then leaving them to feast on the essence of your food afterwards. Finding myself in Chichén Itzá – an ancient Maya city on the Yucatán peninsula – on the day of the spring equinox, when the shadow creeping down the steps of the main pyramid resembles a serpent. Pacing the colonial cobbles of Oaxaca, scrambling up pyramids of the pre-Columbian site of Monte Albán and the Aztec stronghold of Teotihuacán, in awe of these intact relics of mighty ancient civilisations.

Celeste has felt the pull of Mexico herself. She and her husband are considering a move from Oregon to Baja, or even to one of TJ's beachside communities (though that idea is nixed on our first night in Tijuana, when we stay in an apartment in a sketchy part of town, and hear gunshots). As for me, gunshots remind me of my previous stays in TJ, and I stiffen involuntarily with every sharp retort coming out of the dark. There was shouting back then, too. The last time I'd ever see him, Forrest and I had a spectacular fight.

'You can't save me!' he snarled, the two of us facing off against each other across the room, my arguments and entreaties powerless against the demons of his depression, addiction and self-loathing.

'No, perhaps I can't,' I relented, lowering my voice. 'But you can save yourself. And you're worth saving.'

Silently, I reflect that maybe my desire to help Forrest all those years ago wasn't just pure sympathy for someone less fortunate than myself. It was also a desire for atonement. Perhaps, had I succeeded in saving Forrest from himself, it would've somehow made up for my failure to protect my mother and sister from family violence during my childhood and teenage years.

'He did, eventually,' I tell Celeste. 'Save himself, that is.' She nods sympathetically, having heard the whole story about Forrest, and having known people herself who'd struggled with substance abuse. 'But his getting clean had nothing to do with me.'

And in hindsight, my getting banned from the States was a blessing in disguise because coming to TJ was too expensive, too inconvenient. It put a decisive end to what hadn't ever really been a functioning relationship.

Celeste and I spend our few days together admiring TJ's edgy street art, people-watching from hipster taco joints, touring Mexico's compact wine country, loving the friendly wineries but mostly not loving the vinegar-like tipples, discussing future travels, aspirations. Moreover, near our apartment, we stumble across a hole-in-the-wall run by a delightful woman from Oaxaca, who makes the best *mole negro* – a complex, spicy, chocolatey sauce that uses chicken as the vehicle for showcasing its complexity – that I've tried outside the fanciest restaurants in her home town. With Celeste's help – a traveller with whom I'm entirely simpatico – and her easy, uncomplicated companionship, I can feel the tears in my life mending, and new impressions of TJ obscuring my older, darker ones.

* * * * *

'There's someone we'd like you to meet,' John tells me as I sit with him and Christina in Lupita, a casual waterfront eatery in the tiny pueblo of Aticama in Nayarit – a tiny grid of streets hugging the bend of Mexico's Pacific coast highway. Waves splash against the terrace as we tuck into grilled lobster, our elbows sticking to the plastic tablecloth in the heat.

John and Christina – a curly-haired, exuberant, retired American couple – and I met a decade prior in Chile. Since then, we'd kept in touch, and like a number of older friends I'd made on the road, over the years they sent me more than one invitation to come and stay with them.

The 'someone' turns out to be Trilby, a smiling Texan native with a wonderful name, who arrives in a flurry of peasant blouse and long skirt. It transpires that she's the girlfriend of Jimmy, an attorney-at-law who moonlights as a blues guitarist and splits his time between Narayit and Austin, Texas. And who also happened to have been Scharlette Holdman's best friend.

The year before, in 2016, Scharlette emailed me out of the blue.

'I went to Mecca,' she wrote. 'Just call me Hajjah Scharlette.' I could almost hear her chuckling with glee. She explained her reasons for conversion: 'Our Guantanamo clients are Muslim and they take pure joy when they convert someone, plus they trust Muslims but not non-Muslims… We have to do everything possible to be close to our clients whose lives and cultures and histories are not ours for the asking until we demonstrate we might be worthy.'

She never did anything by half, and converting to Islam in order to do her work more effectively was just *so* Scharlette. After the Tsarnaev case that I was unable to join her on, she threw herself into helping British lawyer Clive Stafford Smith (of Reprieve) with the Guantanamo Bay cases, and her travels took her to Saudi Arabia, Jordan, Kuwait, Qatar, Pakistan – destinations she travelled to with her insatiable curiosity, without fear or apprehension. I last saw her in late 2012, in London. I crashed in her hotel room, and we devoured the contents of her minibar and talked late into the night.

Months after Scharlette's email to me, David, my attorney-in-law friend with whom I worked in Ukraine, forwarded me the final email he'd received from her:

'Thank you for carrying this burden and love all these years,' it read. 'I love you. I have stage IV cancer all over the place, inoperable. I have a few months. I want you to know how much you mean to me, you rascal, radical, revolutionary. Thank you for always making my life's work a part of yours.'

On July 12, 2017, Scharlette passed away at the age of seventy, leaving behind a remarkable legacy. When I posted her obituary in *Time* magazine on Facebook, John and Christina got in touch to tell me that they knew someone who knew Scharlette, proving how true the Spanish saying is: 'El mundo es un panuelo' ('The world is a handkerchief').

When Trilby – who's heard so much about Scharlette but never met her – and I get into a long discussion about what she was like as a person, and what it had been like to work for her, Christina and John leave us alone to compare stories. Later, Trilby introduces me to Jimmy. He and I connect via a video link and I finally get to hear about Scharlette's last months from someone who'd known her best, and who was present at the time. Who tells me that my workaholic friend who hardly ever took time off, even when seriously ill, was finally able to have one last beach holiday in Florida, surrounded to the last by her sisters, children and close friends. It provides me with the ending I hadn't realised I'd needed.

* * * * *

After catching up with Christina and John, I head to Mexico City for a few days. There is one last thing I need to do before I depart from Mexico.

Down the nondescript Calle Alfarería in Mexico City's Tepito neighbourhood, known for drug busts and pirated goods, is the original altar to Santa Muerte, Mexico's controversial skeletal saint. She's dressed in bridal white and carries a bouquet of white lilies. La Flaca, La Santísima Muerte – the Skinny One, Holiest Death – is the patron saint of the dispossessed, the one that you turn to when you have nowhere else to go. Drug runners and robbers pray to her for success before doing a job, and her protection extends to Mexico's marginalised LGBT+ community. Her origins are rather obscure, but her followers number in millions, both in Mexico and abroad. I'm not religious, and never have been. But it's the sign of these strange and unsettling times that I feel compelled to seek comfort from a renegade skeletal saint outlawed by the Catholic Church.

Since my time in Mexico City is short, I opt for the small neighbourhood church of Santa Muerte, a few blocks up from the Mercado La Merced. The church is quiet and homey inside, with little statues of Santa Muerte all over the place – in black shrouds and white shrouds, with candles lit in front of them. They are carrying scythes, or the scales of justice, or bouquets of yellow roses or sunflowers. There's the odd Jesus on the Cross as well. The place is completely deserted until a young woman slinks in, shooting me a glance of profound distrust before placing a candle before one of the images, giving a silent prayer and then skulking off again.

Locating the main shrine, where a larger image of Holy Death, dressed in a resplendent embroidered robe, presides over offerings of flowers against a backdrop of tackily painted angels and a trio of saints, I address the church's caretaker, a kindly middle-aged man.

'Where shall I put the tequila?'

He motions to the side of the prayer kneeler, with its cracked leather cushion and grooves worn by hundreds of kneeling petitioners. I place my offering gingerly. Like the Haitian loa, Santa Muerte enjoys a good tipple and so I bought her the best-quality firewater I could find, as well as a bottle of mineral water (she's always thirsty) and a bag of cookies (she has a sweet tooth). When the caretaker retreats to his cubbyhole, I gaze into the skull's impassive eye sockets and drop to my knees.

The hurt and the anger of recent years pour out of me in a silent howl of anguish. As far as my life is concerned, the year 2016 has been a perfect storm. Even as two of my treasured friendships were dissolving, my fellow Brits were voting to leave the EU. Seeing my home of thirty years morph from a liberal democracy that once welcomed my family into a hollow nationalist state where ideological lunacy trumps reason, and where hostility towards foreigners is palpable, really shook me up.

The same year, on the other side of the Atlantic, the presidential elections culminated in an electorate college win for Trump. It's difficult for me to imagine someone less morally or temperamentally fit to hold high office. His presidency has been an attack on everything I hold dear: multiculturalism, the environment, ethnic minorities, immigrants, common decency and fact-based, easily provable truth. When stories emerged of the brutal separation of refugee families from Latin America at the border, alongside images of Latino kids in cages, I couldn't sleep properly for weeks. I remember being left for a few minutes to watch my family's luggage at Frankfurt Airport as a child, and being gripped by the paralysing terror of abandonment, convinced in my heart of hearts that my family would never come back for me. And when my mother and I were in Madrid together, well into my career as a travel writer, and she was late coming back from the Prado, I was unexpectedly hit by that same stomach-clenching terror of separation at the sight of her sensible black shoes, sitting tidily in the corner of our hotel room. With great clarity I foresaw a moment in time when those shoes – and I as well – would be orphaned. When my unhappy task would be to decide what to keep and what to part with, and no amount of modest keepsakes would ever add up to the person that I'd lost. To strip some of the world's most vulnerable people, running from horrors that many of us can't even imagine, of the only thing they have of value – their children, their parents – seemed monstrous. Even I, aware as I am of all the horrific things that human beings do to one another, was taken aback by this deliberate cruelty. The only difference between the sweet, clever, funny boy who's my honorary godson, and those caged children who look like him, is that he's had the good fortune of being born into a middle-class Anglo-Peruvian family, and not to impoverished refugees from Honduras or Guatemala.

Most of my friends and loved ones are overwhelmed by the corrosive politics at home and abroad, which is why I'm reluctant to burden them further with my anger and anxieties. 'Santísima Muerte, I'm exhausted,' I tell her, and it's the truth. I petition her, asking for the refugee children in cages to be reunited with their families and for justice and retribution to befall the perpetrators of evil deeds.

* * * * *

Months later, when the pandemic sweeps the globe and Boris Johnson falls ill first, followed by Trump, I bashfully ask my friend Heather whether she thinks I caused this by way of my communion with a skeletal renegade saint.

'Are you suggesting that you might be responsible for the plague that's infected millions of people?' Even through we're talking on the phone, I can picture the sardonically arched eyebrow. 'Well, there's nothing wrong with your ego,' Heather concludes.

* * * * *

By the time I've finished silently addressing Santa Muerte, I feel completely wrung out. I take a seat in one of the wooden pews to recover a little. A black-and-white cat that's been asleep on the floor rubs itself against my ankles and hops into my lap, where it kneads my thighs and then settles down, purring loudly. I draw immense comfort from that, and take it to be a good omen.

CHAPTER 14
ACCIDENTAL IMMIGRANT

At random intervals, my phone pings. Each message begins the same way:

'Don't forget: you're going to die.'

It's the WeCroak app, inspired by a Bhutanese belief: to lead a happy life, one must contemplate death five times daily.

It's a simple idea: five daily quotes, all on the subject of mortality, lead you to consider whether you are living your best life. If not, then they should jolt you into changing your life for the better. Because no one knows how much time they've got left.

Lately, though, these messages have acquired an ominous feel to them, as the pandemic ventures ever closer.

I've just returned to Spain from New Zealand, and with contagion gathering pace, am looking at months of unemployment. Should I attempt a last-minute dash to Portugal for work? What about contagion? Would it be better to get sick now, while there are more ICU beds, or later? Would I feel like crap for a week, or end up attached to a ventilator?

In the end, the decision is made for me. On March 14, 2020, Spain declares a state of emergency. The country's in full lockdown. Things are changing rapidly. The Czech Republic closes its borders. In northern Italy, Covid patients are fighting for their lives in overwhelmed hospitals. A week prior, I was having coffee by the sea in Torre del Mar with my friend Mike. Seems like a lifetime ago.

I knuckle down in Cómpeta, Andalusia, for the foreseeable future.

*****

On the snowy morning of January 31, 2019, I hightailed it out of the UK with my friend Georgia in tow, going into self-imposed exile. I needed some distance between myself and Brexit, physical and mental. She offered to help me move to Spain. I chose Cómpeta as my destination almost by chance. A quiet village in the mountains, an hour's drive from an international airport, ample hiking opportunities, the chance to rebuild my compromised lungs... Plus, having Mike – one of my oldest and dearest friends – less than an hour's drive from me, and my Lonely Planet colleague John in Cómpeta itself, meant that I wouldn't be completely isolated. Georgia took charge of my passive, shell-shocked self in her firm, no-nonsense way. She drove us up the hairpin bends, installed me in my flat, made me my morning coffee, and took me on my first ramble to the nearby village of Canillas de Albaida.

I'd stay in Cómpeta for a year or so, I figured. Hopefully Brexit would be reversed and I could come back home. Then came the election of December 2019, which brought Boris Johnson to power, and Brexit went ahead. Feeling untethered and unmoored, I found myself grieving for Britain. For the loss of my home, my idea of home, my sense of belonging. Just like my parents, who'd ventured into the unknown in 1990, I had no idea that my move would be a permanent one.

I don't know if it's true of all immigrants, or all misfits, but one of my deepest, most fervent desires, for as long as I've been self-aware, had been to *belong*. To be accepted as part of a community. And my life in the UK provided me with that for the longest time, from friends who'd welcomed me with all my idiosyncrasies to the burgundy passport full of stamps that confirmed that, as a Brit and Her Majesty's subject, I was entitled to assistance and protection abroad.

Brexit stripped me of a sense of security that I'd taken for granted my entire adult life. I finally understood what what my mentor meant when he once told me how ethnic minorities 'lived with their bags mentally packed.' Witnessing the hostile treatment of EU citizens who'd lived in the UK for decades and made a life for themselves there, with untold thousands facing loss of residency and their rights, their families torn apart, I didn't feel safe myself. I could no longer say with confidence that this could never happen to naturalised immigrants.

I fought for the country that I felt slipping out of my grasp, attending all the anti-Brexit marches, knocking on hundreds of doors of ill-inclined strangers on behalf of Dominic Grieve MP, who'd opposed Brexit in spite of death threats. Halfway around the world, my friend Chung-Wah, a mild-mannered yoga teacher, marched for the Hong Kongers' democratic rights, braving beatings and getting tear gassed. But it was all for nought. Coming to terms with the UK no longer being my home took me a very long time. Chung-Wah also contemplated leaving Hong Kong: 'I'm thinking of moving to the UK as a last resort. I still cannot accept that my city has fallen apart…'

* * * * *

WeCroak: *The material of the doomed stars and the material of my doomed body are actually the same material. Literally the same atoms…*

* * * * *

My days vacillate between tedium and terror. The uncertainty is the worst. I have no idea when or if I'll see my loved ones again. Confined to my flat, without work, I pace the floor of my living room, too agitated to focus on any task for long. Unable to shake the ominous feeling in my head, exacerbated by the cold, foggy, rainy weather, fretting every time I develop a bit of a cough, throwing off all my clothes and locking them in the spare room after each fearful dash for groceries, I cut myself off from most human contact for months. My upstairs neighbours provide an unsettling soundtrack to my days, their moody piano sonatas reverberating through my ceiling.

A tense atmosphere reigns in the village. Some expats have had run-ins with the local police for walking their dogs further than 150m from their homes. When I dally by the tiled fountain on the Plaza del Carmen, beneath an ominous, leaden sky, I'm wary of suspicious faces peering through the blinds. I'm pre-emptively suspecting locals of betrayal and denunciation, à la 1930s Soviet Union. The paranoia is setting in. On the Cómpeta expats' page on Facebook, an exchange between two fellow émigrés goes like this:

'I saw four hikers on the trail above the village.'

'Report them to the police.'

Lockdown brings out the Stasi in some people.

Walks to the garbage skip aside, my world has been reduced to my two-bedroom flat and the cul-de-sac in which my house stands. There are exactly ninety-seven paces from my front door to the street corner. I know this because I sometimes pace back and forth in the rain and the fog, for hours on end, for the sake of my sanity, hoping that no one will see me or report me. I'm losing all track of my days.

As if humanity is reverting to a more primitive, dog-eat-dog way of life, early lockdown days are consumed by the frantic hunt for sustenance. Friends in Madrid, Málaga, Cambridge, London, New York share stories of shelves stripped bare. Cómpeta seems a world removed from all the panic. Coviran, my little local supermarket, delivers to my doorstep.

In a strange role reversal – my childhood flipped on its head – the people I'm desperately trying to acquire food for are my parents, because I don't want them risking their lives in a crowded supermarket full of panicked shoppers. They've had no luck with arranging home delivery because British supermarket chains are overwhelmed with demand. I'm trying to impress upon them that this crisis requires flexibility. Shopping less frequently, eating things they wouldn't normally eat, accepting help from a friend of mine who's offered to go shopping for them. Trying to convince two stubborn old folks, who are set in their ways, to alter their normal routine, is akin to herding cats. But after numerous dead ends, and after hitting up foodie friends for information, I finally manage to find a fruit and veg wholesaler in Cambridgeshire that normally supplies restaurants and caterers, and will deliver to their door. Whew.

On Twitter, I'm bombarded by Covid calamities. The impulse to seek out the latest news is strong. Scraps of information temporarily make you feel as if you're in control. But most of the time, I feel as if I'm part of a particularly dissonant Borg collective, my brain jangling with thousands of anguished, angry voices. What I'm trying to come to terms with is my own impotence. With Covid-19, all bets are off. Mindful of my chronic respiratory condition, I'm frightened of becoming cripplingly ill again, of being unable to fend for myself, of being left with lungs the texture of cracked glass, never to climb a mountain again, or even go up a short flight of stairs without wheezing. Of having a loved one fall ill, and not even being able to visit them, or comfort them in their final hours, if it comes to that. I'm angry over Covid sufferers being described by politicians as having 'won the battle' if they recover, or having 'lost the war' if they die, as if they're too lazy or insufficiently committed to living. It's this helplessness that makes me well up at the drop of a hat these days. I've never been a crier, and instantly feel guilty, because I'm spending the pandemic in comfortable surroundings and am not in any immediate danger. 'Likkle but tallawah,' Jamaicans used to call me. 'Little but tough.' Well, not anymore.

I once had a conversation with my friend Jacob, whose Guyanese mother is in her eighties, and who'd emigrated to Britain in the 1960s, about whether the wartime generations were 'tougher' than us. Unlike us, his mother and my grandmother didn't have the luxury of sitting around contemplating their feelings, or devoting their lives to the pursuit of happiness. What makes people more resilient? Being self-aware, and working with one's weaknesses, or not being aware of them and functioning in a semi-permanent state of hyper-alertness and survival mode? The former is psychologically more healthy, but would it make a person more fragile during a massive crisis? Our discussion was inconclusive.

What's sobering is that I'm not the only one who's spiralling out at times. So are various friends who are normally very good at keeping it together. Some rail against the draconian government regulations that keep us confined to our homes: 'We live in a dictatorship.'

On one hand, I'm greatly feeling the strain of being cooped up indoors. But there's a certain naïveté in comparing Western democracies with temporary movement restrictions *under extraordinary circumstances* to brutal totalitarian regimes. Short-term inconvenience is not the same as being stripped of one's freedoms for good. But I appreciate that it feels that way sometimes.

There's little respite from Covid-19 even in my dreams. I'm either running from something dark and evil, or fighting it and losing. Or else I experience a gnawing sense of dread and loss after coming to my parents' house and finding them missing. Some nights, I wake up at 4am – the hour when we are most vulnerable, the time when most natural deaths occur – and contemplate the possibility that I will not live to see the end of the pandemic.

* * * * *

There's a runaway train hurtling down the track, the old ethics dilemma goes. The line splits in two. There are five people lying on one track and one person lying on the other. Do nothing, and five people die. Pull the lever, one person dies. What do you do?

I like dilemmas like these and have my answers firmly in place. Pull the lever, of course. Maximise the number of lives saved.

There are other variations. The five people are high school dropouts and one's a brain surgeon. Or maybe there's one person on each line, and both are your friends. Or your parents. Then you make value judgements based on the person's relative worth – to you, to society. Ethics dilemmas are fun until they cross over into real life. All over the world, medical resources are in short supply. With Covid-19 threatening to overwhelm hospitals, doctors make life-and-death decisions according to age, clinical frailty and pre-existing comorbidities. Evaluating a medical decision by its outcome and given a choice between my 72-year-old mother (of two) and a

27-year-old mother of two, no medical professional would choose my mother in a triage situation.

Why is youth considered more valuable than old age? How do you put a price on a life?

Triage – basing a person's worth purely on age and medical statistics – is heartless. It doesn't take into account things that make individuals precious and irreplaceable to their loved ones. I've come to realise that I've always made a big effort to see the people I care about, in between travel gigs, because I've been stocking up on memories. Of my father, whose abstract ideas about the universe I can't even begin to grapple with and who, at the age of 75, still gets excited about teaching and finding students who have potential, sparks that he can nurture. Of my mother – one of the kindest, most loyal people I know, sturdy and irrepressible with her love of the mountains, and forests, and hiking, and museums. Of my friends. Because their lives are finite, as is mine.

I'm also unlikely to survive a triage decision. My health issues aside, society seems to value people with offspring far more than non-parents. Because the whole point of life is to perpetuate more life, right? If you don't have children – and I don't, by choice – you're seen as deficient, strange, incomplete, a genetic dead end.

When I was younger and more idealistic, I believed that I was doing a public service by encouraging people to travel, interact with other cultures and broaden their minds. When you see more similarities than differences between yourself and cultures different from your own, surely this leads to greater empathy towards humanity in general. Less conflict. I've been privileged to see more of our world than many people get to see in their lifetimes, and still believe that there's great value to travel, though now there's the carbon footprint and the environmental repercussions to consider.

Surely the knowledge that I've accumulated is valuable in the abstract? Surely there are other values beyond youth, health and parenthood, such as furthering our understanding of the world for its own sake, or meticulous record-keeping of what has come to pass, or creative ways of recording what it means to be human? Without all of those, humanity loses its grace, its collective experience.

I think about my own life, and how it had been greatly enriched by individuals without progeny: an award-winning performance poet who mentors inner-city kids; a historian producing original research on the Japanese space program; my former teacher, who spread her wings over the neediest teenagers and always found time to listen to them; and my mentor, who'd shaped the way I look at the world like no other.

* * * * *

WeCroak: *As people come closer to death, only two questions matter to them: 'Am I loved?' and 'Did I love well?'*

* * * * *

In the end, it's not me who dies. It's Marvin.

My pen pal was diagnosed with cancer in 2019 and received emergency medical treatment at the last possible minute, shackled to the hospital bed the whole time. Returning to prison, he was so weak he could barely walk.

His daughters were back in his life, and he wrote to me at length to tell me how proud he was of how his girls turned out. He missed a Christmas visit from his mother and sister due to chemo sessions, though he managed to speak to his mother on the phone before she herself passed away from cancer.

'I can't believe I'm not going to see her again,' he wrote to me. 'I miss her so much.'

He followed her a few weeks later. When I found out, I broke lockdown rules and hiked in the mountains all day under the cover of rain and fog, to the point of exhaustion.

I shall miss him. His sense of humour, his quiet stoicism, how he spelled 'probably': 'proberly'. Though he'd spent almost half of his life behind bars, Marvin never lost sight of who he was and, though bigger and stronger than other inmates, never abused his strength. A big brother figure, he provided guidance and counselling to younger inmates, whose lives had been defined by abuse and violence and who'd never had that kind of stability before. He was my big brother, too. More now than ever, I appreciate that the advice my younger self bristled at came from a good place, and that he was often very perceptive about human relationships.

* * * * *

I watch the Queen's broadcast, having never even watched the Queen's Speech before, and find myself getting emotional over her penultimate words:

'We should take comfort that while we may have more still to endure, better days will return: we will be with our friends again; we will be with our families again; we will meet again.'

No, I'm not crying, dammit. You're crying.

* * * * *

WeCroak: *To die is nothing, but it is terrible not to live.*

* * * * *

Death row inmates and extreme adventurers such as Roald Amundsen and Reinhold Messner alike agree on one thing: if you find yourself in a stressful or monotonous environment, you need a strict routine in order to function and survive a solitary existence mentally intact. So I attempt to structure the endless days spent indoors, taking up yoga, exploring every aspect of coffee nerdery, keeping on top of my death row correspondence, watching reruns of *Frasier*, calling my parents to check up on them. A friend tells me that her own mother, fed up with her children calling her every day to ask how she is, has taken to pre-emptively calling them instead in a display of 'revenge concern'. In the evenings, I try to focus on reading, but perhaps Margaret Atwood's *The Testaments* isn't the best choice, since everything is feeling a bit Under His Eye. At 8pm every day, we pour out on to roof terraces and balconies to applaud the healthcare workers and wave lighters and torches at each other through the fog, grateful to be able to let off steam.

The daily routine sometimes works. Other times, the only travelling I do is from the bedroom to the living room and back again. I don't even bother changing out of my pyjamas. What would be the point?

In the end, it's cooking that helps to preserve my sanity. I may not be able to travel – or even set foot outside – but through recreating authentic dishes of various countries, at least I can retrace landscapes familiar to me via my taste buds. I work my way through Ottolenghi's *Simple*, learning to make preserved lemons and harissa paste from scratch, since those are just a couple of the Middle Eastern ingredients that you can't get in Cómpeta for love nor money.

I move on to comfort food: potatoes dauphinoise; Greek-style lamb chops. Make stock from scratch. Then I turn to the flavours of my childhood, and attempt *kholodets* – the classic that my aunt used to make for New Year's Eve celebrations, with its slivers of meat suspended in a cold, translucent, meaty jelly. The project takes two pig's feet and about nineteen hours of prep and cooking, and my flat smells like boiled pig's feet for days. I eat half the *kholodets*, and feed the rest to stray cats.

Fuchsia Dunlop's *The Food of Sichuan* arrives, along with care packages of authentic ingredients from the UK, courtesy of my friend Sara. I love the way Dunlop writes, instructing readers to stir-fry chillies not 'for two to three minutes' but 'until they smell wonderful.' I recreate double-cooked pork in the style of Seven Days restaurant in Cambridge; gung bao prawns; cumin lamb…

Becoming a pandemic cliché, I learn to make my own sourdough, then master Montreal-style bagels. I also try my hand at smoking oysters in my stovetop smoker, trying to imitate what I'd savoured at the Orford smokery in Suffolk. 'They taste like the best orgasm of your life,' I enthused to fellow foodie Sonia, back then. The ones I smoke do not. They taste like a very modest orgasm. But it's a start.

Apart from the satisfaction that I get from building a dish from its elementary components, I find that while concentrating intensely on the slicing, the mixing, the kneading and the stirring, I'm able, for a time, to put aside the uncertainty and the existential fear.

But it's not enough. Culinary experimentation serves as a pleasant distraction, but what I'm really missing, with a fierce ache, are the rituals of eating. Sharing food with people whose company I enjoy, and in whom I'm emotionally invested. I find myself wishing away the curse of my good memory. I'm haunted by recollections of memorable meals spent with 'fungry' ('fun when hungry') companions. Melt-off-the-bone oxtail and curry goat, with Kala and my other friends from the Caribbean Riddims Society at university. Seafood feasts with the Leongs in Bangkok. *Rape rape* (small lobster) with Christina and Simon – fellow backpackers I met while crossing the Chile-Argentina border on foot and by boat – by the waterfront in Rapa Nui, Easter Island. Being taught to eat curry with my right hand by Niresh and his grandmother while staying in their home in Kandy, Sri Lanka. Consuming chilli crab with Shawn and Wyn in Singapore, splattered head to foot in chilli sauce. Tearing chunks of Patagonian grilled lamb with my bare hands at a raucous barbecue in Puerto Natales. My mentor bringing down the blade of his hand on a poppadum in a curry house. Dawn, Sara, Steve and Heather diving into the heaped dish of crispy-skinned salt-and-chilli chicken drumsticks at Hakka, our scruffy local Chinese place in Cambridge, and picking slivers of crisped garlic from the wreckage.

While I'm used to meals for one while on the road, they tended to be consumed amidst the merry hubbub of other diners. For the first time in my life, I find myself eating my meals completely, utterly alone.

* * * * *

Several months after Marvin's passing, I get a text message out of the blue.

'Hello, I'm a friend of Rasheed Simpson. He is no longer on death row. His conviction was overturned by the federal courts. His lawyer is now in talks to get him home. He really wanted you to know…'

And because I spring a leak so very easily these days, I burst into tears.

Rasheed and I had lost touch in 2016. Too consumed by my own problems, I abandoned all correspondence for over a year. When I finally replied, my letter to Rasheed bounced back. I assumed that he no longer wanted to hear from me.

Cautiously, I send a short note, expressing my joy at this positive development, having previously almost given up hope that my pen pals proclaiming their innocence would ever get justice.

'I hope that we can meet up in future in person, as regular friends, and not behind plexiglass. Hug each other, and go out for pizza,' I write.

Rasheed writes back.

'This will happen! However, I'm not too keen on trying those delicacies that you seem to try without any fear...'

I resolve to take it slow when it comes to introducing a guy from inner-city Philly to some of the more exotic foodstuffs.

Another death row letter arrives. Paul's legal appeals have also borne fruit:

'I'm getting a retrial this summer... Best-case scenario: I'll walk out a free man.'

He sounds optimistic about his chances, and asks whether he can come crash on my couch in Spain. Of course, I say yes. Because it looks like I'll be staying in Spain for the foreseeable future.

* * * * *

WeCroak: *Whatever you're meant to do, do it now. The conditions are always impossible.*

* * * * *

The change, when it comes, is so subtle that I cannot pinpoint when exactly it occurs. It creeps up on me on an old cat's paws. I think that much of the time we make critical, life-changing decisions during seemingly inconsequential time frames. Or else we assign specific moments to decisions, perhaps in order to fool ourselves that our choices were conscious ones, made as a direct result of rational thought, rather than of complex feelings seeping through over time.

The pandemic has given me ample time to contemplate my transient life. My having been in constant motion for a decade, doing back-to-back gigs, and not giving myself breathing space. Never really taking the time to contemplate what gave my life value, or genuinely trying to find a true work–life balance, for all my talk of it. It's ironic that it had taken an actual plague to slow me down.

I don't want to be transient forever, I conclude. I no longer want to live out of a bag. I want to have a home. Perhaps not a forever home, but at least a for-a-while home. The year before, when I was in Porto for work, amidst the bustle of humanity, and culture, and restaurants, and river views, I got struck by a bout of FOMO and almost made the decision to move to Portugal, right there and then. What am I doing, stuck in a small mountain village in Andalusia? And yet proximity to other people's busy, full lives is not the same as living that life yourself. With considerable dismay, I realise that I cannot find a life – the sort of life that I want to lead – with the skills that I've learned so far.

Months into the pandemic, Spain lifts its restrictions a little. Cautiously, I venture out. First on solo loop walks between Cómpeta and Canillas, masked up and shying away from other hikers. Then, occasionally, to my colleague John's terrace, for coffee and a chat. His cats come and sit on me, purring. I hadn't realised how much I'd missed casual physical contact until I find myself on the receiving end of uncomplicated feline affection.

My pattern of solitary hikes is broken by an ascent of Lucero, the higher peak in our immediate vicinity, with Sol, the superfit fifty-something red-haired 'Estonian ibex' to whom John introduced me when I first moved to Spain. With Sol's encouragement, though still wary of contagion and being around a group of people, I join the Ladies Wot Walk, a 'walkie talkie' group that combines gentle rambles in the surrounding hills with tapas lunches by the sea in El Morche, or in the 'lost' village of Acebuchal. Sol teaches me to recognise edible plants and I trade recipes with Deborah, Wendy, Jill, Kay, Alison and others – mostly retired old-timers, who've all been here a while and who treat me with kindness.

Slowly, very slowly, the thought emerges that perhaps it isn't my geographical location that's been the problem. That my restlessness isn't a result of where I am, but rather of who I am. And that unless I do something about it, my baggage will follow me wherever I go. That perhaps it's my attitude that requires tweaking. Instead of seeing Cómpeta as a place of exile – as somewhere that I got stuck, grudgingly – and instead of wryly referring to myself as a 'Brexile', maybe I can come to view Cómpeta as my proper base, and cut the melodrama.

Concerned whether I'll be able to keep up, but keen to shake off the long months of hermiting and couch potato inertia brought on by no-deal Brexit fears, in March 2021 I tag along with the Strollers, the more hardcore hiking group in our village, which includes Sol and her partner Mark, my colleague John, Tony and Ruth from Skipton, Yorkshire. Again, in spite of my reservations, I find myself welcomed.

My second hike with the Strollers involves the toughest ascent of La Maroma – Andalusia's highest peak. The youngest, yet the slowest and the least fit, I lag behind and fail to summit. But I manage to make it to the pass and then finish the hike with the rest. In time, I'll be able to keep up, I decide.

We then go away for a weekend, to climb Andalusia's second highest peak – La Torrecilla. The evening after we summit, we go out to paint the village of Burgos red. For the first time in a decade, I get properly inebriated and end up telling half the hiking group a moderately scandalous story from my days in Kingston, involving me, another legal intern and a gay British Airways steward – not an anecdote I'd ever tell my mother or even some of my old friends. You're never sure, with new people, where their boundaries lie, so I'm relieved when Mike and Lorna and Marieke are such good sports about it. They laugh, and I laugh – a proper belly laugh – more than I've laughed in a very long time. I must've felt safe with them, I realise later, because I never allow myself true inebriation when alone on the road, and they justify this feeling by steering my wobbly form clear of traffic.

My fear of Covid is abating. It's not that I'm any less likely to die if I were to fall ill, but I have a more realistic view of the odds of catching it in a village with a very low case load. When I take the steep steps and alleyways down into the heart of the village, I realise how much I enjoy going about my weekly chores. I like that there is predictability and shape to my days, to my weeks. That when I shop for fruit and veg in the village grocery, Marisol the greengrocer always throws in something extra for free – some courgettes, or tomatoes or oranges – and always has time to chat about recipes. When I sit on my balcony and look down the valley from my lofty vantage point at the top of this *pueblo blanco* amphitheatre, I can see the all the way to the

Mediterranean. In the evenings, there's the ever-changing light show as the setting sun illuminates the clouds with crimson. On the clearest days, I can see Africa's shadow on the horizon.

On April 22, 2021, for the first time since moving to Spain more than two years earlier, I have guests over for dinner: fellow Lonely Planet writer John; Sol and Mark, the hardcore cycling couple; new hiker friend Mike. In my former life, in Cambridge, I'd always had dining companions in the form of my housemates, and other friends would come over – for dinner, for brunch. But by now, I've been alone for several years – living out of a bag and then keeping to myself when not on the road. My social skills are rusty. I haven't cooked for other people in years. I'm nervous as hell.

I care a great deal what they'll make of the food, and get to cooking with a vengeance. The dinner is preceded by a frenetic dim sum-making session and the fermentation of two types of kimchi. I dust off *The Food of Sichuan*, marinate prawns in Shaoxing rice wine and soy sauce for that 'drunken prawn' effect, and stir-fry them with handfuls of *erjingtiao* chillies and cashews, toss battered squid with slivers of garlic and chopped chillies, flash-fry lamb cubes with cumin and heaven-facing chillies. I consult my wine expert friend Terry about wine pairings, figuring that it's about time I learned that skill. He duly obliges, and in spite of things going awry during dress rehearsal, the food and wine are a success.

I pour the wine, then step back to finish cooking and to observe my guests from the kitchen nook. There's John, my bearded colleague with wild grey hair, who was already researching Lonely Planet guidebooks when I was still a kid in the Soviet Union, and who's written for LP longer than any other writer. 'Do you see yourself as an LP legend?' I asked him once. 'That's for others to decide,' he responded, with characteristic modesty. I hadn't really known John before moving to Cómpeta, though we'd worked on the same books over the years, and whenever I'd inherited one of his chapters, I appreciated the mapwork and the research being spot on. The gruff appearance is deceptive: every now and then, there's a glimpse of a crooked grin, and it'd hard not like a man who gets colonised by a hierarchy of cats whenever he lies down on the sofa at home. I'm not quite sure at what point the shift from 'colleague' to 'colleague/friend' has taken place, but it has.

Next to him is Mark, with short-cropped hair and goatee. His sunburned face and hoop earring put me in mind of a jolly pirate. He's the teenager who never grew up. During our hikes, he makes it his business to tease me and take advantage of my gullibility, his eyes dancing with mirth, like some of the guys that I've grown up with. Like them, and like me, he appreciates lowbrow humour and slapstick comedy and, as I've told him, being on the receiving end of his mockery and abuse has made me feel right at home. In spite of playing the fool, he's very sharp, genuinely takes me by surprise, and occasionally makes me laugh till I cry.

Diagonally across is Sol, his partner, whom he introduced to off-road mountain biking when she was in her early fifties. She's very athletic, fearless, self-sufficient and all-round capable – whether scrambling up a steep slope to find a hiking trail, identifying and gathering edible plants, making lemon marmalade, or fixing broken plumbing. Sol challenges me to push my own boundaries and her no-nonsense attitude and direct manner remind me of one of my oldest friends. Plus, she and I were born in the same country – the one that no longer exists – and she both understands Russian and gets my Soviet cultural references.

On her other side is Mike – a dapper, immaculately turned out, aquiline-nosed, silver-haired gentleman in his trademark monochrome get-up, who wouldn't look out of place in *The Godfather*. He's cultured, well spoken, perceptive, with a well-argued opinion on many subjects. Someone who takes a genuine interest in people. It's rare for me to meet someone who loves good food as much as I do. Turns out we've been to some of the same restaurants over the years – in Barcelona, in New Orleans – and we both have fond memories of the Caribbean and an appreciation of 'di holy herb'. I'm intrigued. Not sure what to make of him yet. Which is a fine dilemma to have: most of the time, I often have little trouble when it comes to pigeonholing people.

Naturally, conversation turns to travel. Of the places we've been, and where we'd like to go, post-pandemic. John and I have both hiked in Nepal and would like to return. Mark and Sol want to cycle the Pamir Highway. I want to drive it. Mike's got Chile on his bucket list, and I'd like to see my beloved land of ice and fire again, outside of work. Much of the time, I'm content to listen to my dining companions. John and I have swapped work stories over coffee, and have friends and colleagues in common. The others also know many of my travel stories by now, since I've shared part of my life during our walks: the death row inmates, the aspirations to a career in criminal law that didn't come to fruition, the adventures and misadventures in Papua New Guinea, Haiti, Jamaica.

As I look around the table, and the relaxed, happy hikers who've eaten all my food – the highest compliment a chef can get – I acknowledge to myself that I feel comfortable around them, and feel the tension drain out of my body. Over my cooking, over whether I'd fit in. I'm glad to have them here, in my house. And just as the meals consumed while travelling have been my tangible links to other countries, this pan-Asian spread connects me to this place. To my home.

It's the first time I've ever used that word in my head in relation to Cómpeta.

'I'm sorry it's taken me such a long time to return your invitations,' I tell Sol, John and Mark, who've been very hospitable from the very beginning of my life in Spain, inviting me over and doing their best to make me feel included. I wasn't ready for it, back then, and actively resisted getting attached – to the people, to the place. I saw Cómpeta as somewhere I was just passing through.

'My attitude needed to change,' I confess to them. 'I needed to get over myself.'

They assure me that friendship was always on the backburner but never extinguished.

We hug each other goodbye – the first proper human, physical contact I've had since the beginning of the pandemic. I sit out on my balcony for a while, revelling in the silence, watching the stars, the bats flitting past. I'm reminded of another night, in a garden in Haiti, other stars, other bats. I think about those absent from my table tonight – the cherished dead, the others. Those whom I still miss, and think about often.

Then, a startling thought.

What if Haitians don't actually see their dead as separate entities, carrying on in death as they did in life? What if they just mean that our dead are always with us, because they are part of our memories that shape our time on this earth?

As all signs of life subside in the dark streets around me, I address my ghosts, past and present. Your voices and insights are an established presence within me, I tell them. What I need of you is here, in my head, subject to no one's judgement but my own. Perhaps we shall never meet again, or at least not as we once did, but my door is always open. Recollections of our intertwined lives are a part of me, as vital as my limbs, until it's my time to go.

And I think about my guests who've just left – good people whom I'd like to get to know better, who have come to embody my connection to this unusual half-Spanish, half-expat community. They are not a replacement for old friends I left behind, but rather a welcome new addition to my life, an enhancement of what I already have. It dawns on me that by virtue of this connection, of finding this particular *pueblo blanco*, and being accepted by this motley crew of travellers and adventurers, I am finally able to see the UK and Russia as places that are a part of me also. Still. And in time, I may be able to work out how these disparate parts of me fit together.

I no longer wish to view myself as an involuntary immigrant buffeted by mercurial fate, I realise. I want to make conscious choices: that I'm going to live here, and put down roots here, and have a life here.

I'm ready to let people into my life. A little. Cómpeta won't hold me forever, but for now, I'll stay.

JOIN
THE TRAVEL CLUB

THE MEMBERSHIP CLUB FOR SERIOUS TRAVELLERS
FROM BRADT GUIDES

Be inspired
Free books and our monthly
e-zine, packed with travel tips
and inspiration

Save money
Exclusive offers and special
discounts from our favourite
travel brands

Plan the trip
of a lifetime
Access our exclusive concierge
service and have a bespoke
itinerary created for you
by a Bradt author

Join here:
bradtguides.com/travelclub

Membership levels to suit all budgets

Bradt GUIDES

TRAVEL TAKEN SERIOUSLY